KEY ISSUES IN TAX REFORM

Other Books by FISCAL PUBLICATIONS

Administrative and Compliance Costs of Taxation, 1989

Practical Tax Administration, 1993

Successful Tax Reform: Lessons from an Analysis of Tax Reform in Six Countries, 1993

KEY ISSUES IN TAX REFORM

Cedric Sandford (Editor)

Andrew Dilnot
Claudia Scott
Sijbren Cnossen
David King
Ian Wallschutzky
Frank Cassells
Don Thornhill
Michael Foers
Chuck Brown
Stephen Smith
Donald Brean

FISCAL PUBLICATIONS
1993

336.205
K44

British Library Cataloguing-in-Publication Data

A catalogue record for this book is available from the British Library.

ISBN 0 9515157 2 1 Hardback

Printed in Great Britain by
Redwood Books
Trowbridge, Wiltshire

Published by Fiscal Publications,
Old Coach House, Fersfield, Perrymead,
BATH BA2 5AR

CONTENTS

THE CONTRIBUTORS

DONALD J. S. BREAN is Associate Dean and Professor of Finance and Economics in the Faculty of Management, University of Toronto. He has advised numerous international agencies and governments, including the European Community, the World Bank, the International Monetary Fund, the United Nations Development Programme, USAID, the Canadian Government and a number of developing countries. He has published widely, particularly on international finance and investment, taxation, industrial organisation and economic policy.

CHUCK BROWN was Professor of Economics at Stirling University and had specialised in research on the disincentive effects of taxes. As well as the study outlined in Chapter 9, he had previously directed national surveys on taxation and work incentives funded by the Social Science Research Council and HM Treasury and had published widely on this subject.

FRANK CASSELLS is a career civil servant who has served in virtually all parts of the Irish Revenue organisation. In 1986 he was appointed an Assistant Secretary with particular responsibilities for legislation and inputs to policy formulation; during this period he was closely involved with the introduction of self assessment in Ireland. In 1989 he was appointed a Revenue Commissioner – one of three members of a Board with responsibility for the care and management of all inland revenue taxes and customs and excise duties in Ireland. He is Vice Chairman of the OECD Committee on Fiscal Affairs.

SIJBREN CNOSSEN is a Professor in the Economics Faculty of Erasmus University, Rotterdam. Prior to his appointment, he served on the staff of the International Monetary Fund. Professor Cnossen is the author or editor of several books and numerous articles on tax harmonisation, value–added taxation, excise duties and corporation taxes. He has advised more than a dozen countries on the design of their tax systems, most recently the newly emerging market economies of Eastern Europe.

ANDREW DILNOT is the Director of the independent London based research institute, the Institute for Fiscal Studies. He has taught at the Universities of Oxford and London and published widely on taxation, social security and the distribution of income. He is a regular broadcaster and contributor to the national press.

MIKE FOERS is an Inspector of Taxes with the United Kingdom Inland Revenue. He was Head of the Department's Form Design Unit, 1980–85, when he was awarded a Civil Service travelling fellowship to make an international comparative study of administrative forms. He lectures on forms design and plain language and has run workshops and seminars for, amongst other organisations, OECD and UNESCO. He has recently undertaken form design projects in Budapest and Colombo for the International Monetary Fund.

DAVID KING is a Senior Lecturer in Economics at the University of Stirling. He has had two one–year periods working for the British Government, once as Consultant Economist to the Royal Commission on the Constitution and once – on secondment from Stirling – as Economic Adviser on local tax reform. He has worked on the reform of local taxes in Portugal and recently he has worked with the OECD on the reform of local government finance in Eastern Europe. His publications include *Taxes on Immovable Property*, prepared for the OECD, and *Fiscal Tiers: the Economics of Multi–Level Government*.

CEDRIC SANDFORD is Professor Emeritus of Political Economy at the University of Bath and formerly Director of the Bath University Centre for Fiscal Studies. His specialist research areas are the compliance costs of taxation, wealth taxes and tax policy–making, on all of which he has published widely. In recent years he has undertaken consultancies for the International Monetary Fund, World Bank, United Nations and OECD as well as national governments and the United Kingdom National Audit Office.

CLAUDIA SCOTT is Professor of Public Policy at Victoria University of Wellington, New Zealand and is Director of the Master of Public Policy Programme. She holds a PhD in Economics from Duke University and is the author of several books and monographs in the areas of economic and social policy. She initiated and continues to contribute to a major project on taxation through the Institute of Policy

Studies at Victoria University. Specific interests in recent years have included family taxation, the goods and services tax (VAT) and the fringe benefit tax.

STEPHEN SMITH is Deputy Director of the Institute for Fiscal Studies, London, an independent research institute. He is also Jean Monnet Senior Lecturer in European Economics and Integration at University College London. Prior to joining IFS in 1985, he was an Economic Adviser at the Department of Trade and Industry. His research interests include tax policy and the environment, European public finance, tax reform in Eastern Europe and local government finance. He has recently been a consultant to both the European Community and the OECD on the subject of environmental taxation.

DON THORNHILL is Assistant Secretary for VAT and Capital Taxes in the Office of the Irish Revenue Commissioners. Prior to joining the Revenue in 1985, he worked in the Irish Departments of Finance and Foreign Affairs. He is a member of the European Community VAT Committee and of the EC Committee of Senior Officials on the Abolition of Fiscal Frontiers. A former participant in the UK Fulbright Program, he was a Guest Scholar at the Brookings Institution, Washington DC in 1987.

IAN WALLSCHUTZKY is Associate Professor in Taxation at the University of Newcastle, NSW, Australia. He completed his PhD at the University of Bath in 1983 and, in 1988–89, was a Visiting Scholar at the Harvard International Tax Program. He has published widely in the field of taxation specialising in tax compliance. He is author of *Australian Income Tax Law* (2nd ed.) 1988 and *Australian Income Tax Questions* (5th ed.) 1990. He is currently working as a consultant to the Australian Taxation Office on a Cost of Compliance to Small Business project.

H20   1-6

βк Title

INTRODUCTION   ed.

In the 1980s major restructuring of the tax system - usually referred to as tax reform - dominated tax policy-making in many countries in the world. Whilst there were significant differences amongst countries in measures, methods, emphasis and their degree of success, world-wide tax reform was remarkable for the common elements. Lower marginal rates of personal income tax and fewer steps in the income tax scale; lower rates of corporation tax; a broader base for income and corporation tax; often a move from taxes on income to taxes on spending and from a classical to an imputation system of corporation tax - these were the main characteristics of world-wide tax reform in the 1980s.

Whilst simplifying the tax system and improving horizontal equity were subsidiary motives for tax reform in many countries, the philosophical under-pinning of the tax reform movement was the drive for efficiency or tax neutrality. Save in the case of clear market imperfections (which taxation might help to remedy) efficiency meant minimum interference with prices and the free workings of the market. Thus, taxes should impinge as little as possible on producers' choices of what products to make, what factors of production to use, what form of finance to employ and what kind of business organisation to adopt. Similarly, the choices of individuals between work and leisure, between different goods and services to consume, between saving and consumption and between alternative forms of saving, should be subject to minimum tax distortion. Minimising tax distortions could be expected to promote economic growth and increase consumer welfare.

Whilst the extent and range of tax reform has been impressive, its dynamic remains unexhausted. Not even in countries where tax reform went farthest and fastest - of which New Zealand is perhaps the prime example - can tax reform be said to have been completed. Nor in any country could the tax reform implemented be said to have been wholly successful. Thus, tax reform remains very much on the agenda. Indeed, for some countries, notably those of central and eastern Europe and China, where western type tax systems have to be created almost from scratch, the task of tax reform is only just beginning.

1

Thus, this book, which examines key issues in tax reform, drawing on the experience of a number of different countries, should prove of widespread value. It should be useful for policy-makers and administrators in their search for better tax systems; and of value to all who are, in the broadest sense, students of taxation, to give a fuller understanding of some of the central issues which will dominate the tax agenda in the 1990s and beyond.

The book is divided into three parts. The first and longest is concerned with issues of tax structure. We have already mentioned that one feature of the tax reforms of the 1980s was a reduction in the number of steps of the income tax. How far should this process go? In several countries the number of bands was reduced to two positive rates. Does such a reduction seriously inhibit the progressiveness of the tax? In Chapter 1, Andrew Dilnot, Director of the Institute for Fiscal Studies in London, argues that it does not; that a two rate band structure leaves considerable flexibility in determining the progressivity of the tax system and carries other advantages such as lower administrative and compliance costs and possibly less disincentive effects.

One way of reducing tax distortions and effectively broadening the income tax base, adopted by many tax reforming administrations, is to tax fringe benefits. In principle, the most appropriate way is to tax the value of the benefit in the hands of the recipient, at his or her marginal tax rate, and that is what most countries attempt to do, but with limited success. An alternative, adopted by New Zealand and Australia in the mid 1980s, was to impose a fringe benefit tax (FBT) on the employer. The FBT has the practical advantage that the revenue authorities have to deal with fewer people, the valuation problems are less and administrative and compliance costs can be expected to be much lower. This approach to taxing fringe benefits has aroused much international interest and Ireland is considering following the Australasian example. Chapter 2, by Professor Claudia Scott of the Victoria University of Wellington, New Zealand, describes the working of the FBT in both New Zealand and Australia and analyses the response of business in each country to the tax.

Corporation tax is notable for the variety of forms that it takes. The most appropriate relationship between corporation tax and the personal income tax continues to be debated. Should corporate profits be taxed twice or should some form of dividend relief be provided? Should dividend relief be provided at corporate or at shareholder level? How much weight should be given to the international repercussions of partial integration? In 'What Kind of Corporation Tax?', Chapter 3, Professor Sijbren Cnossen of Erasmus University, Rotterdam, provides a searching analysis of these issues.

A notable feature of tax reform in many countries was a switch from direct to indirect taxation either by introducing a value added tax (VAT) or by increasing an existing VAT. Indeed, the widespread adoption of VAT around the world should probably be considered the most important event in the development of tax structure in the last half of this century. As with corporation tax, however, the structure of VAT differs widely between countries. Thus not only countries where the adoption of a VAT is under consideration, like Australia, the United States, China and many developing countries, but also those which have already implemented a VAT, but look to improve its form, will find Sijbren Cnossen's analysis invaluable to any understanding of the nature of the tax, its social and economic effects and the practical issues of design and operation.

The first part of the book concludes with a paper by David King of the University of Stirling on local government finance. For its one local tax, Britain has recently moved from a property tax to a poll tax and back to a modified form of property tax. David King draws out the lessons from British experience which are of relevance to the many other countries where the form and level of local taxation is a subject of concern and debate.

Part II of the book concentrates on issues centred on tax administration. One of the motivations for tax reform in many countries, of which the United States is a notable example, (see, for example, Birnbaum and Murray, 1988) arose from the concern that tax avoidance and tax evasion were widespread and growing and in danger of undermining the integrity of the tax system. Perhaps nowhere was concern on these issues more prevalent than in Australia, where some notorious avoidance/evasion schemes had currency in the 1970s and early 1980s. In 1985, the Treasurer, Paul Keating, could refer to 'an avalanche of avoidance, evasion and minimisation' (Keating, 1985). As the author of Chapter 6 puts it: 'Because successive Australian governments and tax administrations had to deal with evasion and avoidance on a large scale ... a number of options have been considered or tried and in some instances a number of unique solutions have been found'. Professor Ian Wallschutzky of the University of Newcastle, New South Wales, draws on this Australian experience as his main source of reference, but also offers a theoretical structure within which the issues of tax avoidance and evasion can most usefully be examined.

Despite a comprehensive blueprint for reform provided by a Commission on Taxation, the Republic of Ireland saw less reform of the structure of its tax system in the 1980s than many other English speaking countries. However, it has been in the forefront of administrative reform including the introduction and extension of schemes of self assessment to tax. In an informative and lively paper, two senior revenue officials, Frank Cassells and Don Thornhill, discuss how Ireland used innovative methods to tackle the problem of poor compliance and heavy administrative and compliance costs.

Finally, in this part of the book, Michael Foers, formerly head of a forms design unit at Inland Revenue in the United Kingdom, examines the issue of forms design and comprehensibility. In many countries tax reform failed to bring a simplification of the tax system, even though this was often one of its specified objectives. Whilst simplification comprises more than improved tax literature, designing forms so that they are easy to use and minimise taxpayer compliance costs (a highly skilled art) is a vital component of any programme of simplification.

The final part of the book considers some general issues of tax reform. One important component of the argument for tax reform was the disincentive and distorting effects which were believed to follow from high marginal rates of personal income tax. These effects were stressed, and the anticipated benefits of tax reduction lauded, by the United Kingdom Chancellor of the Exchequer, Mr Nigel (now Lord) Lawson in 1988, when he cut the top rates of personal income tax from 60 to 40 per cent. Chapter 9, after a brief analysis of the theoretical issues, and a review of earlier research, outlines the findings of a study designed to test the Chancellor's claims. The research was directed by Professor Chuck Brown of Stirling University. He was an acknowledged expert in this field and had previously undertaken a series of studies of the effect of taxation on labour supply. He had agreed to write this chapter, but, tragically, he died after a short illness before he was able to do so. In the event, the editor, who collaborated with Professor Brown in the study on the 1988 income tax cuts, has written the chapter. In the process he has drawn heavily not only on Professor Brown's contribution to this research study, but also on his earlier work; and it was only just to include Professor Brown as joint author. The findings of the study serve as a warning against over-optimistic assessment of supply side benefits from cuts in marginal rates of income tax.

With Chapter 10 we move to an aspect of tax reform which did not figure prominently in the world-wide tax changes of the past ten or fifteen years, but will prove increasingly important in the future: the use of taxation as an instrument for dealing with environmental problems. Stephen Smith, Deputy Director of the Institute for Fiscal Studies in London, examines the scope for 'green taxes' and the arguments for using taxes as compared with regulative instruments. On the face of things using taxes may seem contrary to the philosophy of the 1980s tax reform of minimum price distortion; but this is not so. Taxation for environmental purposes is generally designed to correct distortions inherent in the free price system - its failure to take account of certain 'externality effects' as a result of which the free market price fails to reflect the true social costs.

In the 1980s tax reform in many countries was heavily influenced or even conditioned by what was happening to taxes in their larger neighbours. The globalisation of the economy has imposed and will increasingly impose both requirements and constraints on individual countries, particularly with the taxation of the most mobile factor of production, capital. In the final chapter Professor Don Brean, of the University of Toronto, analyses this vital international dimension and assesses its significance for tax policy.

References and Further Reading

Birnbaum, J. H. and A. S. Murray, *Showdown at Gucci Gulch: Lawmakers, Lobbyists and the Unlikely Triumph of Tax Reform*, Vintage Books, Random House, New York, 1988.

Keating, P. J., *Reform of the Australian Tax System: Statement by the Treasurer, The Hon Paul Keating, September 1985*, AGPS, Canberra, 1985.

KEY ISSUES IN TAX REFORM

PART I
TAX REFORM - STRUCTURE

CHAPTER 1

THE INCOME TAX RATE STRUCTURE

Andrew Dilnot*

Introduction

All developed countries use income taxes as a part of their revenue raising process, but there remains enormous diversity of structure and size. Throughout the 1980s reform of income taxes was common and there was a clear trend towards fewer rates, a lower maximum rate and (less uniformly) a higher initial rate, as shown in Table 1.1.

Table 1.1 Tax Schedules Internationally

	Number of rate brackets		Initial rate		Maximum rate	
	1975	1988/9	1975	1988/9	1975	1988/9
Australia	7	5	20	24	65	49
Canada	13	3	9	17	47	29
France	13	13	5	5	60	57
Germany	—[1]	—[1]	22	19 (1990)	56	53 (1990)
Ireland	6	3	26	32	72	56
Italy	32	7	10	10	72	50
Japan	19	5	10	10	75	50
Netherlands	10	3 (1990)	27	35[2]	71	60 (1990)
New Zealand	22	2	19	24	57	33
Sweden	11	3	7	5	56	42
UK	10	2[3]	35	25	83	40
US	25	3	14	15	70	33

[1]Not applicable: the German tax schedule is based on a polynomial formula.
[2]Not comparable: includes social security contributions.
[3]Increased to 3 in 1992.
Source: Cnossen and Messere (1989)

*Director of the Institute for Fiscal Studies. The author wishes to thank the ESRC for funding under grant number W100281002.

9

This trend seems set to continue and we have even seen countries such as New Zealand and Ireland considering a move to an income tax with only one positive rate. Since it is rare to see such uniformity of action, it seems important to examine the issues surrounding the choice of income tax rate structure.

Three groups of issues dominate. The first is progressivity and in particular the relationship between the number of tax rates and the degree of progressivity in a tax system. The growing realisation that progressivity does not require a multiple rate structure has been a powerful force in the world–wide reform process.

The second set of issues relates to administration, simplicity and the compliance costs of taxation. The third set of issues relates to the interaction between tax rates and work effort. As the 'supply side revolution' swept around the world, concern grew about the potential disincentive effects of high rates of taxation.

Each of these areas is discussed below.

Progressivity – What It Is and How to Achieve It

Although income taxes form only a part of the overall tax system, and in many countries a fairly small part, they typically provide a disproportionately large share of the progressivity of any country's overall tax system. Since we define progressivity in terms of the relationship between tax payment and gross income, it is not surprising that income tax is a popular vehicle for achieving progressivity.

Unfortunately, the term progressivity has become widely used but almost as widely misunderstood or misapplied. In this chapter we use 'progressive' to describe a tax system which imposes an increasing average tax rate as income rises, that is one which takes a larger share of income from those with higher income. A 'proportional' tax system is one which takes in tax the same proportion of income, whatever the level of income. And a 'regressive' tax system is one which takes a lower share of income in tax as income rises. These definitions of progressive, proportional and regressive are straightforward and convey the meaning that they are typically understood to have.

The crucial issue for us is the relationship between the rate structure for income tax and the degree of progressivity. The most common confusion in this area is the belief that a progressive tax system requires a graduated rate structure, that is one with multiple rates which increase with income. While it is true that progressivity does require at least two rates, one of those rates can be zero. A tax system with a tax free allowance and a single positive tax rate is a progressive tax system and may be more or less progressive than a tax system with multiple rates. In a tax system with a single positive rate, the progressivity is produced by the tax free allowance, whereas with multiple rate systems both the allowance and the structure of positive tax rates can produce an effect.

To clarify these points we show in Table 1.2 the levels of tax and average tax rates produced by two different tax systems for a hypothetical population of ten individuals, each with different incomes. The two tax systems are:

Tax system A		**Tax system B**	
Tax free allowance	2000	Tax free allowance	1100
Tax rate	25%	Tax rate on first 2000	
		of taxable income	15%
		Tax rate on next 2000	20%
		Tax rate on next 2000	25%
		Tax rate on further income	30%

The two tax systems are designed to raise as nearly as possible the same amount of revenue. The tax free allowance is lower in the case of the graduated tax system since the lower starting rate of tax reduces revenue which must be compensated for. There are in principle an infinite number of multiple rates structuring which would raise the same amount of revenue as tax system A, but that selected as system B seems to be a fair reflection of such systems in practice.

We can see that both these tax systems are clearly progressive; the average tax rate rises continuously with income. The rate at which the average tax rate rises is greater for system A than system B over the first half of the income distribution and slower over the second half. Anyone with income of less than 3560 pays more under system B than system A; those with incomes between 3560 and 8600 pay more under system A than system B; those with incomes in excess of 8600 pay more under system B than system A.

The general characteristic of multiple rate systems that those in the middle do best can be seen more clearly in the figures below, which show actual tax liabilities (Figure 1.1), average tax rates (Figure 1.2) and marginal tax rates (Figure 1.3).

Table 1.2 The Impact of a Single Rate and Multiple Rate System

Income of individual	Tax system A	Tax system B	Average tax rate system A %	Average tax rate system B %
1000	0	0	0	0
2000	0	135	0	6.8
3000	250	285	8.3	9.5
4000	500	480	12.5	12.0
5000	750	680	15.0	13.6
6000	1000	925	16.7	15.4
7000	1250	1175	17.9	16.8
8000	1500	1470	18.8	18.4
9000	1750	1770	19.4	19.7
10000	2000	2070	20.0	20.7
Total	9000	8990	16.36	16.35

It is clear in Figure 1.2 that the average tax rate in a single positive rate system climbs much more slowly as it nears the marginal tax rate (25 per cent in this case). This flattening of the average tax rate at higher incomes is one of the main attractions of imposing at least one higher rate on a small number of high income individuals, as is done in the United Kingdom, United States, New Zealand and Ireland.

We might reasonably want to ask which of the two hypothetical systems outlined above is most progressive. The answer is that we simply cannot say in any general way. Over the first half of the income distribution system A is more progressive, over the second half system B is more progressive. There is no unambiguously correct answer and any that is given will be a function of the relative weights attached to different parts of the income distribution. The attraction of unambiguous statements is obvious, but they will often simply not be possible when we are comparing the overall progressivity of two income tax rate structures.

The difficulty of comparing whole rate structures emphasises the point that we may do better to think in terms of specific objectives for income tax reform. The effectiveness of two systems at reducing or

Figure 1.1 Tax Payments under Systems A and B

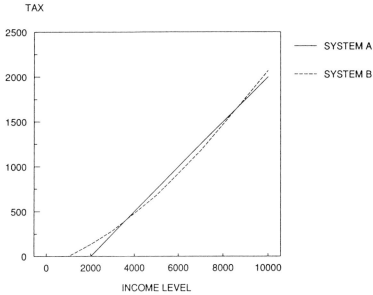

Figure 1.2 Average Tax Rates under Tax Systems A and B

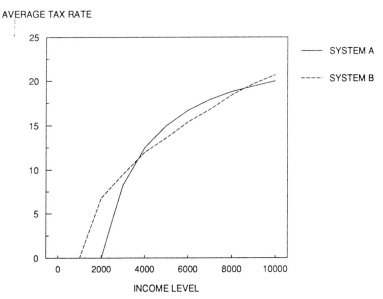

Figure 1.3 Marginal Tax Rates under Tax Systems A and B

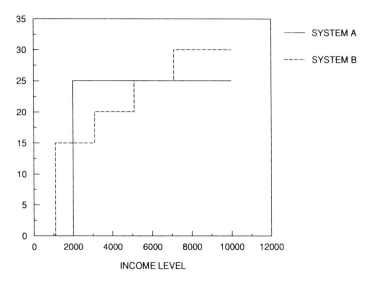

MARGINAL TAX RATE

increasing the number of taxpayers, reducing or increasing the tax liabilities of those on low or medium or high incomes, reducing administrative costs, improving work incentives, or making tax revenue more buoyant can be discussed more sensibly and with more hope of some useful conclusion than generalisation about progressivity.

It is clear that if the main aim is to minimise tax liabilities for those on low incomes, a structure with fewer tax rates and with a relatively high starting rate will dominate a multiple rate structure, although this has not prevented politicians from claiming the reverse. In 1980 the then Conservative Chancellor of the Exchequer, Sir Geoffrey (now Lord) Howe, seemed to understand these arguments and abolished the low starting for income tax introduced by the preceding Labour Government in 1978, saying,

> 'The case for the lower rate tax band was never at all clear. The 25 per cent rate was not the effective marginal rate for more than a small number of full–time adult workers. For those on lower

incomes an increase in the personal allowance would always have been more valuable than the lower rate band. And the existence of the lower rate band added significantly to the complexity of the tax system. Its disappearance will simplify and shorten the PAYE tables and reduce the administrative burden on employers and the Inland Revenue, where there will be a valuable staff saving of 1300 posts.'

Twelve years later, a succeeding Conservative Chancellor, Norman Lamont, reintroduced a reduced rate, presumably having forgotten his predecessor's remarks. This action, immediately before a General Election, demonstrated once again that the political importance of taxation can lead to decisions that have little justification from an economic or analytical point of view, but seem politically attractive. In this case, the awareness that a reduction in the starting rate of tax from 25 per cent to 20 per cent was far more memorable than an equal cost increase in allowances led to the lower rate band, although low income taxpayers would, as Sir Geoffrey Howe explained, have done far better from an allowance increase.

Perhaps the strongest argument which can be put forward in favour of a multiple rate strategy is not that it is better at achieving progressivity, which is not obviously true, but that it allows more complex distributional aims to be achieved than can be, using a simpler structure. It is certainly true that a multiple rate structure confers some additional flexibility, but is unfortunately true that the distributional objectives of income taxes are rarely set out sufficiently clearly for it to be obvious how to implement them using a simple structure; a more complex structure would only be needed if objectives were set out far more clearly than they typically are at present.

Progressivity in income tax does require more than one rate, but two is enough and one of these two can be the zero produced by tax free allowances. A growing awareness of this in the 1980s was one of the reasons for the world–wide drift towards fewer tax rates.

Administrative Issues and the Rate Structure

A further area where the rate structure will have an impact is on the administration of the tax system for revenue authorities and for taxpayers. Related to these issues are questions of simplicity.

It is straightforward to see that, as a general rule, more tax rates must mean more administrative cost, more complexity and higher compliance costs. But it is also true that there are circumstances in which the size of such additional costs will be quite small.

Perhaps the clearest case in which multiple rates of tax add complexity is that where individuals have more than one income source. With a simple tax system of a tax free allowance and a single positive tax rate, withholding the correct amount of tax from secondary income sources, whether additional employment income or investment income, is relatively easy. The allowance can be offset against the main source of income, and tax withheld at the single positive rate on all other income sources. In such a world, no end of year adjustments will be necessary provided annual income exceeds the tax free allowance.

, The introduction of additional rates of tax begins to complicate matters, although the extent of the complication is a function of where in the income distribution the additional tax rates apply. If higher rates are imposed on a small group of those on high incomes, relatively few problems should ensue, since although end of year adjustment of tax liability will typically be necessary, this group would probably be in contact with the Revenue anyway. If, on the other hand, additional rates are added at low incomes, considerable problems can arise, particularly in countries where only a small proportion of taxpayers are required to fill in annual tax returns. If a self–assessment type system operates, as in, for example, the United States or Australia, and indeed the great bulk of developed countries, some additional administrative problems arise, but it is in countries such as the United Kingdom, where most do not fill in tax returns, that most difficulties will be seen.

The introduction in the 1992 Budget in the United Kingdom of a new lower rate of 20 per cent on the first £2000 of taxable income (£2000 is roughly 12.5 per cent of average earnings), compared with the 25 per cent standard rate, is a good example of some of the problems that can be caused. Some four million individuals will find that their marginal tax rate is 20 per cent, out of around 27 million income tax payers. Many of these will have investment income in the form of bank or building society interest on which tax will be withheld at 25 per cent. Very few of these four million individuals will generally complete tax returns and yet many of them will now be entitled to rather small tax refunds. UK experience of non–taxpayers reclaiming tax withheld on investment income suggests that many of those affected will not succeed in reclaiming this tax, either because they do not know that they may be entitled to, or because the effort involved seems disproportionately great relative to the sums to be reclaimed.

Although a self assessment system, with tax returns compulsory, solves some of these problems, it can be a way of substituting increased administrative costs for the revenue services and compliance costs for individual taxpayers for the possibility of over–taxation which exists in systems like that seen in the United Kingdom. It is worth noting that improvements in the technology of data manipulation and transfer have already reduced revenue service administrative costs in this area and should continue to do so.

Related to this issue is the question of the time period, over which the rule for income taxes, although not for social security taxes, is that tax should be assessed over a period of a year. A year seems a long enough period to give a good idea of the 'typical' income level of a taxpayer and not so long as to provide serious delays in payment, or for inflation adjustment of allowances and thresholds to be required. With a simple system with one positive rate, fluctuation of income from year to year (provided the rate remains the same) will have no impact on aggregate tax liability provided that annual income never falls below the tax free allowance. With a multiple rate system, varying income from year to year will lead to variation in aggregate tax liability.

Consider a three–year period in which individual 1 earns 6000 every year, while individual 2 earns 2000, 6000, 10,000. In Table 1.3 we apply the same tax systems as were outlined earlier in the section on progressivity.

Under tax system A, with a single positive rate the total tax paid is the same with the two different income streams. Under tax system B, with multiple rates the total tax due is far higher for the fluctuating income stream than for the constant income stream. This dependence of tax liability on the time path of income is a relatively small problem for most employees, but for the self–employed, whose income is typically more volatile, it may give rise to serious inequity.

A slightly different version of the same problem arises where the income tax base includes items which are by their nature likely to be irregular receipts. The most obvious example is capital gains. If capital gains form part of the income tax base, the tax charged under a multiple rate system on realised capital gains may seem excessive if the capital gain has accrued over many years and the proceeds are to be consumed over a lengthy period.

**Table 1.3 Comparison of Tax Liability under Systems A and B
for Individuals with Constant and Fluctuating Income Streams**

Income	Tax system A	Tax system B	Income	Tax system A	Tax system B
6000	1000	925	2000	–	135
6000	1000	925	6000	1000	925
6000	1000	925	10000	2000	2070
Total	3000	2775		3000	3130

It seems fair to assume that the greater the number of tax rates a
system employs, the higher will be administrative and compliance costs,
the greater the likelihood of under– or over–payment of tax will be, and
the less clear the understanding of the impact of the system will be. But
if the administration of the tax system has been designed with a multiple
rate system in mind, as is the case in many jurisdictions, these costs
should not be too great. And if there are powerful non–administrative
arguments for a multiple rate system, administrative arguments should
not be adequate to prevent the introduction of such a system, even where
the tradition and current administration is rather different.

Incentives Issues and the Rate Structure

The final major area of debate over the impact of the rate structure is
over the effect of tax rates on incentives to work. Throughout the
developed world the 1980s saw reduction in top rates of income tax
which were defended in terms of their beneficial impact on work
incentives. These issues are discussed at length in Chapter 9 of this
book, but they are closely related to the rate structure and so merit some
discussion here.

It is in general true that for a given distribution of pre–tax income
and a set revenue requirement, a multiple rate tax system will impose
higher marginal tax rates on the higher end of the income distribution,
lower marginal rates on most of the lower end of the income
distribution, but higher marginal rates on a small number of very low
incomes who would be non–taxpayers in a single positive rate system.

Evidence on the relationship between tax rates and incentives to work is still somewhat confusing, although consensus does seem to be emerging. For 'core' groups in the labour market, incentive effects from changes in tax rates seem relatively unimportant, but for groups whose attachment is more marginal, relatively strong effects can be found as a result of very high marginal tax rates. A typical core group is that of 30– to 40–year–old men, while a group less attached to the labour market might be lone parent mothers with very young children. These latter groups tend to face much higher costs of work than core groups and be under less social pressure to be in paid employment.

Multiple rate systems will impose higher marginal rates on those on higher incomes. Whether this will have a serious effect on incentives is to some extent a function of the level of marginal rate. Marginal rates of 98 per cent, as existed in the UK in the late 1970s for investment income, or 83 per cent on earnings, make the return to tax avoidance or evasion so great or the loss from reducing gross income so small that some behavioural effects seem inevitable. When top rates are 40 or 50 per cent, such effects seem less likely. It is also important to note that for groups at the top of the income distribution the measurement of incentive effects is quite difficult. It may, for example, be the case that the main effect of reducing high marginal tax rates is to encourage the taking of entrepreneurial risks, since the returns are so great, or to encourage new graduates to take jobs in industries with high gross incomes in return for very hard work. Measuring hours worked is unlikely to pick up the effects that matter here.

Overall, it seems unlikely that at currently prevailing levels of income tax rates much damage is done to work incentives for high earners, but some must be done and to that extent a multiple rate system does more damage than a single or few rate system.

While multiple rate systems impose higher rates on many on higher incomes, they do impose lower marginal rates than a single routine rate system on many on low incomes. This is often argued to have a beneficial effect on incentives. But this seems an odd suggestion. If the disincentive effect of a marginal tax rate of 40 or 50 per cent is small, we might expect that of a marginal tax rate of 25 or 30 per cent to be even smaller and the positive incentive gain from introducing a lower rate very dubious. This is especially clear when we remember that a lower rate at low incomes necessarily implies some increase in rates at higher incomes. One response to this point is often made: that the combination of income tax and social security system produces marginal tax and benefit withdrawal rates that are very high and produce disincentives. This is certainly true; most clearly discernible and large incentive effects are seen amongst social security benefit recipients. But it is the social security system, not the tax system, which imposes these high marginal withdrawal rates. Small reductions in the marginal income tax rate will do little to help; if anything can be done through the tax system, a move to higher tax free allowances funded by a higher tax rate might be best, since this would remove some on low incomes from tax altogether. Even this would be much less effective than reconsidering social security.

The impact of income tax rates on incentives to work is easily and frequently overstated. To the extent that there are incentive effects, a system with fewer rates will dominate one with more.

Conclusion

The world–wide move towards fewer rates of income tax was driven by worries about work incentives which may have been overstated, a genuine desire to increase simplicity in the tax system and an awareness that progressivity could be achieved without large numbers of tax rates. We seem likely to see those countries that retain structures with more than five tax rates move towards the simpler structures that became so much more common in the 1980s.

References and Further Reading

Cnossen, S. and K. Messere, 'Survey and evaluation of personal income tax systems in OECD member countries', in eds. S. Cnossen and R. M. Bird, *The Personal Income Tax: Phoenix from the Ashes?* North Holland,Amsterdam, 1989.

Dilnot, A. W. and C. N. Morris, 'Progressivity and graduation in income tax', *Fiscal Studies*, Vol. 5, No. 4, pp.23–29, Nov. 1984.

Kesselman, J. R., *Rate Structure and Personal Taxation: Flat Rate or Dual Rate*, Institute of Policy Studies, Victoria University of Wellington, 1990.

Slemrod, J., 'Do Taxes Matter? Lessons from the 1980s'. *American Economic Review, Papers and Proceedings*, Vol. 82, No. 2, pp.250–256, 1992.

OECD, *The Personal Income Tax Base*, OECD, Paris, 1990.

New Zealand
Australia

H224 H25 J32

H32

CHAPTER 2

TAXING FRINGE BENEFITS:
THE NEW ZEALAND AND AUSTRALIAN
EXPERIENCE

Claudia Scott*

Introduction

This article reviews the experience of New Zealand and Australia with regard to the taxation of fringe benefits (FBT). Both countries introduced a fringe benefit tax in the mid-1980s as part of a wider package of tax reform measures. A distinguishing feature, in relation to that in other OECD countries, is that the tax is levied upon employers rather than employees.

Following a brief examination of the features of the fringe benefit tax and the reasons for introducing it, consideration will be given to the impact of the tax on the level and composition of fringe benefits. The information reported on the behavioural response of firms in New Zealand and Australia to the introduction of the FBT relies on data provided by management consultants and other organisations concerned with trends in remuneration levels within the private and public sectors. The criteria of efficiency, equity and administrative simplicity will be used to discuss the merits and demerits of introducing a comprehensive fringe benefit tax - including the case for it being levied on employers rather than employees.

The Tax Treatment of Fringe Benefits

Fringe benefits consist of all non-monetary advantages which an employer provides to an employee for services rendered and form an important component of remuneration packages. Because fringe benefits commonly enjoy favourable tax treatment, they lead to an erosion of the

*Professor of Public Policy, Victoria University of Wellington, New Zealand.

tax base. Revenue authorities often subject the taxation of fringe benefits to review within the context of tax reform strategies aimed at broadening the income tax base. Over recent years, many OECD countries have implemented tax policy measures which are aimed at the more comprehensive and effective tax treatment of fringe benefits.

There is neither universal agreement nor consistency as regards a definition of fringe benefits. One common approach is to define fringe benefits as all advantages, other than monetary salary and wages, in consequence of services rendered or to be rendered by an employee. While in many cases fringe benefits do not take the form of cash payments, there are notable exceptions - which include various kinds of reimbursement allowances, bonuses, joining payments and the like. Employee share schemes are classified as fringe benefits and statutory obligations to provide benefits (e.g. contributions to superannuation schemes or social security funds) may or may not be included in the definition of fringe benefits.

Countries vary according to whether they define fringe benefits in terms of a comprehensive code (which lists kinds of benefits commonly received and their tax treatment) or whether they use a general provision. Whatever the system there are usually some borderline problems in defining fringe benefits for taxation purposes. Fringe benefits are usually defined in an agreement between the employer and the employee.

Governments may provide preferential tax treatment for fringe benefits in order to support another policy goal - for example, encouraging employers to provide pensions and employee share schemes. The policy may support a government's objective of providing assistance to particular industries or sectors (e.g. motor vehicles). Sometimes fringe benefits are treated favourably because the administrative or compliance cost of collecting them would be too high in relation to revenue raised.

Preferential tax treatment of fringe benefits provides an important reason why employees and employers support the substitution of fringe benefits for wages and salaries. Employees benefit from a lower level of income tax and firms benefit from a lower overall cost of labour. Fringe benefits reduce the level of income earned by an employee and this can be advantageous if it gives greater access to income support benefits and reduced rates of contribution into social security funds. Fringe benefits may enhance the quality of the work environment for employees and give enhanced status within the firm or within society. Employers may use them to overcome government constraints or other inflexibilities within salary structures. Fringe benefits such as employee share schemes may encourage firm loyalty and commitment and increased productivity.

The Fringe Benefit Tax in New Zealand and Australia

A quarterly fringe benefit tax was introduced in New Zealand on 1 April 1985 under which all employers who provide their employees with benefits, either directly or indirectly, were liable for fringe benefit tax. An employer is defined as a person who pays 'source deduction payments' (i.e. salary, wages, extra emoluments or a withholding tax payment). Included in this employer definition are the partners in a partnership, managers of unincorporated bodies and the trustees of estates or trusts. An employee is defined as all persons who receive income from salary, wages, extra emoluments or withholding payments. Included in the definition are shareholder employees, future and past employees and associated persons (i.e. an employee's spouse or child). If employers file four consecutive 'nil' returns, or satisfy the Inland Revenue Department that they do not provide or intend to provide taxable fringe benefits, they can apply to file annual rather than quarterly 'nil' returns.

The fringe benefit tax was initially calculated at 45 per cent of the taxable value of fringe benefits. On 1 April 1986 it increased to 48 per cent in line with the top personal tax rate. The 17 December 1987 Statement removed the previous exclusion of fringe benefit tax from life and health insurance, superannuation schemes, accident, sickness or death benefit funds and school fees. When it was introduced, FBT was not allowed as deductible expenditure for income tax purposes. However, since 1 April 1989 the costs incurred in the provision of fringe benefits, including FBT itself, have been tax deductible to the employer on an accruals basis. This measure places FBT on the same footing as PAYE, which has always been deductible.

On 1 April 1989, a new deductible FBT rate of 49 per cent was established. The FBT rate is higher than the top personal tax rate of 33 per cent because FBT is calculated as a proportion of the value of the net fringe benefit, whereas PAYE is calculated as a proportion of gross salary.

The New Zealand FBT identifies five main categories of taxable fringe benefit: the private use of motor vehicles; low interest loans;

free and discounted goods and services; employer contributions to superannuation, sickness, accident and death benefit funds; and lump sum retiring allowances and some categories of redundancy payments.

**Table 2.1 Revenues from the Fringe Benefit Tax
in New Zealand 1985/86-1990/91**

	Fringe benefit tax revenue ($000s)	Percentage of total revenue
1985/86	104503	0.9
1986/87	167761	1.3
1987/88	213931	1.6
1988/89	523431	3.5
1989/90	483451	2.3
1990/91	485011	2.3

Source: Annual Reports, Inland Revenue Department

Table 2.1 shows the pattern of revenues from FBT between 1985/86 and 1990/91. Growth in revenues was rapid over the first four years and peaked in 1988/89. The decline in revenue since 1989 reflects the weak economy and also some tendency for a cashing out of benefits particularly once greater tax neutrality had been achieved.

The Australian FBT

The fringe benefit tax was introduced in Australia to apply as from July 1 1986 to be levied at a rate of 46 per cent for the first nine months and 49 per cent thereafter. Over the past few years it has comprised about 2.5 per cent of government revenue. Its introduction followed vigorous debate and objections from the public and serves as a remnant of a more ambitious pattern of tax reform. Like New Zealand provisions, the tax is levied on employers rather than employees and is paid quarterly. In Australia the first three payments of the year comprise instalments towards an annual assessment.

The legislation for the Australian Fringe Benefits Tax was much broader than the New Zealand legislation (although subsequent changes have served to remove some of the earlier exemptions in New Zealand). All fringe benefits were subject to tax unless specifically exempted and the main benefits nominated were private use of employer-provided vehicles, interest free or low interest loans, release of employee debts, payment of private expenses, free or subsidised rental accommodation or board, living-away-from-home allowances and discounted goods or services (including air travel). Several benefits were excluded such as employee share acquisition schemes, employer-provided recreational facilities, employer contributions to superannuation schemes, free or discounted travel to and from work and relocation and recruitment expenses.

The Impact of Fringe Benefit Tax on Economic Behaviour in New Zealand and Australia

While there is widespread belief that tax regimes have a substantial impact on the utilisation of fringe benefits as a form of remuneration, empirical studies have not demonstrated strong relationships. There is also limited information on the behavioural adjustments by employers and employees to the introduction of an FBT.

It is difficult to measure the separate impact of fringe benefit tax on remuneration packages. A number of factors influence the level and mix of fringe benefits - including changes in income tax rates, incomes policies and market conditions for labour and commodities. As a means of exploring some of these impacts it was decided to examine trends in remuneration packages around the time of the introduction of the tax. It was decided that consistent and reliable results could be obtained by drawing upon the information derived from the regular salary surveys which are conducted by various management consultants. The firms of PA Consulting Group, Price Waterhouse and Deloittes, assisted this research by providing access to their survey information on remuneration trends.

While PA conduct the most comprehensive and reliable salary surveys in New Zealand, certain limitations of the data should be outlined. Fluctuations in the sample size caused difficulties and the analysis excluded individual positions where the sample size was below 25 in any one year. Deriving trends in the composition of fringe benefits by making comparisons over time based on costs may be deceptive. For example, in New Zealand there have been significant changes to previous trends which have arisen from sharp movements in the levels of remuneration, rates of inflation and above average cost increases in some benefits such as low interest loans and motor cars.

In New Zealand, the predominant view is that the tax has led to a reduction in the use of fringe benefits. The Price Waterhouse surveys over the period 1985-88 show a distinct move away from fringe benefits as a result of the FBT - particularly following the December 1987 tax changes which increased the comprehensiveness of coverage. The lowering of personal tax rates relative to the FBT rate provided strong financial incentives for employees and employers to cash out of perks.

The Price Waterhouse survey reports that the introduction of FBT in New Zealand has affected the firm's willingness to provide low interest loans and motor cars. Survey trends have shown some reduction in many fringe benefits with the exceptions of medical insurance and education allowances - which were initially exempt from FBT. Over the 1985-88 period the Price Waterhouse survey sample reported percentage decreases in the take up of fringe benefits ranging from 2 per cent for representation allowances to 13.4 per cent for motor cars. At the time the FBT was introduced it was suggested that those at the top of the organisation might be unaffected by the FBT; however, actual patterns have shown that this is not the case and that reductions have occurred both at the top and further down the organisational structure.

The December 1987 tax changes neutralised the tax advantages of most fringe benefits and later changes to the provisions for FBT together with personal tax modifications provided further disincentives to employees and firms. It is anticipated that as the financial impacts become more widely understood, the trend to move away from benefits to cash alternatives will be even stronger. There is a growing view that fringe benefits are administratively cumbersome and costly. While firms may continue to offer fringe benefits to their top executives and to groups which are hard to recruit and retain, there is some evidence that firms may - in the name of administrative efficiency - wish to limit the coverage of smaller perks.

A significant increase in public sector participation in the 1988 and 1989 PA Salary Surveys has affected the overall trends. Fringe benefit provision within the public sector has increased in recent years in response to the creation of the commercially oriented State-Owned Enterprises, the establishment of a Senior Executive Service within the core state sector and the greater autonomy given to departmental chief executives in negotiating wage settlements.

The relationship between the personal income and fringe benefit tax rates is the most critical determinant of the economic incentives associated with their provision. In the early 1980s when the top marginal income tax rate exceeded 60 per cent and fringe benefits were tax exempt, employers had strong financial incentives to increase the proportion of non-taxed benefits in remuneration packages. Even after the imposition of FBT in April 1985, fringe benefits were still a tax effective form of remuneration, as the top marginal income tax rate remained at 66 per cent, whereas the new FBT rate was 45 per cent and only applied to the net value of fringe benefits. The 1986 tax reform package flattened the personal tax scale and reduced the number of personal tax rates to three. These have subsequently been modified to two rates - 24 per cent and 33 per cent. While the FBT tax rate and top personal tax rate were equalised in October 1986, this did not create a completely tax neutral environment, as fringe benefits were still taxed at their net rather than grossed-up rate. Fringe benefits only became truly tax neutral in April 1989, when a tax-deductible FBT rate of 49 per cent established parity of treatment with the income tax base.

The incremental changes made in the relationship between the FBT and income tax regimes suggests that FBT has had a gradual rather than instantaneous effect on fringe benefit practices. Perhaps the most significant non-tax factor influencing fringe benefit practices was the introduction of the wage and price freeze regulations on 22 June 1982 as part of the National Government's disinflationary strategy. The wage freeze was subsequently lifted by the Labour Administration on 9 November 1984 and was immediately followed by a wage round in which key awards settled at a modest 6-7 per cent. The freeze gave employers considerable incentive to provide additional fringe benefits in lieu of salary increases - given that cash compensation was the primary target of the freeze.

Using data from the PA salary survey for 4 top chief executive positions, there was negative CPI adjusted salary growth recorded from 1982 to 1985, followed by positive growth in the range of 5.5 to 6.2 per cent in 1986. Yet, there is no evidence that companies immediately moved to grant additional fringe benefits to their employees as a means of circumventing the wage freeze. Statistics reveal a slow-down in the annual growth of fringe benefits and this may be attributable to the restraining influence of the freeze. However, the acceleration in fringe benefit growth in 1984 and 1985 points to a substitution of fringe benefits in place of salary adjustments, albeit after a substantial time-lag. The contractions in the inflation adjusted value of fringe benefits recorded in 1986 and 1989 point to the influence of FBT.

Despite the problems associated with isolating the effects of FBT on fringe benefit practices, it is clear that FBT has affected the provision of fringe benefits to top level executives. These results challenge the view that personnel at the top of an organisation were unaffected by FBT. (For instance, Hart (1987, p.9) argues that most companies were 'retaining upper-level executive benefits exactly as they have always been, but reducing the incidence of benefits, such as cars, for lower-level managers.')

Because FBT was introduced as companies were still adjusting their remuneration practices to the post-wage freeze environment, it is difficult to isolate the influence of FBT on fringe benefit practices. A better picture of the effects of FBT can be gained by analysing the impact on benefits which were affected by the December 1987 tax changes. The 17 December 1987 Economic Statement removed the previous FBT exemption enjoyed by life and medical insurance, superannuation schemes, accident, sickness or death benefit funds and school fees. FBT was also extended to lump sum redundancy payments and retirement allowances. In the 1988/89 financial year superannuation contributions and redundancy payments accounted for $373.5 million (67 per cent) of FBT revenue, demonstrating that they substantially expanded the FBT base.

Between 1980 and 1987 the percentage of selected executives receiving medical benefits grew steadily. However, since the September 1987 survey this upward trend has been arrested and a small but discernible downward trend in the provision of medical benefits is apparent. Similar trends emerge after 1987 in the general staff surveys, where a downward movement in the percentage of staff receiving medical benefits can be observed for most positions. The tax treatment of superannuation has been subject to considerable change in the last few years. FBT on superannuation was replaced by a withholding tax in April 1989, which appears to have altered the economic incidence of the tax payments. Price Waterhouse comment in their September 1989 Salary Survey:

'While employers may increase their rate of contribution to existing superannuation schemes in order to meet the same net contribution as previously, the majority have clearly opted for a reduction in the net contribution, i.e. the employee is actually paying the price of the 33% withholding tax.'

On the other hand, Price Waterhouse note that the diminishing role of the Government's Guaranteed Retirement Income scheme may increase the obligation on employers to provide incentives for employees to save for retirement.

The percentage of selected top executives in receipt of employer contributions to superannuation schemes has generally declined since 1985, with a marked downward trend emerging since the 1987 survey. The general staff survey results also show an across-the-board downward movement in the percentage of staff receiving superannuation benefits after 1987, though seven of the thirty positions surveyed showed little change. The removal of FBT exempt status reduced superannuation's use within remuneration packages. The results are all the more significant given that many employers would have responded by reducing the monetary value of superannuation benefits, rather than cutting superannuation out altogether. The trends suggest that employers responded immediately to the removal of the tax exempt status enjoyed by superannuation contributions and medical benefits, in sharp contrast to the lagged response which was apparent with FBT's introduction in 1985. The differences in response to the tax changes underpins the influence of non-tax factors on fringe benefit utilisation.

The provision of company cars to employees warrants detailed examination, given that up to December 1987 cars were the dominant source of fringe benefit tax revenue. The survey found that most companies had made no significant response, with only 8 per cent of the companies having changed their policy in respect of top management and 15 per cent in respect of senior and middle management.

There is a widespread belief that the provision of company cars has been relatively unaffected by the imposition of FBT. Hart (1987, p.11) comments that the company car is a 'New Zealand institution' and has high 'emotional' value, thereby creating conditions of inelastic demand. Further, there is considerable anecdotal evidence of organisations enhancing the provision of company cars despite the imposition of FBT. For instance, all members of the Government's new Senior Executive Service were offered cars, despite the disincentives associated with FBT.

In September 1985 PA Consulting Group surveyed companies to determine the extent to which the introduction of FBT had changed their policies or practices towards the provision of company cars. Despite the reluctance of most employers to move away from the provision of company cars, an analysis of salary survey data suggests that the changed tax environment has had some influence.

From 1983 there was an increase in the average proportion of executive remuneration packages taken up by company cars. However, the lifting of the wage freeze and introduction of FBT may have contributed to an arrest in this growth after the 1985 survey. Since 1987 cars have steadily declined as a proportion of executive remuneration, with the October 1987 share market crash possibly contributing to the downward shift as companies replaced luxury cars with more conventional models. It should also be noted that recent cuts in excise tax have reduced the purchase prices of imported cars.

There have been only minor changes in terms of the percentage of top executives receiving company cars. A small downward trend is apparent for many executive positions after the 1987 survey. An analysis which was undertaken on the percentage of general staff receiving company cars produced inconclusive results. PA's data provides little evidence of a significant move away from the provision of company cars to general staff.

Employers may have reacted to FBT by providing a lower standard of vehicle rather than cutting company cars out completely. However, in their September 1988 survey PA suggests that there is no evidence to suggest that companies are providing a lower standard of vehicle. In cases where employers have cut out the provision of company cars, employees have often been compensated with car allowances. The percentage of top executives receiving car allowances has grown since 1987. This is indicative of an acceptance by employers that in a tax-neutral environment cash is superior to fringe benefits and provides an opportunity for each employee to get better value from a remuneration package.

An analysis was undertaken of trends in fringe benefit provision for top executive staff in selected industry groups. Due to the small sample sizes used in the analysis the results should be interpreted with considerable caution. However, the results do establish that some industry groups have been more responsive to the changed tax environment than others.

Of particular interest has been remuneration trends within the financial service industries. Hart (1987, p.1) noted a two-tier response to fringe benefits - with a grouping of 'new wave' investment, financial and property companies offering remuneration packages which traditional companies were unable to match. The increased demand for qualified personnel which followed the deregulation of the financial sector forced these 'new wave' industries to concentrate on the provision of tax-effective income packages. Accordingly, in the mid-1980s the financial sector led a rapid expansion in fringe benefit provision which other industry groups were forced to emulate in order to retain staff.

The PA data shows a rapid growth in fringe benefit trends upward within the financial services sector until the September 1985 salary survey. In 1986 and 1987 there was a significant fall off in the proportion of total cash compensation comprised of fringe benefits. However, these patterns of fringe benefit utilisation have not been unique to the financial services sector. Similar trends were observed in the construction, contracting and chemicals sector groups.

Salary survey data over the past decade reveals general reductions in fringe benefits in response to the introduction of FBT, particularly following the December 1987 tax changes. However, it is clear that these reductions have not been as significant as may have been expected. A number of factors could account for this. Firstly, the on-going effects of the wage-price freeze saw the value of fringe benefits continue to grow in the PA September 1985 salary survey. Secondly, demand for some fringe benefits appears to have been relatively inelastic, with company cars being the most obvious example. Finally and most importantly, fringe benefits continued to be a tax effective form of compensation despite the imposition of FBT in 1985. Complete tax neutrality between cash income and fringe benefits was not finally achieved until April 1989. All of these factors contributed to a lagged and muted reaction to the imposition of FBT.

With the recent attainment of a tax neutral remuneration environment, significant movement away from the provision of fringe benefits can now be expected. Further, there is growing evidence that firms are changing their institutional practices to accommodate the new tax environment. The September 1989 Price Waterhouse survey argues that the most notable trend relating to fringe benefits over the past two years has been the movement towards flexible benefit packages and total remuneration policies - where employees are set a notional base salary and then negotiate between cash and preferred benefits. Between September 1988 and March 1989 7 per cent of participants in the Price Waterhouse executive remuneration survey had moved on to a total remuneration packaging concept, or intended doing so. Institutional measures such as these will be just as critical as economic incentives to achieving further reductions in the utilisation of fringe benefits.

The Impact of FBT in Australia

Information compiled from the December 1984 Price Waterhouse and Associated Pty Ltd *Top 5 Plus* Executives Compensation Report gives a clear indication that the money equivalent of most benefits rises with the size of earnings and forms a substantial part of total remuneration at higher levels of income. Individuals higher up the income scale stand a better chance both of receiving a range of fringe benefits and of enjoying them at more generous levels. For example, a Data Processing Executive with a total package of $42,692, received about one seventh in fringe benefits whereas a chief executive whose total remuneration package was $85,530 received just over one quarter of it in benefits.

Reactions from the business community to the FBT were strong and in late October, 1986, a number of modifications to the tax were announced which reduced revenue estimates by $75 million. The system was streamlined administratively in terms of the bookkeeping required by employees and employers, some new exemptions were introduced and a higher threshold was introduced on free or discounted goods.

A 1986 Australian Bureau of Statistics survey of fringe benefits indicated that the most common types of benefits enjoyed by employees were in the area of goods and services, with 18.9 per cent of all employees receiving such benefits. Telephone (7.8 per cent) and transport (7 per cent) benefits were the next most popular fringe benefits. About 3.9 per cent received holiday expenses and less than 3.3 per cent enjoyed benefits in the areas of housing, medical, low-interest finance, entertainment, union dues, electricity, shares and club fees. Between 1984 and 1986 there was a 2.5 per cent drop in the proportion of employees receiving goods and services benefits and a small overall drop in all other categories mentioned above - apart from holiday expenses which remained at 3.9 per cent.

The most commonly received fringe benefit, goods and services, experienced a large increase of 15.5 per cent in the year 1983/84 but dropped away again in 1984/85 by 3.8 per cent and in 1985/86 by 2.9 per cent. Similarly, other categories of benefit experienced significant increases in the year 1983/84 ranging from 25.9 per cent for union dues at the high end to 4.8 per cent for shares at the low end. The trend across the two following years is rather one of reduction in employee numbers receiving benefits than of increase. The reduction of 57.4 per cent in entertainment allowances in 1985/86 is the largest. It was suggested that the sharp downturn in numbers of employees receiving fringe benefits between August 1984 and August 1985 and which continued for several categories of benefit over the August 1985/86 period, can be attributed to the anticipation and implementation of the fringe benefit tax.

The August 1986 ABS Employment Benefits Survey indicates that about 21 per cent of all employees in Australia received one or more taxable benefits, 8 per cent receiving more than one such benefit. There are clear indications that most benefits are more frequently enjoyed by employees on higher incomes. The survey categorised employees in four income groupings: under $200, $200-360, $360-520 and over $520 per week. There was a fairly even spread of the proportion of employees who received goods and service benefits over these four income groups, with a slight weighting towards the two lower income groups. However, in all other areas of benefit there was a weighting of benefits towards the two higher income groups with 17.9 per cent of the top group and 8.8 per cent of the $360-520 group being in receipt of transport benefits. A greater proportion of the top two income groups also enjoyed telephone benefits at 7.4 per cent for the over $520 group and 10.1 per cent for the other. Other benefits ranged from nil to 2.3 per cent in the bottom income range, in comparison with 2.9 per cent to 6.6 per cent for the top income range. Other benefits included entertainment allowances, housing holiday expenses, medical, low-interest finance, union dues, electricity club fees and shares.

The Australian experience shows some substantial modifications to behaviour around the time of the introduction of the FBT. However, a report (*Australian Financial Review*, 16 November, 1988) has suggested that the proportion of the workforce receiving fringe benefits has stabilised after a sharp fall in the wake of the fringe benefit tax.

Because of the privileged position of superannuation in the Australian scheme there has been a tendency for superannuation benefits to grow. While 39.5 per cent received super benefits in 1984 and 39.9 per cent in 1987, the share increased to 41.4 per cent in 1988. Almost two thirds of public sector and one third of private sector workers have superannuation benefits. Benefits such as sick leave, long-service leave and annual leave are also more prevalent among public servants.

Private sector employees are more likely to receive taxable fringe benefits such as company cars, entertainment allowances, subsidised loans and the payment of school, club or other fees. The company car receives concessional treatment under the tax arrangements and has been the least affected of fringe benefits. The 1988 survey shows 15.4 per cent of workers received this benefit, compared with 14.7 per cent in the previous year.

The demise of entertainment allowances at the time the tax was introduced has continued, with only 1.7 per cent of employees receiving this form of benefit. This is in sharp contrast to the 4.7 per cent who received it in 1984. Discounted shares to employees are not affected by the fringe benefit tax and have grown slightly, receiving some stimulation from the introduction of dividend imputation. Benefits have risen from 1.5 per cent of the workforce in 1984 to 1.8 per cent in 1988. The overall share of workers receiving some form of benefit has stabilised - moving from a decline from 89.6 per cent in 1984 to 88.9 per cent in 1985 to 87.7 per cent in 1986 and 87.3 per cent in 1987, with a small increase to 87.5 per cent in 1988.

The survey indicates that employers are narrowing the range of fringe benefits offered and are specialising in goods and services they can provide 'in house'. For example, of the 2.9 per cent of employees who received low-interest finance, 64.6 per cent were employed in the finance sector, while of the 15.5 per cent receiving discounted goods and services, 45.4 per cent were employed in retailing and wholesaling.

The evidence available suggests that the response to FBT in Australia was much stronger than in New Zealand, Australian employers reacted more harshly to the fringe benefits tax and certain modifications and a softening of the provisions was introduced - for example, the FBT on cars was lowered as a response to opposition to the rate.

The impact of the Australian FBT appears to have been felt hardest by middle level executives. While earlier trends suggested that this group had experienced a significant rise in benefit levels over the past 15 years, the Australian FBT appears to have created incentives for firms to withdraw fringes. Remuneration packages have become less complex and there has been a tendency to shift into non-taxable forms of fringe benefit.

The Rationale for Taxing Fringe Benefits

It is widely accepted that when fringe benefits are not subject to tax, there will be substantial distortions to the form of employee compensation. Employees will receive a larger share of remuneration in the form of fringe benefits (and less cash income) which will create substantial economic distortions and erode the income tax base. In countries where separate social security taxes are levied on wages, these distortions extend from the tax to the social security system.

Tax policy reforms can be judged having regard to the criteria of economic efficiency, horizontal and vertical equity and administrative simplicity. Collins (1987) provides a clear exposition of the efficiency and equity case for fringe benefits based on the need to maintain the comprehensive taxation of income. The definition of comprehensiveness lies in the Haig-Simons concept of income which embodies the 'accretion' principle - the accretion in the taxpayer's command over economic resources measured over a period of time. All receipts should be included in this definition of comprehensive income including wages, salaries, capital gains, non-pecuniary income, bequests, gambling winnings and fringe benefits. Any preferential treatment of one element of comprehensive income will lead to inefficiency as resources are reallocated to the more favoured form. Erosion of the tax base leads to the need to have higher rates to reach any revenue target and this creates larger tax wedges (and deadweight losses) between pre- and post-tax prices for goods and services in the economy.

Failure to tax fringe benefits comprehensively also leads to losses of both horizontal and vertical equity. Opportunities to exploit the tax advantages of preferential treatments of fringe benefits are not evenly distributed either within or across income group(s) resulting in a different assignment of tax burdens from that intended by the legislators. Evidence suggests that higher income groups have greater access to fringe benefits and this means that failure to tax fringe benefits comprehensively will reduce the progressivity of the overall tax burden.

The issue of administrative simplicity concerns the administrative and compliance costs associated with the tax. The case for imposing fringe benefit taxes on firms rather than on individuals is based on the fact that this will lead to lower administrative and compliance costs and higher revenue. The higher revenues result both from higher rates of compliance by firms than by individuals and the fact that the company tax rate is at a level which exceeds the personal tax rates of at least some workers.

In addressing the issues of where the tax should be imposed, it is important to consider the economic incidence (or burden) of the tax. Legal incidence identifies who is legally responsible for paying the tax whereas economic incidence shows how real incomes are reduced as a result of imposing the tax. Economic and legal incidence need not be the same because the economic liability of the tax may be shifted. For example, if employers are liable for fringe benefit tax, they may suggest to their employees that these increased costs have led to profit reductions and make some adjustment to the remuneration levels of the employees. If this occurs, then the burden of the tax is shifted or shared, meaning that the employee has accepted some of its burden arising from a reduction in remuneration levels. Conversely, if the tax is imposed on the employee, the employer may be asked to compensate for the reduction in real income caused by the tax. If this is granted, then the tax will have been shifted, in part, to the employer.

Quite apart from where the tax is originally imposed, the economic burden of it will depend on the sensitivity of the employers' demand for labour when total labour costs increase, in relation to the sensitivity of the employees' supply of labour with respect to changes in their real after-tax income. If employers are likely to reduce labour demand if costs rise, then this will result in forces which encourage employees to bear more of the burden. If employees are likely to reduce labour supply if remuneration levels fall, then this will encourage employers to bear more of the burden.

Summary

There have been some noticeable similarities and differences between the Australian and New Zealand experiences with the FBT. While the Australians appear to have reacted to a greater degree, evidence from both countries shows a trend away from fringe benefits towards cash income. Also in common is an increase in the availability of flexible packages of fringes, together with an increase in performance-oriented packages - which contain elements such as profit sharing and open-ended bonuses. There is a growing tendency to provide inducements to attract people into key positions. Increasingly remuneration is being negotiated to provide an individual package based on total remuneration cost rather than salary plus standard fringes.

The levying of an FBT on employers in New Zealand and Australia has received considerable support from revenue authorities but questions remain as to the incentive effects of levying tax on the employers rather than the employee. The approach has provided greater security of the revenue base and lower administrative and compliance costs. However, so long as more than one marginal tax rate exists, it is clear that the administrative efficiency gains from imposing the tax on employers has been achieved at some cost in terms of the greater neutrality which would result from imposing the tax on individuals.

References and Further Reading

Adamache, K. W. and F. A. Sloan, 'Fringe Benefits: To Tax or Not to Tax?', *National Tax Journal*, Vol. XXXVIII, No.1, pp.47-64, March 1985.

Collins, D. J., 'Taxation of Fringe Benefits - An Economist's Perspective', *Australian Tax Forum: a journal of taxation policy, law and reform*, Vol. 4, No. 1, 1987.

Elmgreen, J., *Reform of Fringe Benefits Taxation*, Australian Tax Research Foundation, Sydney, 1986.

Hart, R. A., *The Economics of Non-Wage Labour Costs*, George Allen & Unwin, London, 1984.

Hart, Simon, *Executive Remuneration Packages,* New Zealand Society of Accountants, May 1987.

Katz, A. and N. G. Mankiw, 'How Should Fringe Benefits be Taxed?', *National Tax Journal*, Vol. 38, No. 1, 1985.

Long, J. E. and F. A. Scott, 'The Impact of the 1981 Tax Act on Fringe Benefits and Federal Tax Revenues', *National Tax Journal*, Vol. XXXVII, No. 2, pp.185-94, June 1984.

Long, J. E. and F. A. Scott, 'The Income Tax and Non-wage Compensation', *Review of Economics and Statistics*, Vol. 64, pp.211-18, May 1982.

Norman, Neville R., *FBT and the Way We Pay*, Information Paper No. IP25, Committee for Economic Development in Australia, 1988.

Owens, J., 'The Tax Treatment of Fringe Benefits', *OECD Observer*, No. 150, pp.25-27, 1988.

Rigby, M. P., 'The Taxation of Fringe Benefits', *Victoria University Law Review,* Vol. 15, pp.301-332, 1985.

Sloan, F. A. and K. W. Adamache, 'Taxation and Growth of Non-wage Compensation', *Public Finance Quarterly,* Vol. 14, No. 2, pp.115-137, April 1986.

Turner, R. W., 'Are Taxes Responsible for the Growth in Fringe Benefits?', *National Tax Journal*, Vol. XL, No. 2, pp.185-94 & 205-220, June 1987.

Woodbury, S. A., 'Substitution Between Wage and Non-wage Benefits', *American Economic Review*, Vol. 73, pp.166-82, March 1983.

OECD, *The Taxation of Fringe Benefits*, Paris 1988.

CHAPTER 3

WHAT KIND OF CORPORATION TAX?

Sijbren Cnossen*

Introduction

Corporation taxes are important because corporations are social and economic institutions of great impact. As separate legal entities, corporations have the power to contract, the right to hold and convey title to property, the capacity to sue and to be sued, and the authority to make rules and bylaws. Corporations have a life independent of the lives of their shareholders, they beget offspring, called subsidiaries, and, in principle, corporations are legally immortal. The power of a large transnational corporation approximates that of the government of a medium-sized country. Although no doubt there are exceptions, the total impact of a corporation is truly more than the sum of the influence of the constituent parts.

The social and economic importance of the 'finding' of the corporate form of business organization has rightly been compared to the discovery of steam and electricity[1]. Corporations have reshaped the world in which we live. In most countries, a large part of the national product is generated in the corporate sector and its activities exercise a profound influence on the remainder of the economy. Modern industrial development is absolutely unthinkable without the corporate business form in which capital and labour are combined for mutually beneficial

---

[1]For the reference, see Goode (1951), p.11.

*Professor in the Economics Faculty of Erasmus University Rotterdam. This paper is an updated and expanded version of two earlier publications: 'The Imputation System in the EEC', in Sijbren Cnossen (ed.), *Comparative Tax Studies: Essays in Honor of Richard Goode*, Amsterdam, North Holland, 1983, and 'Corporation Taxes in OECD Member Countries', in *Bulletin for International Fiscal Documentation*, Vol. 38/11, November 1984. The author is grateful to Lans Bovenberg for his comments on an earlier draft.

productive purposes. Without exaggeration, the corporation may be characterized as 'the central economic institution of modern society[1].

This paper surveys and evaluates the various forms of tax that are imposed on corporate profits. As a tax on the return on equity, the corporation tax interacts with the individual income tax of shareholders entitled to corporate profits. In tax law and theory, such interaction may be denied or explicitly recognized and reflected in the form of the tax.

The second section, therefore, delineates the various forms of corporation tax and reviews their role in the countries that are members of the Organization for Economic Cooperation and Development (OECD).

The third section discusses the two poles of the corporation tax philosophy: the classical system that views the corporation as an entity distinct from its shareholders, and the conduit system that regards it as an extension of those shareholders. In practice, the corporation tax and the income tax are integrated only with respect to the taxation of distributed profits. Consequently, the fourth and fifth sections examine the schemes for such integration at corporate level and at shareholder level. The sixth section compares the various systems, noting the degrees of dividend relief and the remaining discrimination of payout decisions and methods of finance. Finally, the seventh section evaluates the various systems.

The Role of the Corporation Tax

The role of the corporation tax in various countries, particularly as regards its relationship to the income tax, is reflected in the forms of the tax. Forms differ as shown by a survey of corporation taxes in OECD member countries.

Forms of Corporation Tax

Figure 3.1 presents the various forms of corporation tax that can be distinguished depending on whether and to what extent they are integrated with the income tax of shareholders. At one extreme, the corporation is regarded as an entity entirely separate from its

---

[1]See Mason (1968), p.396, in International Encyclopedia of the Social Sciences.

shareholders and taxed as such (classical system).[1] At the other extreme, the corporation is viewed as a pass-through, a conduit, of all corporate source income of shareholders - distributed as well as undistributed earnings. The corporation tax, if retained, serves solely as a prepayment for the income tax, just like a wage withholding scheme.

Figure 3.1

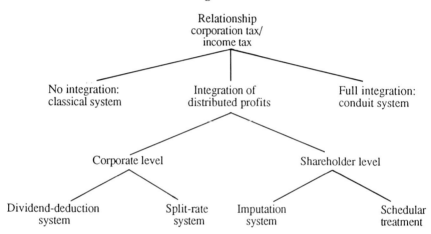

In practice, the integration of the corporation tax with the income tax of shareholders is limited to distributed profits (dividends). This form of partial integration, often referred to as dividend relief, can be achieved at either corporate level or at shareholder level. The most obvious method of dividend relief at the corporate level is to permit a deduction for dividends from taxable profits, as is commonly done for interest. This is called the dividend-deduction system. Another approach that can achieve

[1]The label 'classical system' was introduced by Van den Tempel (1970, p.7). It should be noted, however, that, contrary to what the terminology suggests, the imputation system, discussed below, is of older date. In the 19th century, some German states already had some form of imputation and in 1922 it was incorporated as the withholding method in the Model Income Tax Ordinance of the United Kingdom, which was introduced in many colonies. For the classic treatment of the separate entity system, see Goode (1951).

the same result is the split-rate system, under which a lower rate of tax is levied on distributed profits. At shareholder level, dividend relief may be achieved systematically under the imputation system, which permits shareholders a full or partial credit for the corporation tax that can be imputed to the dividends received by them. Alternatively, dividend relief may be provided by taxing dividend income on a schedular basis, e.g. by applying a separate flat tax to it or by allowing shareholders a tax credit against their income tax without regard to the underlying corporation tax. The workings of all of these systems will be discussed below.

The concern over the appropriate form of corporation tax arises because, under the classical system, corporate source income is taxed twice if it is distributed: once at corporate level and again at shareholder level. In the tax literature, this phenomenon is referred to as the 'economic double taxation of dividends.'[1] The existence of a separate corporation tax means that dividends will be 'overtaxed' compared to other capital income, such as interest. The label is pejorative, however, in the sense that retained corporate source income may be 'undertaxed' if the rate of corporation tax is lower than the rate of income tax at which dividends would be taxed at shareholder level under full imputation. In the latter case, the separate corporation tax may be said to be biased in favour of retained profits. In a broader (and more correct) view, the real issue is not that dividend income is taxed twice or that the separate corporation tax exhibits a tax bias, but that corporate source income, distributed as well as retained earnings, is not taxed in accordance with the marginal income tax rates of shareholders.

Survey of Corporation Taxes

Table 3.1 shows the various corporation tax systems in OECD member countries, their rates (including the corporation tax, if any, levied by subordinate units of government) and contribution to revenue, and particulars about the way and the extent to which dividend relief is provided. Out of 24 countries, four countries levy the corporation tax in its pure classical garb: dividend income is subject to the twin yoke of the corporation tax and the personal income tax. In contrast, 20 countries permit some form of dividend relief either at the corporate level (3 countries) or at the shareholder level (17 countries). At the corporate level, the dividend-deduction system is found in three countries, while

---

[1]The classic treatment of the double-taxation issue is McLure (1979).

Table 3.1 Corporation Taxes in OECD Member Countries, 1992

System and countries covered	Total CT-rate[1]	Mitigation of economic double taxation[2]	Revenue contribution[3]	
			As percent of total tax revenue	As percent of GDP
I. Classical Systems				
Luxembourg	39.4	Relief for newly issued shares[4]	16.2	8.2
Netherlands	35	None.[5]	7.6	3.4
Switzerland	30.3	None.	6.5	2.1
United States	38.3	None.	7.3	2.2
II A. Dividend Relief at Corporate Level				
1. Dividend deduction				
Greece	46(40)	Generally, 50% withholding tax is final.	5.6	2.1
Ireland	45	Deductible and exempt from PT (up to maximum) up to 15% of share value.[4]	2.8	0.9
2. Split-rate (None)				
Sweden	30	Deductible up to 10% of share value.	3.1	1.8
II B. Dividend Relief at Shareholder Level				
1. Imputation				
a. Full				
Australia	39	Gross-up and credit of $39/81$ of net dividend.	13.9	4.3
Finland	40.2	Gross-up and credit for CT at 40%.	5.5	2.1
Germany	58.1/45.5	Gross-up and credit for CG-CT of 36%	4.7	1.8
Italy	47.8	Gross-up and credit for CG-CT of 36%.	10.0	3.9
New Zealand	33	Gross-up and credit of $33/67$ of net dividend.	6.5	2.5
Norway	28	Gross-up and credit of $7/18$ of net dividend.	8.9	4.1
b. Partial				
France	34/42	Gross-up and credit of 50% of net div dend.[5]	5.4	2.3
Ireland	40(10)	Gross-up and credit of $1/3$ ($1/18$) of net dividend.[5]	5.0	1.8
United Kingdom	33	Gross-up and credit of $1/3$ of net dividend.	11.0	4.0
2. Schedular treatment				
a. Separate Tax				
Austria	39	Dividends taxed at one-half of PT-rate.[4,5]	3.3	1.4
Belgium	39	Generally, 25% withholding tax is final.[6]	6.4	2.9
Denmark	38	Dividends taxed at 45% (30% up to DKr 30,000).	3.3	1.6
Japan	51	Generally, 35% withholding tax is final.[6]	21.5	6.7
Portugal	39.6	Generally, 25% withholding tax is final.[6]	7.4	2.6
Turkey	49.2	Dividends exempt.	6.7	1.9
b. Tax Credit				
Canada	44.3(38.3)	Gross-up and tax credit of approximately 25%.	6.8	2.5
Spain	35.3	Tax credit of 10% of dividends received.	8.8	3.0

Notes:
[1] See Appendix.
[2] CG = Central Government; SG = Subordinate Government; CT = Corporation Tax; PT = Personal Income Tax.
[3] Revenue figures relate to fiscal years 1990 as reported in OECD (1992).
[4] Subject to maximum, newly issued shares are deductible from taxable income.
[5] Basic PT-exemption applies to dividend and interest income (usually doubled for married couples).
[6] At the choice of the taxpayer. Credit for withholding tax if dividend included in taxable PT-income.

Source: See Appendix. Revenue figures are from OECD (1992).

the split-rate system, as such, is not employed any more. At the shareholder level, nine countries have a full or partial imputation system. Eight countries tax dividend income on a schedular basis. Germany has a mixed imputation/split-rate system: distributed profits are taxed at a lower rate than are retained profits, and the corporation tax attributable to distributed profits is fully eliminated at shareholder level (at least if the local corporation tax is ignored). In contrast, France taxes distributed profits at a higher rate than retained profits. The domestic degree of integration or dividend relief can be made the same under the dividend-deduction system, the split-rate system, and the imputation system (but not the schedular methods), if it is assumed that the choice of the integration system does not affect the payout rate[1].

As Table 3.1 indicates, most (total) corporation tax rates lie in the 35-45 per cent range. The unweighted average rate (on retained profits, if differentiated) for all OECD countries is 39.7 per cent. Since 1983, when the previous survey was undertaken, the average rate has fallen by some eight percentage-points, reflecting the worldwide move of rate-lowering and base-broadening that occurred in the late 1980s.[2] Not surprisingly, the average corporation tax rate is somewhat higher in countries with some form of dividend relief than in countries with a pure classical system. Norway has the lowest overall tax rate of 28 per cent.

In addition to the national corporation tax, several countries, often with federal forms of government, have local corporation taxes (see Appendix) which, if differentially applied, are generally condemned in the professional literature because of their distorting effects on the location of investment. The case is also weak for levying lower rates of tax, as many countries do, on small amounts of profits that are not necessarily characteristic of small companies. Such rates do impart a slight degree of progressivity to the corporation tax but, except by coincidence, this does not have to reflect the tax burden distribution at shareholder level. It should be noted that effective rates of tax, i.e. actual tax payments expressed as a percentage of 'economic income,' may vary widely, within countries as well as between countries, on account of differences in the way in which taxable profits are determined.[3]

Several countries have changed their corporation tax system in the past decade. Australia and New Zealand moved away from the classical system to the full imputation system; Finland and Norway did so from

[1]For the formal proof, see the Appendix in Cnossen (1983).
[2]For an overview, see Cnossen and Bird (1990), Table 1.1.
[3]See OECD (1991) for an overview and analysis.

the dividend-deduction system. The split-rate system was abandoned in Austria, Japan, and Portugal in favour of some form of relief at shareholder level. Perhaps the most interesting development in the past years is the increasing schedular treatment of dividends under the personal income tax. Most changes reflect concern with the domestic effects of the corporation tax on payout and investment decisions rather than considerations pertaining to international neutrality.

With few exceptions, the corporation tax is not a major source of revenue. In 1990, the corporation tax, on average, contributed 7.7 per cent of total tax revenue, or 2.9 per cent of Gross Domestic Product (GDP), when total tax revenue, on average, was 38.8 per cent of GDP. (Comparable figures for 1982 were 7.8 per cent, 2.8 per cent, and 36.2 per cent, respectively). The yield of the corporation tax, of course, depends not only on the rate and the method and degree of dividend relief, but also on the extent of incorporation. Without further analysis, a comparison of inter-country yields, therefore, makes little sense. It should be noted that the yield of imputation systems includes the (creditable) 'income tax' portion, whereas integration systems at corporate level, of course, leave the income tax out of account. Although in most countries the corporation tax is not a negligible source of revenue, its yield seems disproportionately smaller than the attention, also in this paper, devoted to its form and structure. One reason may be that the corporation tax acts as a backstop to the income tax. Whatever the case, even corporations that pay little or no tax are still subjected to all its complexities, attendant compliance costs, and excess burdens.

Classical System versus Full Integration

The essence of the corporation tax debate can best be illustrated by contrasting the classical system with the conduit or full integration system. The case for full integration can be made on equity as well as efficiency grounds.

Classical System

Four OECD member countries have the separate entity system of corporation tax (Table 3.1), including a major economy such as the United States. (The Netherlands exempts a small amount of dividend income at shareholder level, but this does not really affect the classical nature of the system). In computing taxable profits, classical systems do not allow a deduction for profit distributions (dividends) to shareholders. Moreover, those distributions are taxed again in full in their hands at rates that differ from one shareholder to another - depending on the dividend amount and their other income - but that may range from the lowest to the highest marginal rate of the progressive income tax.

The workings of the classical system are illustrated in Example 1. It is assumed that the profits of a corporation before dividend distribution and corporation tax are £300, which are taxed at a rate of 40 per cent. Remaining profits of £180 are distributed in full and taxed again at shareholder level at individual income tax rates of, say, 30 per cent or 50 per cent, resulting in income tax liabilities of £54 and £90, respectively. Combined corporation and income tax payments are £174 or £210. When expressed as a percentage of original corporate source income, these payments translate into effective tax rates of 58 per cent for the 30 per cent bracket and 70 per cent for the shareholder whose dividend falls in the 50 per cent bracket. If these effective rates, in turn, are compared to the appropriate marginal tax rate of each shareholder, the dividend income of the 30 per cent shareholder is 'overtaxed' by 93 per cent and that of the 50 per cent shareholder by 40 per cent.

Example 1
Classical system

		(£)	
A.	Corporate level		
	1.Profits before corporation tax	300	
	2.Corporation tax: 40% (1 x 2)	120	
B.	Shareholder level		
	3.Income tax rate	30%	50%
	4.Dividend income (1 − 2)	180	180
	5.Income tax (3 x 4)	54	90
C.	Combined tax burden		
	6.Total tax (2 + 5)	174	210
	7.Effective tax rate (6 + 1)	58%	70%
	8.Overtaxation [(7 − 3) + 3]	93%	40%

However, this is not the only possible outcome. As noted above, corporate source income, if retained, may also be undertaxed compared to the marginal tax rate of the shareholder. If, in Example 1, all profits would have been retained in the corporation, the effective tax rate for both shareholders would have been 40 per cent. In other words, the 30 per cent shareholder would still be overtaxed, namely 33 per cent, but the 50 per cent shareholder would be undertaxed by 25 per cent. Furthermore, if half of profits after tax had been distributed (probably a more realistic situation than either no or full distribution), the 50 per cent shareholder would be taxed roughly in accordance with his marginal income tax rate, but the 30 per cent shareholder would still be overtaxed by 63 per cent.

Proponents of the classical system deny the relevancy of the interaction between the two taxes. They point out that ownership and control functions have been completely divorced from each other in the large public corporation and that shareholders, except in rare instances, have no legal claim on earnings until dividends are declared by management. In their view, shareholders are little more than subordinate creditors. However, this argument does not provide an explanation for the difference in tax treatment of retained profits, dividends and interest.

Economic Distortions

Whatever the argument that the separate personality of a corporation justifies a separate tax, the systematic overtaxation of distributed profits under the classical system brings a number of undesirable economic effects in its train, which deserve to be taken seriously.

The distortionary effect on investment of taxing profit distributions twice depends on the marginal source of equity finance, which may be retained profits or newly issued shares. If firms finance their investments through profit retention rather than new shares, they have to reduce dividends that would otherwise be available for distribution. Accordingly, the role of dividends is crucial. In this connection, the literature has developed two hypotheses, which are known as the 'traditional view' and the 'new view,' respectively[1].

The traditional view argues that dividend payouts offer non-fiscal benefits. Dividends may provide a signal to shareholders that all is well with the company, or they may limit financial discretion and, hence, potential misuse of funds by management. At the margin, therefore,

[1]For a review and analysis, see Poterba and Summers (1985), Sinn (1985) and, more recently, Zodrow (1991).

companies equalize the tax advantages of profit retention and the non-fiscal disadvantages of reducing profit distributions. Accordingly, a new investment will in part be financed by issuing new shares, because dividends cannot be lowered without cost. This implies that the double tax on dividends discourages new investment and distorts the dividend-payout decision.

The 'new view' denies the existence of nonfiscal advantages associated with profit distributions. Accordingly, the double tax on dividends should cause corporations to prefer profit retention over new share issues as the marginal source of finance. Profit retention enables shareholders to enjoy the return on the new investment in the form of tax-preferred capital gains. Moreover, they save on the personal income tax on dividend income that they would have had to pay if profits had not been retained but distributed. The capitalized value of this tax saving is exactly equal to the discounted value of the tax on distributed profits that must be paid in the future. Therefore, the argument goes, the tax on dividends does not distort investment decisions - at least not as long as the company generates sufficient profits to finance marginal investments through retained profits and the tax rate on dividends is expected to remain constant over time.

Most empirical studies support the traditional view[1]. Companies clearly have alternative means of distributing funds other than taxable dividends. This weakens the new view. Furthermore, an important implication of the new view is that the market value of corporate assets exceeds existing share values. This does not seem to be the case. Whatever view is adopted, the double tax always harms investment by new businesses, which have to rely on new share issues to provide for their equity needs.[2] The discrimination against new equity under the classical system, therefore, contributes to the concentration of market power. The double tax is especially detrimental to small, growing firms that face difficulties in attracting debt, as they do not yet enjoy a high credit rating or generate sufficient taxable profits to be able to deduct interest. Consequently, these firms, which provide an important impetus to technological innovation, have to incur higher capital costs on account of taxation than do older, established firms with easier access to debt financing, or with sufficient retained profits to finance new investments.

[1] See Zodrow (1991) for a review of empirical work.
[2] It applies also to firms in which management is far removed from shareholders and a dividend reduction in any one year would thus be costly to management.

Full Integration

The economic distortions caused by the classical system should not occur in a fully transparent, competitive world in which the corporation tax would be integrated with the income tax of shareholders. The corporation would then serve only as a conduit, a pass-through, of corporate source income, which would be taxed fully at the appropriate marginal income tax rate in the hands of shareholders. Example 2 illustrates the workings of full integration. For income tax purposes, it is irrelevant whether a corporation distributes profits and, if so, to what extent. Retained as well as distributed profits are fully taxed according to the partnership method; that is, they are allocated in proportion to each shareholder's holding in the corporation's equity. The corporation tax is simply a prepayment for the income tax. It follows, of course, that effective rates are equal to respective bracket rates; there is no overtaxation.

Example 2
Full integration

		(£)	
A.	Corporate level		
	1. Profits before corporation tax	300	
	2. Corporation tax: 40% (1 x 2)	120	
B.	Shareholder level		
	3. Income tax rate	30%	50%
	4. Attributed profits (1)	300	300
	5. Income tax (3 x 4)	90	150
	6. Corporation withholding tax (2)	120	120
	7. Net income tax (5 – 6)	–30	30
C.	Combined tax burden		
	8. Total tax (5 or 2 + 7)	90	150
	9. Effective tax rate (8 ÷ 1)	30%	50%
	10. Overtaxation [(9 – 3) ÷ 3]	0%	0%
	11. Tax relief [(classical overtaxation – 10) ÷ classical overtaxation)]	100%	100%

Full integration is one of the normative implications of the accretion concept of income, as formulated by Schanz, Haig, and Simons (S-H-S concept). Its advocates point out that ability-to-pay, being an equity notion, can only be related to natural persons. It follows that if income is chosen as the best index of that ability, the equal treatment rule requires that income should be defined all-inclusive. For tax purposes there should be no difference between corporate profits and other capital income, such as interest and rents, or labour income, such as wages and salaries, which is solely subject to the individual income tax. There is no place, therefore, for an extra tax on distributed profits nor, it should be added, for the preferential treatment of profits retained by the corporation and taxed below the marginal income tax rate of shareholders.

Full integration of retained as well as distributed profits has been proposed by the Royal (Carter) Commission in Canada, the United States Treasury (*Blueprints*), and the Campbell Committee in Australia. Under both the voluntary and mandatory plans, all corporate source income would be included in the income of shareholders, while a full credit would be permitted for the corporate tax paid on their behalf. To prevent double taxation of retentions, the basis for corporate shares would be written up by the amount of retained profits. These plans, however ingenious, have never left the drawing board, primarily because they are considered impractical. In particular, it has been pointed out that full integration would be costly to the treasury, that delays in completing corporation tax assessments would have repercussions on the filing of shareholders' income tax returns, that it would be difficult to deal with different types of equity, that an undesirable side-effect might be that preferential income items would be passed through to shareholders, and last but not least, that shareholders might have to pay additional income tax, although no cash had in fact been received[1].

Full integration has been characterized as the search for a perfect solution in an imperfect world. Yet at the same time it has been considered important to eliminate or mitigate the economic distortions of the classical system. As a halfway house to the ideal, various dividend relief systems have been introduced under which at least distributed profits can be taxed in accordance with the shareholder's marginal income tax rate. These dividend relief systems are discussed in the following sections[2].

---

[1] See, especially, McLure (1979), ch. 5.
[2] A useful discussion of the nature and history of various dividend relief systems may be found in Norr (1982). For an up-to-date analysis, see also United States Department of the Treasury (1992).

Dividend Relief at Corporate Level

The most obvious approach to the double-taxation issue is to permit dividends as a deduction from taxable profits, as is the case with interest. An alternative would be to tax distributed profits at a lower rate. The dividend-deduction system and the split-rate system are analyzed in turn.

Dividend–deduction System

As shown in Table 3.1, the dividend-deduction system is found in Greece, Iceland, and Sweden. Finland and Norway also had a dividend-deduction system before these countries moved to (full) imputation. Greece allows profit distributions to be deducted in full subject, however, to withholding rates (creditable against the personal income tax at the choice of the taxpayer) ranging from 42-50 per cent (depending on the nature of the shares and on whether they are quoted on the Athens Stock Exchange), which exceed the usual corporation tax rate on large, open companies of 40 per cent. Hence, the country's corporation tax is still biased in favour of retained profits.

Example 3 shows the workings of the dividend-deduction system. As in the previous examples, the illustration is based on profits before corporation tax of £300 and a corporation tax rate of 40 per cent. It is assumed that the intention is to provide dividend relief for all shareholders at a rate of 50 per cent measured against the overtaxation under the classical system (Example 1, line 8). To achieve this, one-half of profits marked for distribution should be made deductible in determining taxable profits. It is possible, of course, to vary the degree of dividend relief. A full deduction makes the system equivalent to an undistributed profits tax with which the United States briefly, and not altogether favourably, experimented in the late thirties. A small deduction moves the system closer to the classical corporation tax.

Iceland and Sweden limit the dividend deduction to what might be called a normal or primary dividend of 15 per cent of the value of the shares or 10 per cent of the paid-up capital, respectively[1]. The

---

[1]For a description of the arrangements, see OECD (1991), pp.351, 354-55 and 418. The primary dividend-deduction system receives a favourable review in a recent study of the Institute for Fiscal Studies (1991).

corporation tax becomes then akin to an excess profits tax. Conceptual difficulties arise in determining the base on which the relief must be computed. Equity capital placed and paid up, the Swedish criterion, has only historical significance. Certainly, it does not represent the amount that subsequent shareholders have paid for the acquisition of their holding. Another base, namely equity for tax (book) purposes (including retained profits and reserves), implies that the primary dividend is calculated by reference to an accounting item which may differ markedly from the market value of equity. The relief is then an arbitrary reduction of the corporation tax rate which varies with the (accounting) relationship between the business's equity and its total worth.

Example 3
Dividend-deduction system

		(£)	
A.	Corporate level		
	1. Profits before corporation tax	300	
	2. Dividend deduction (0.5 x 1)	150	
	3. Profits after deduction (1 – 2)	150	
	4. Corporation tax: 40% (3 x 4)	60	
B.	Shareholder level		
	5. Income tax rate	30%	50%
	6. Dividend income (1 – 4)	240	240
	7. Income tax (5 x 6)	72	120
C.	Combined tax burden		
	8. Total tax (4 + 7)	132	180
	9. Effective tax rate (8 + 1)	44%	60%
	10. Overtaxation [(9 – 5) + 5]	47%	20%
	11. Tax relief [(classical overtaxation		
	– 10) + classical overtaxation)]	50%	50%

In Sweden, the relief is limited to dividends paid on newly issued shares for a maximum of 20 years (the total deduction cannot exceed the paid-in capital). In 1979, the American Law Institute also suggested a limited deduction at the corporate level for dividends on new equity, as well as a corporate excise tax on redemption, in order to achieve a more even handed treatment of dividend and interest payments. An able lawyer, who compared the proposal to the imputation system, however, concluded that the latter was 'preferable in theory and workable in practice.'[1] Moreover, some arbitrary line must be drawn in deciding when shares stop being 'newly issued'. Also, there is always the danger that old equity will be liquidated and converted into new issues. In 1992, in sharp contrast to its previous position, the American Law Institute issued a study favouring the imputation system.

Unless the goal is to stimulate domestic investment, a drawback of the dividend-deduction system is that the relief is automatically extended to foreign shareholders (and exempt entities) who do not pay the (additional) national income tax incurred by domestic shareholders. To prevent this, the dividend withholding tax for profits transferred abroad might be increased, but experience in Germany has taught that it is nearly impossible to get such an increase incorporated in existing or new treaties for the prevention of double taxation. Another possibility is to disallow the deduction for dividends paid to (foreign) shareholders, who are not subject to the national dividend withholding tax. This does not require a renegotiation of treaties. It is the route followed by Sweden under the coupon tax. A final objection to the dividend-deduction system is that the corporation tax cannot serve as a means to verify the correct return of dividend income for the income tax. Its major advantage, of course, is that dividends are clearly treated at par with interest.

Split–Rate System

The split-rate system used to be employed in Austria, Japan, and Portugal. Currently, under the German imputation system, distributed profits are taxed at a lower rate than are retained profits. Just as under the dividend-deduction system, it has been proposed in the literature in these countries to limit the lower rate to a so-called normal or primary dividend, or, more generally, to a specified part of distributed profits. Of course, if the rate differential is small, the split-rate system resembles the classical corporation tax, and if the differential is large it again becomes an undistributed profits tax. In contrast to usual practice, France taxes distributed profits at a higher rate in order to stimulate retentions.

[1] See Warren (1981), commenting on American Law Institute (1979).

Example 4 gives an illustration of a split-rate system that taxes distributed profits at a lower rate of 20 per cent (and retained profits at 40 per cent). Following, profits after corporation tax are distributed. At shareholder level, they fall in either the 30 per cent income tax bracket: £72 tax, or the 50 per cent bracket: £120 tax. The combined liability (line 6) is £132 or £180, and the corresponding effective rates are 44 per cent and 60 per cent. If the degree of overtaxation is now compared to the overtaxation inherent to the classical system, then a dividend relief of 50 per cent has been extended, the same as under the dividend-deduction system.

Example 4
Split-rate system

		(£)	
A.	Corporate level		
	1. Profits before corporation tax	300	
	2. Corporation tax: 20% (1 x 2)	60	
B.	Shareholder level		
	3. Income tax rate	<u>30%</u>	<u>50%</u>
	4. Dividend income (1 – 2)	240	240
	5. Income tax (3 x 4)	72	120
C.	Combined tax burden		
	6. Total tax (2 + 5)	132	180
	7. Effective tax rate (6 + 1)	44%	60%
	8. Overtaxation [(7 – 3) + 3]	47%	20%
	9. Tax relief [(classical overtaxation		
	– 8) + classical overtaxation)]	50%	50%

A disadvantage of the pre-1977 German split-rate system (without imputation) was that foreign parent companies with German subsidiaries could avoid the high split-rate on retained profits by first distributing the subsidiary's earnings and then channeling them back as equity for reinvestment purposes. The effect might have been considered less serious if other countries, such as the United States, levied corporation tax on profits transferred from Germany, while crediting the corporation tax paid in Germany. After all, the American Treasury would then recoup the difference between its tax and the German tax. But aside from the question whether this effect was intended by the German legislator, it could be avoided by placing a Dutch or Swiss holding between the subsidiary and the parent. As a remedy, Germany attempted to negotiate increases of dividend withholding taxes on earnings transferred abroad, but this required changes in treaties already agreed to - always a laborious exercise.

Dividend Relief at Shareholder Level

As noted, there are two basic approaches to the integration of the corporation tax and the personal income tax at shareholder level: the imputation system and various schedular methods of dividend relief.

Imputation System

The imputation system appears the most important form of dividend relief. It is, therefore, reviewed in somewhat greater detail than are the other systems.

1. Workings. The imputation system has long been dominant in the European Community (EC). The most important member states, namely, France, Germany, Italy, and the United Kingdom (together accounting for 80 per cent of the Community's GDP) all employ this system. In the EC, economic rather than equity considerations played an important role in the decision to adopt the imputation system. Foremost among these was the desire to promote profit distributions in order to stimulate stock markets and, to a lesser extent, to reduce the tax-induced preference for the corporate form of doing business. The fact that the relief was not automatically extended to foreign shareholders strengthened the grip of many countries on their international tax rights and obligations[1]. Since 1983, the imputation system has also been introduced in Australia, Finland, New Zealand, and Norway.

---

[1]The interest in the imputation system was also stimulated by the 1975 draft directive of the European Commission on the most appropriate harmonized form of corporation tax for the Community. The directive proposed that the corporation tax rate should be harmonized between 45 per cent and 55 per cent and that member countries should agree on a tax credit of 45 per cent to 55 per cent of dividends paid. Source countries would bear the revenue cost of cross-border tax credits. The directive was withdrawn in 1990.

As shown in Example 5, imputation is achieved by requiring the shareholder to partly gross up his net dividend of £180 (line 4) by one-third, representing the corporation tax attributable thereto. This achieves the same degree of dividend relief as under the dividend-deduction system and the split-rate-system. The grossed-up dividend of £240 is then added to his other income and subjected to the progressive income tax. Next, the gross tax: £72 or £120 (line 7), is credited with the corporation tax, with which the net dividend was grossed up in the first place. The balance represents the net tax payable (or refundable). Imputation, therefore, has the same gross-up and tax credit features as a dividend withholding tax. Moreover, it provides the tax administration with a similar means of checking the income tax return for the proper reporting of dividends. The withholding technique works as an anti-evasion device because nationals holding stock through nominee accounts do not benefit from the relief.

Example 5
Imputation system

		(£)	
A.	Corporate level		
	1. Profits before corporation tax	300	
	2. Corporation tax: 40% (1 x 2)	120	
B.	Shareholder level		
	3. Income tax rate	30%	50%
	4. Net dividend (1 – 2)	180	180
	5. Imputed corporation tax (1/3 x 4)	60	60
	6. Dividend income (4 + 5)	240	240
	7. Income tax (3 x 6)	72	120
	8. Tax credit (5)	60	60
	9. Net income tax (7 – 8)	12	60
C.	Combined tax burden		
	10. Total tax (2 + 9)	132	180
	11. Effective tax rate (10+ 1)	44%	60%
	12. Overtaxation [(11 – 3) + 3]	47%	20%
	13. Tax relief [(classical overtaxation – 12) + classical overtaxation)]	50%	50%

The tax credit under an imputation system may be expressed as a percentage of the net dividend, indicating the usual legal form of the dividend relief, or as a percentage of the corporation tax, showing the extent to which the double tax is mitigated. The tax credit may also be calculated as a percentage of the grossed-up dividend, representing the comparable tax-inclusive income tax rate. In Ireland and the United Kingdom, the latter percentage equals the basic rate of income tax. A tax assessment is then not required if taxpayers' other income is also subject to the basic rate.

 2. Technical Aspects. Table 3.2 shows details of the various imputation systems. Because they do not want to provide a tax credit for profit distributions on which national corporation tax has not been collected, most countries levy a compensatory tax at the company level on dividends paid out of earnings that are wholly or partially exempt from corporation tax, such as profits remitted from abroad, earned under a tax incentive scheme, or arising in the form of lower taxed capital gains. Alternatively, as in Australia, the tax credit is reduced or denied at shareholder level. In France, the compensatory tax applies also to profits retained longer than five years, even though corporation tax has already been paid thereon at the full rate. In Ireland and the United Kingdom, the withholding tax for the 'mainstream' corporation tax, called advance corporation tax (ACT), has been assigned the role of compensatory tax, because the offset is limited to 25 per cent of a corporation's taxable profits. Although the imputation system is meant to promote profit distributions, the compensatory tax, of course, forms an inducement to retain exempt profits in the corporation as a means to minimize the corporate tax liability. Also, to the extent exempt profits are distributed, the tax nullifies the intended effect of tax holidays and other tax incentives.

 Countries with a compensatory tax must provide rules for the sequence in which profits are presumed to be distributed (Table 3.2). In order to mitigate the effect of the compensatory tax, profits that have been subject to the highest rate of corporation tax are generally deemed to be distributed first when dividends are paid. In addition, in France, current profits are presumed to be distributed before retained profits, and among retained profits, the latest profits are deemed to be paid out first. In Germany, profits are allocated to three accounts: profits to which the 50 per cent rate has been applied, profits that have been subject to the 36 per cent rate, and profits fully exempt from tax. Profits subject to an intermediate rate must be apportioned between a higher- and a lower-rated account.

In five countries, domestic corporate portfolio shareholders are treated the same as individual shareholders, i.e. they are permitted to deduct the tax credit attached to dividends received from other companies from their own corporate tax liability. In Germany, the lower rate on distributions implies that an additional 20 per cent tax is charged on the receiving company if the dividend is not passed on to individual shareholders. In fact, the introduction of the imputation system made the old 'affiliation privilege' for domestic companies obsolete. Ireland, NewZealand, and the United Kingdom exempt all intercompany dividends in the hands of receiving companies. Under the legislation in Ireland and the United Kingdom, however, the tax credit on 'franked investment income' slumbers and may be used to offset the compensatory tax payable upon redistribution of that income to individual shareholders. That arrangement applies also in other countries; France, for example, exempts dividends received from subsidiary companies under an affiliation privilege (Table 3.2). The use of such a privilege is necessary because if imputation is partial, deduction of the tax credit attached to a subsidiary's dividend from the parent's tax liability would result in a higher aggregate corporate tax liability than if the total profit had been wholly earned by the parent company.[1]

No country permits foreign shareholders to share automatically in the relief. France, Ireland, and the United Kingdom, however, extend the tax credit on a bilateral basis to individual and corporate portfolio investors in a large number of countries (listed in Table 3.2). Thus, under its double taxation agreements, France provides an additional payment (which is generally subject to withholding tax) to foreign shareholders who, in turn, make the appropriate gross-up adjustment with respect to the individual or corporate income tax liability in their country of residence. As regards Germany, France makes a direct payment to the German government, and German shareholders in French companies apply the regular gross-up and credit procedure. Under other treaties, corporate portfolio shareholders receive a refund of the compensatory tax, if any, that has been paid by a French distributing company; in that case, however, shareholders are not entitled to the tax credit.

[1]To illustrate, assume a rate of corporation tax of 40 per cent, while half of dividends are grossed up and credited if profits are distributed. Then, if an affiliation privilege would not apply, a parent and its subsidiary would have to pay £46 tax on each £100 profits (before tax) earned by the subsidiary and paid out to the parent. Of course, this does not make sense.

Table 3.2 Imputation Systems in OECD Member Countries, 1992

Country	Compensatory tax on exempt or partially taxed profits	Ordering rules for profit distribution	Tax credit for domestic corporate shareholders		Tax credit for foreign shareholders (under bilateral treaties)			Refund to domestic shareholder if tax credit exceeds income tax	
			Portfolio	Direct	Individual	Corporate Portfolio	Corporate Direct	Individual	Exempt entity
Australia	Yes, at shareholder level.	Divs. required to be franked to the maximum extent possible.	No. But rebate of tax for domestic divs. received by resident companies (rebate equal to the tax on this income) except for unfranked divs. received by private companies.	No.	No. However, no div. withholding tax is payable on full divs.	No.	No.	No.	No.
Finland	Yes	Highest-in-first-out.	Yes	Yes	No.	No.	No.	Yes	No.
France	Yes, also on profits retained more than 5 years.	Current profit; previous four years profits; profits subject to compensatory tax.	Yes	No, but divs. from 95% + holding exempt. Tax credit deductible from compensatory tax on re-distribution.	Yes: Australia, Austria, Belg., Fin., Germany, Japan, Lux., Neths., Norway, Spain, Sweden, Switz., UK, US.[1]	Yes: Austria, Fin., Germany, Japan, Lux., Neths. NZ, Norway, Spain, Sweden, Switz., UK. US.	No.	Yes	No.
Germany	Yes	Highest-in-first-out.	Yes	Yes	No.	No.	No.	Yes	No.
Ireland	Yes. Profits of manufacturing companies taxed at the special rate of 10% carry a reduced credit.	Proportional to corporate tax.	No, divs. exempt. Tax credit deductible from compensatory tax upon redistribution.	No, except UK.	Yes: Australia, Austria, NZ, Sweden, Switz., UK	Yes: Australia, Austria, NZ, Sweden, Switz., UK.	No.	Yes	Yes
Italy	Yes, at 56.25%.	Highest-in-first-out.	Yes	Yes.	No, except UK.	No, except UK.	Half credit:UK.	Yes	No.
NZ	Yes	Div. to be franked to the maximum extent possible.	No, divs. exempt.	No, divs. exempt.	No.	No.	No.	No.	No.
Norway	No.	Not necessary.	Yes	Yes.	No.	No.	No.	No.	No.
UK	Yes, through Advance Corporation Tax (ACT).	Not necessary.	No, divs. not liable to corporation tax, tax credit franks ACT on re-distribution. No ACT on intra-group divs.	No, divs. exempt. Tax credit deductible from ACT on re-distribution. No ACT on intra-group divs.	Yes: Australia, Austria, Belg., Can., Denmark, Fin., France, Ireland, Italy, Japan, Lux., Neths., Norway, Spain, Sweden, Switz., US.	Yes: Austria, Belg., Can., Denmark, Fin., France, Ireland, Italy, Japan, Lux., Neths., Norway, Spain, Sweden, Switz., US.	Yes: Belg., Can., Denmark, Fin., Italy, Lux., Neths., Switz., US.	Yes	Yes

[1]Refund of compensatory tax under all other treaties, and to all direct corporate shareholders under any treaty.
Source: Updated from S. Cnossen, Table 4.1, pp.90-92, in S. Cnossen ed., 1983.

Generally, tax credits are not granted with respect to foreign direct investments. Only the United Kingdom has concluded a number of treaties under which profits on such investments, when remitted, are entitled to a tax credit at half the rate available to portfolio shareholders. The half rate is based on the argument that the credit should be extended only to non-resident direct investors to the extent earnings are redistributed to individual shareholders. Since it is estimated that approximately one-half of corporate profits are so distributed, the tax credit for direct investments has been set at one half of the credit for portfolio shareholders.

Finally, most countries with an imputation system give a refund to individual shareholders if the tax credit exceeds the gross income tax liability. On the other hand, exempt entities, such as pension funds and educational and charitable institutions, are not entitled to a refund, except in Ireland and the United Kingdom.

Schedular Methods

The separate tax on dividends received and the tax credit method (Table 3.1) are less structured forms of dividend relief. Under the separate tax, all corporate source income, including profit distributions, is taxed at the normal corporation tax rate, but dividend income is partially exempted from the shareholder's income tax by taxing it at a lower (flat) rate. Austria achieves this by taxing dividends at one-half of the shareholder's income tax rate, other countries by applying a final 'withholding' tax. Turkey exempts dividends fully in the hands of shareholders. Alternatively, Canada and Spain permit shareholders a tax credit, specified as some fraction of dividends received, against their income tax. Unlike the imputation system, the tax credit is available regardless of whether or not corporation tax has been levied, usually the net dividend is not grossed-up before the income tax rate is applied, and no refund is given if the tax credit exceeds the gross income tax liability.

Example 6 shows the arithmetic of the tax credit method. Clearly, an objection to this form of dividend relief, as well as the separate tax approach, is that the benefit is distributed regressively with respect to income. As the example makes clear, a dividend relief from classical overtaxation of one-half for the shareholder in the 50 per cent bracket corresponds to a relief of only 35 per cent in the 30 per cent income tax bracket. Essentially, the goal of dividend relief (the prevention of double taxation) interferes with the objective of progressivity (tax increases that rise proportionately faster than income). The effect would not occur if the income tax is levied at a proportional rate. Belgium, Japan, and Portugal mitigate the resulting regressivity by permitting low-income shareholders to include the dividend in income with a credit for the withholding tax against the gross income tax liability.

Example 6
Tax credit method

		(£)	
A. Corporate level			
1. Profits before Corporation tax		300	
2. Corporation tax: 40% (1 x 2)		120	
B. Shareholder level			
3. Income tax rate	30%		50%
4. Dividend income (1 – 2)	180		180
5. Gross income tax (3 x 4)	54		90
6. Tax credit (1/6 x 4)	30		30
7. Net income tax (5 – 6)	24		60
C. Combined tax burden			
8. Total tax (2 + 7).	144		180
9. Effective tax rate (8 ÷ 1)	48%		60%
10. Overtaxation [(9 – 3) ÷ 3]	60%		20%
11. Tax relief [(classical overtaxation – 10) ÷ classical overtaxation)]	35%		50%

Note: The tax credit has been computed by assuming a total combined tax liability of £180 in the 50% bracket (line 8), equal to the liability in the other examples. The corresponding net income tax levied at the rate of 50% can then be calculated, as well as the tax credit itself. Next, the same amount of tax credit has been taken for the shareholder in the 30% bracket, which in turn forms the basis for computing the combined tax figures in this bracket.

Another, in some respects similar, concession permits a deduction from income of a specified net amount spent for the purchase of (new) shares. Austria, Iceland, and Luxembourg have this kind of scheme to stimulate share ownership. However, a similar relief scheme in France in the 1980s, usually referred to as the Monory-deduction, appears hardly to have had any influence on the volume of new share issues or on the number of shareholders, particularly if it is considered that 75 per cent of all new shareholders preferred investments in participation trusts, or so-called Sicav's-Monory. Moreover, small and medium-sized companies usually do not benefit from these kinds of measures.

Cross–country Comparison[1]

This section assesses the degree of dividend relief under the various corporation tax systems on a comparative basis. Dividend relief is rarely provided in full. Also, income tax rates applicable to dividends received are seldom the same as corporation tax rates applied to profits. Hence, various nonneutralities remain.

Degrees of Dividend Relief

Table 3.3 shows the degree of dividend relief, or the absence thereof, under the various corporation tax systems. For the computations, the following simplifying assumptions were made:
- the corporation tax is fully borne by profits;
- all profits after corporation tax are distributed;
- distributed profits are taxed in the hands of individual shareholders who face the top marginal income tax rate; and
- the effective income tax rate on capital gains is nil.

As in the Examples in the previous sections, the degree of dividend relief is computed as the ratio of the difference between the classical overtaxation and the actual overtaxation over the classical overtaxation (all in percentage terms). Simplified, this can be expressed by the following formula:

$$\text{Degree of dividend relief} = \frac{\text{Total CT+PT if no relief} \quad minus \quad \text{Actual CT+PT}}{\text{Total CT+PT if no relief} \quad minus \quad \text{PT if full relief}}$$

---

[1]This section draws on OECD (1991), Annex 2.

Table 3.3 shows the data and the various degrees of dividend relief. For the calculation of the total tax burden under the no relief situation, i.e. the classical tax burden, the figures for 'Total PT' in the Appendix are used rather than the reduced schedular rates shown in Table 3.3. Obviously, the same applies to the PT-figures in the above formula. As expected, the degree of dividend relief varies widely, from 0 percent in countries with classical systems to 100 percent in Greece, Australia, Finland, and New Zealand. In contrast to what the classification suggests, relief is not provided in full under the imputation systems in Germany and Italy, because noncreditable local taxes have to be taken into account. Full relief is considered provided if the total tax on dividends equals the top income tax rate. Judged against this benchmark, Norway, Belgium, and Denmark provide more than full relief.

Remaining Discrimination

As indicated above, the central issue in the debate over the most appropriate corporation tax system is the normative rule that corporate profits, whether retained or distributed, should be taxed like all other income at the marginal personal income tax rates of shareholders. In other words, dividends, interest, and retained profits should bear the same total tax burden. If so, the choice between new share issues, debt, and retentions to finance new investments would not be influenced by the tax system. The corporation tax would be neutral regarding financing and payout decisions and, by extension, investment location decisions.

In the real world, corporation taxes, in conjunction with income taxes, discriminate against financing and payout decisions. Three measures of discrimination may be distinguished. First, the dividend/retention differential measures the percentage excess by which profit distributions are overtaxed compared with retentions. This measure is important for the choice between new shares and retained profits. Second, the dividend/interest differential measures the percentage excess by which profit distributions are overtaxed compared with interest. It is relevant for the choice between new shares and debt. Third, the retention/interest differential measures the percentage excess by which retentions are overtaxed (or, as often, undertaxed) compared with interest. This measure, which can readily be deduced from the preceding measures, affects the choice between retained profits and debt.

Table 3.3 OECD: Dividend Relief and Potential Distortions of Corporation Tax Systems, 1992
(in Percentages)

System and countries covered	CT on retentions	CT + top PT on dividends	Top PT on interest	Degree of dividend relief[1]	Degrees of discrimination		
					Dividends/ retentions[2]	Dividends/ interest[3]	Interest/ retentions[4]
I. Classical Systems							
Luxembourg	39.4	70.5	51.3	0	79	37	30
Netherlands	35	74	60	0	111	23	71
Switzerland	30.3	60.8	43.8	0	101	39	45
United States	38.3	60.5	36	0	58	68	-6
II A. Dividend Relief at Corporate Level							
1. Dividend deduction							
Greece	46(40)	50	25	100	9	100	-46
Ireland	45	Varies	0	—	—	—	-100
Sweden	30	Varies	30	—	—	—	0
2. Split-rate (None)							
II B. Dividend Relief at Shareholder Level							
1. Imputation							
a. Full							
Australia	39	48.3	48.3	100	24	0	24
Finland	40.2	56.2	10	100	40	462	-75
Germany	58.1/45.5	61.7	55	67	6	12	-5
Italy	47.8	58.1	30	66	22	94	-37
New Zealand	33	33	33	100	0	0	0
Norway	28	28	28	179	0	0	0
b. Partial							
France	34/42	63.4	18.1	69	86	250	-47
Ireland	40(10)	61.6	52	50	54	18	30
United Kingdom	33	46.4	40	68	41	16	21
2. Schedular treatment							
a. Separate Tax							
Austria	39	54.3	50	78	39	9	28
Belgium	39	54.3	10	129	39	443	-74
Denmark	38	65.9	57.8	117	73	14	52
Japan	51	68.2	20	82	34	241	-61
Portugal	39.6	54.7	25	38	38	119	-37
Turkey	49.2	49.2	10	93	0	392	-80
b. Tax Credit							
Canada	44.3(38.3)	64.5	49.1	31	46	31	11
Spain	35.3	65.1	56	42	84	16	59

Notes: [1] Dividend Relief = $\dfrac{CT + PT \text{ if no relief } minus \text{ } CT + Top\ PT}{CT + PT \text{ if no relief } minus\ PT}$

[2] Dividends/Retentions = $\dfrac{CT + Top\ PT\ minus\ CT \text{ on Retentions}}{CT \text{ on Retentions}}$ Differential

[3] Dividends/Interest = $\dfrac{CT + Top\ PT\ minus\ Top\ PT \text{ on interest}}{Top\ PT \text{ on interest}}$

[4] Interest/Retentions = $\dfrac{Top\ PT \text{ on interest } minus\ CT \text{ on Retentions}}{CT \text{ on Retentions}}$ Differential

Source: See Appendix. CT = Corporation Tax; PT = Personal Income Tax. Figures have been rounded to nearest decimal. Degrees of Discrimination are shown in full figures.

The calculations for the dividend/retention differential in Table 3.3 indicate that most corporation tax systems, particularly if classical in nature, discriminate heavily against profit distributions. Basically, the systems favor established firms that have sufficient profits to finance new investments and discriminate against starting firms that need new equity. Exceptions are the corporation taxes of New Zealand, Norway, and Greece, where the differential is nil because dividends bear the same tax as retentions. Basically, the computations for the dividend/interest differential carry the same message. Some countries, such as Finland, France, Belgium, Japan, and Turkey, discriminate heavily in favour of debt, however, because interest is taxed at a mere 10 or 20 per cent under the personal income tax. The interest/retention differential varies most. The number of corporation taxes that is biased against debt is the same as the number that favors debt over retentions. Three countries (Sweden, New Zealand, and Norway) are neutral as regards the choice between debt and retained profits.

The figures indicate that hardly any corporation tax system achieves neutrality in the taxation of the returns to current equity (retained profits), new shares (dividends), and debt (interest). For neutrality to occur (in other words, for all differentials to be zero), dividend relief should be given in full and the top rate of the income tax at which dividends and interest are taxed should equal the corporation tax rate. The corporation and personal income taxes in New Zealand and Norway meet these requirements, but only for the top marginal rate.

Although the figures form a useful indication of the remaining nonneutralities under the various corporation tax systems, it should be emphasized that they cannot explain why investors do not use opportunities for arbitrage. Thus, returns may not be taxed at shareholder or debtholder level because they are channeled through tax havens or received by tax exempt entities, such as pension funds. Financial liberalization and innovation have greatly increased the opportunities for tax arbitrage. As a result, remaining nonneutralities may be accentuated or, more likely, mitigated in comparison with the figures shown in Table 3.3.

Evaluation and Conclusion

The appropriate place of the corporation tax in an equitable and efficient tax system plays an important role in the tax debate in most OECD member countries. Should corporations be taxed as such or should their earnings be allocated to shareholders? If full integration is not feasible, is integration of the corporation tax on distributed profits a second-best alternative? If so, should dividend relief be provided at corporate or at shareholder level? How much weight should be given to the international repercussions of partial integration? And above all, even if some form of dividend relief appears desirable in theory, are the transition costs worth the trouble?

In an equitable tax system, the case for a separate corporation tax (classical system) is somewhat uneasy. Surely, corporations have an independent legal existence, as well as the capacity to pay tax in the sense that the corporation tax does not force them into bankruptcy. But the conclusion that they also have ability-to-pay is a *non sequitur*. The incidence of all taxes, whatever their name and form, is always on natural persons. The search for the answer to the question of who bears the tax burden must start and end with individuals of flesh and blood. The more nearly tax burdens are imposed on them in line with the ability-to-pay principle and government's redistributive objectives, the better the tax system is. Also, the classical corporation tax does not appear a particularly efficient tax. There are indications that the tax distorts the optimal allocation of resources because it (a) stimulates the retention of profits, thus interfering with competitive conditions and hampering the entry of new firms; and (b) discriminates against new shares by treating interest favorably compared to dividends, thereby imposing relatively higher capital costs on starting firms that have difficulty attracting debt. In short, financing and payout decisions are distorted.

The equity shortcomings and economic distortions of the classical system, therefore, appear to point the way to integration. Full integration and retention of the corporation tax as a withholding device - to protect the workings of the income tax and to levy tax on foreign companies whose shareholders do not fall under the national income tax - does not appear feasible. Partial integration or dividend relief seems a viable alternative, however, as evidenced by the experience of 20 OECD member countries. Moreover, it has been pointed out that full integration might then, in practice, be achieved if the top marginal rate of the income tax would be set at the same level as the corporation tax rate, as in New Zealand and Norway. Shareholders in low-income tax brackets would then push for profit distribution, while high-income shareholders would not benefit from profit retention[1].

[1] See McLure (1979), pp.219-23.

If payout rates would not be influenced by the choice of the integration system, the degree of dividend relief can be made the same under a dividend-deduction system, a split-rate system, and an imputation system. Any one of these systems distributes the tax on distributed corporate source income more systematically in line with marginal individual income tax rates than does the classical system. If the objective is to stimulate the stock market, relief at the shareholder level would seem most appropriate. If the goal is to increase the liquidity position of corporations (as an indirect investment incentive), a dividend-deduction or split-rate system might be called for. An advantage of the imputation system is that it functions as a withholding device, which should further taxpayer compliance with the income tax.

It should be noted that the case for or against dividend relief is not contingent upon the assumption made with respect to the incidence of the corporation tax[1]. If, as some argue, the tax is borne by consumers (in the form of higher prices) or workers (in the form of lower wages either immediately or, more likely, in the long run through the reduced availability of capital), it should be considered an inferior sales tax or payroll tax: inferior because its burden distribution varies arbitrarily from one corporation to another depending on the ratio between profits and sales or between profits and payrolls. Of course, there is no rationale for such taxes in an equitable tax system. Similarly, the efficiency case for integration does not depend on incidence assumptions.[2] Dividend relief, like other tax changes, cannot be imposed on a *de novo* basis. Changes in the existing tax burden distribution, transition costs, and revenue effects must be accounted for. In classical countries, shareholders have long become accustomed to the system and it is likely that the tax, including its double levy, has been capitalized in earlier years in the form of reduced share prices. In other words, the tax has been borne by original shareholders who are not necessarily the same persons as present holders. Removal of the tax would then result in unwarranted windfall gains to existing shareholders. Nonetheless, this does not mean that change should not be contemplated, because distorting effects linger on. Dividend relief mitigates these effects.

---

[1]For a review of the literature on the incidence of the corporation tax, see Ballentine (1980).
[2]For the equity argument, see Musgrave and Musgrave (1980), p.401, and for the irrelevancy of the incidence issue for efficiency, Mieszkowski (1972).

Whatever the advantages of dividend relief in the domestic context, however, its international implications are a drawback.[1] Without corrections effected through double taxation treaties, the dividend-deduction or split-rate system unduly favors foreign investors, and the imputation system discriminates against them. This is not equitable and detrimentally affects cross-border ownership of equity. Indeed, the growing internationalization and liberalization of capital markets, which increases opportunities for tax arbitrage and tax evasion, may force the focus of attention on schedular systems under which corporate profits would be taxed in full in the source country, while distributed profits (and interest) would be subject to a final flat low-rate income tax (deducted at source), which might be reduced on a bilateral basis.[2]

---

[1]For a good treatment, see Doernberg (1992).
[2]For a further analysis in the U.S. context, see the excellent study of the U.S. Treasury (1992). For reflections on the place of the corporation tax in the EC, see also Cnossen and Bovenberg (forthcoming).

References and Further Reading

Ballentine, J. G., *Equity, Efficiency and the U.S. Corporation Income Tax*, American Enterprise Institute for Public Policy Research, Washington, 1980.

Campbell Committee, *Final Report of the Committee of Inquiry into the Australian Financial System*, AGPS, Canberra, 1981.

Cnossen, S., 'The Imputation System in the EEC,' chapter 4 in S.Cnossen, ed., *Comparative Tax Studies: Essays in Honor of Richard Goode*, North Holland, Amsterdam, 1983.

Cnossen, S., 'Corporation Taxes in OECD Member Countries,' *Bulletin for International Fiscal Documentation*, Vol. 38, Nov., p.483, 1984.

Cnossen, S., and R. M. Bird. *The Personal Income Tax: Phoenix from the Ashes?* Amsterdam: North-Holland, 1990.

Cnossen, S., and L. Bovenberg, 'Harmonization of Corporation Taxes in the European Community: The RudingCommittee Report,' forthcoming.

Doernberg, R. L. 'International Aspects of Individual and Corporate Tax Integration', *Tax Notes International* , March, p.535, 1992.

Goode, R., *The Corporation Income Tax*, John Wiley, New York, 1951.

McLure, C. E. Jr., *Must Corporate Income Be Taxed Twice?* Brookings Institution, Washington, 1979.

Mieszkowski, P., 'Integration of the Corporate and Personal Income Taxes: The Bogus Issue of Shifting,' *Finanzarchiv*, Vol. 31, p.286, 1972.

Musgrave, R. A. and P. B. Musgrave, *Public Finance in Theory and Practice*, McGraw-Hill, New York, 3rd ed., 1980.

Norr, M., *The Taxation of Corporations and Shareholders*, Kluwer, Deventer, The Netherlands, 1982.

Poterba, J. M., 'Tax Policy and Corporate Policy,' *Brooking Papers on Economic Activity*, Vol. 2, p.455, 1987.

Poterba, J.M., and L. Summers, 'The Economic Effects of Dividend Taxes,' in eds. E. Altman and M. Surahanyam, *Recent Advances in Corporate Finance*, Irwin, Homewood, Ill., 1985.

Royal Commission on Taxation *Report*, Queen's Printer, Ottawa, 1966.

Sato, M. and R. M. Bird, 'International Aspects of the Taxation of Corporations and Shareholders,' *IMF Staff Papers*, Vol. 22, p.384, 1975.

Sinn, H. W., *Capital Income Taxation and Resource Allocation*, North-Holland, Amsterdam, 1985.

Van den Tempel, A. J., *Corporation Tax and Individual Income Tax in the European Communities*, Commission of the European Communities, Brussels, 1970.

Warren, A., 'The Relation and Integration of Individual and Corporate Income Taxes,' *Harvard Law Review*, Vol. 94, p.719, 1981.

Zodrow, G. R. 'On the 'Traditional' and 'New' Views of Dividend Taxation,' *National Tax Journal*, Vol. 44, Dec., p.497, 1991.

American Law Institute, *Income Tax Project*, Tentative Draft No. 2, Subchapter C: Corporate Distributions, 1979.

American Law Institute, *Federal Income Tax Project*, Tax Advisory Group Draft No. 21, Reporter's Study, 1992.

Commission of the European Communities (1975) 'Proposal for a Directive of the Council Concerning the Harmonization of Company Taxation and of Withholding Taxes on Dividends,' *European Taxation*, 2-3-4, p.52, 1976.

Institute for Fiscal Studies, *Equity for Companies: A Corporation Tax for the 1990s*, Fourth Report of the IFS Capital Taxes Group, Commentary No. 26, London, 1951.

OECD, *Taxing Profits in a Global Economy: Domestic and International Issues*, Paris, 1991.

OECD, *Revenue Statistics of OECD Member Countries 1965-1990*, Paris, 1992.

U.S. Department of the Treasury, *Blueprints for Basic Tax Reform*, U.S. Government Printing Office, Washington, 1992.

U.S. Department of the Treasury, *Integration of the Individual and Corporate Tax Systems: Taxing Business Income Once*, U.S. Government Printing Office, Washington, 1992.

APPENDIX to Chapter 3   OECD: Corporation Tax Rates and Income Tax Rates in 1992

Country	Rates of corporation tax (CT)			Top rates of personal income tax (PT)				
	Central gov.(CG)[1,2]	Subord. gov.(SG)[3,4]	Total CT	Central gov.(CG)[3]	Subord. gov.(SG)[3]	Total PT	Top PT on dividends	Top PT on interest
Australia	39	—	39	48.3[5]	—	48.3	48.3	48.3
Austria	30	14.8	39	50	—	50	25	50
Belgium	39	—	39	55	7	58.9	25	10
Canada[6]	28.8 (23.8)[7]	15.5 (14.5)[7]	44.3 (38.3)	34	63	49.1	49.1	49.1
Denmark	38	—	38	40	28	68	45	57.8
Finland	23	17.2[8]	40.2	39	17.2[8]	56.2	56.2	10
France	34/42[9]	—	34/42	57.9[10]	—	57.9	57.9	18.1
Germany	51.9/37.4[11]	15	58.1/45/5	55	—	55	55	55
Greece	46(40)[7]	—	46(40)	50	7	50	50	25
Iceland	45	—	45	32.8	—	39.8	39.8	0
Ireland	40(10)[7]	—	40(10)	52	—	52	52	52
Italy	36	16.2	47.8	50	15	50	50	30
Japan	38.5[12]	12+6.5	51	51.3[14]	—	65	35	20
Luxembourg	33.3[13]	10	39.4	60	—	51.3	51.3	51.3
Netherlands	35	—	35	60	—	60	60	60
New Zealand	33	—	33	33	—	33	33	33
Norway		28	28	13	28	41	28	28
Portugal	36	3.6	39.6	40	—	40	25	25
Spain	35.3[15]	—	35.3	56	—	56	56	56
Sweden	30	—	30	20	31	51	30	30
Switzerland[16]	8	24.2	30.3	11.5	32.3	43.8	43.8	43.8
Turkey	49.2[17]	—	49.2	47.5[18]	—	47.5	0	10
United Kingdom	33	—	33	40	—	40	40	40
United States	34	6.5	38.3	31	5	36	36	36

Notes:

[1] Corporations are also liable to net wealth or capital tax in Austria, Canada, Germany, Iceland, Luxembourg, Norway, Switzerland, and Turkey.

[2] Lower or graduated CT-rates are applied to lower amounts of profits or to small businesses in Belgium, Canada, Finland, Japan, Luxembourg, Portugal, Switzerland, the United Kingdom, and the United States. The Netherlands levies a higher rate.

[3] Taxes, surcharges or surtaxes differ between subordinate units of government. Therefore, an average or representative rate has been chosen. Italy has a uniform SG-CT rate and Iceland has a uniform SG-PT rate.

[4] In Austria, Germany, Japan (12%) and Luxembourg, the SG-CT is formulated on a tax-exclusive basis. In these countries, as well as in Italy (3/4), Switzerland, and the United States, the SG-CT is deductible in ascertaining profits for the CG-CT.

[5] CG-PT includes 1.25% surtax.

[6] SG-rates are for Ontario. Rates include 5% CG-PT surcharge and 10% SG-PT surcharge. SG-PT applied to basic CG-PT of 29%.

[7] Rates between brackets apply to manufacturing corporations.

[8] SG-rates include church tax of 1.2%.

[9] Higher rate applies to distributed profits.

[10] CG-PT includes CSG-surtax of 1.1%.

[11] Lower rate applies to distributed profits.   CG-rates include 3.75% surcharge.

[12] CG-CT includes 2.75% surcharge.

[13] Rate includes 1% CG-PT surcharge.

[14] Rate includes 2.5% CG-PT surcharge.

[15] CG-CT includes 1.5% deductible surcharge.

[16] All typical rates, SG-rates are for Zurich.

[17] Rate includes CG-CT surcharge of 7%.

[18] Rate allows for CG-PT rebate of 5%.

Source: International Bureau of Fiscal Documentation, *Taxation of Private Investment Income,* Guides to European Taxation, Vol. 111 (Amsterdam: Loose-leaf). Updated from *Tax News Service.* Percentages have been rounded to nearest decimal.

73 – 10?

CHAPTER 4

ISSUES IN ADOPTING AND DESIGNING
A VALUE–ADDED TAX

Sijbren Cnossen*

Why a VAT?

The widespread introduction of the value–added tax (VAT) in the latter half of this century is one of the most significant events in the evolution of tax structure. Of the twenty–four member countries of the Organisation for Economic Co–operation and Development (OECD), for instance, twenty–one have accepted the VAT as their main consumption tax. Switzerland, the United States and Australia are the only OECD countries that have not yet done so. The Swiss have repeatedly rejected a government proposal to replace their current retail sales tax (RST) by a VAT. In the United States, the pros and cons of the VAT are the subject of an ongoing debate. Finally, Australia still clings to its wholesale sales tax, but the Liberal Opposition Party was committed to introduce one had it been successful in the 1993 General Election. Outside the OECD area, a VAT is levied by approximately 40 countries in Africa, Asia and Latin America. Interestingly, the VAT, as it exists today, was unknown some 25 years ago.

The VAT was pioneered in France and was adopted by the other original member states of the EC. Because the tax was made a condition for membership, the new entrants to the EC introduced it as well. From

*Professor in the Economics Faculty of Erasmus University Rotterdam. This paper has been adapted from the author's 'Key Questions in Considering a Value-Added Tax for Central and Eastern European Countries', IMF *Staff Papers*, Vol. 39, No. 2. Parts of the earlier paper have been reproduced by kind permission of the editor.

the beginning, the EC has attached great importance to the VAT, because, unlike the cascade type of turnover taxes levied earlier, it is very successful in treating intra–Community trade, as well as trade with third countries, according to the destination principle. A VAT enables the precise identification and rebate of the tax on exports, so that they can leave a country free of tax, while imports can be taxed on exactly the same footing as domestically produced commodities. Obviously, this form of neutrality is essential for the proper functioning of a common market. More generally, the border tax adjustments under a VAT agree with the tax provisions of the General Agreement on Tariffs and Trade (GATT).

In addition to being neutral with respect to foreign trade, the VAT does not distort domestic production and distribution. Thus, under the VAT, it makes no difference how often a product is traded before it reaches the consumer or whether its value is added earlier rather than later in the production–distribution process. The VAT is neutral regarding the production technique that a business adopts. In other words, it makes no difference for the tax liability whether a product is manufactured with capital– or labour–intensive technology. Also, the VAT is not influenced by the forms or methods by which business is conducted. Other things being equal, the tax bill is the same whether a product is made in the corporate or non–corporate sector, or whether it is made by integrated or specialised firms. It will be appreciated that these features are important attributes of a 'good' tax in economies that leave the optimal allocation of resources to the free play of market forces.

Another reason why so many countries have adopted the VAT is that it is an exceptionally stable and flexible source of government revenue. The revenue yield of a broadly based VAT with few exemptions, as found in the OECD, exceeds on average 0.4 per cent of gross domestic product (GDP) for every one percentage point of the rate. Since consumption as a share of GDP fluctuates little, by implication the VAT is a stable source of revenue. For much the same reason and because the VAT is collected on a current basis, it is a flexible tax instrument: a change in the rate translates immediately into more or less revenue. As a simple transactions–based tax, moreover, the VAT is a certain levy and relatively easy to understand. Because the tax is broadly based, applying to all sales in the business sector, its base is rarely subject to differing interpretations. Opportunities for tax avoidance and tax evasion are more limited than under the income taxes.

In subsequent sections, this paper looks at various key issues that countries must consider in adopting, designing and operating a VAT under three headings: conceptual aspects; social, economic and political considerations; tax coverage and base.[1] The paper concludes with a summation of the basic requirements for a 'good' VAT. The paper draws on the experience of EC member states and other OECD countries with VATs.

Conceptual Aspects

The VAT used in the EC and in nearly all countries elsewhere, is a multistage, destination–based, net consumption VAT. It includes all goods and services in its base (except those explicitly exempted), covers the retail stage and grants registered firms a credit or deduction for the tax paid in respect of purchases from registered suppliers against their own tax payable on sales. This section examines the workings and nature of this type of VAT. It is shown that a VAT is economically identical to a retail sales tax (RST), although technical differences commonly tilt the choice in favour of the VAT. Finally, some indication is given of how the aggregate VAT base can be computed from national accounts.

How can Value Added be Computed?

The net tax liability of the type of VAT defined above is not difficult to compute. Every taxable entity is required to charge tax on its sales, stating the exact amount on sale invoices. Conversely, that entity pays a VAT on its taxable purchases, which, in turn, is shown on suppliers' invoices. For any tax period, the net VAT liability is then the difference between the total amount of VAT shown on all sale invoices and the total amount of VAT shown on all purchase invoices. (Sales and purchases comprise all taxable goods and services, including raw materials, intermediate products, ancillary supplies, finished goods, plant and equipment.) Although it would be sufficient for VAT accounting purposes to have one spike on which to skewer purchase invoices and another spike for sale invoices, as a rule net VAT liability is ascertained from books of account that need to be maintained to check compliance.

---

[1] For a consideration of legal and administrative features, not considered in this paper, see Cnossen, 1992.

Although the VAT does not enter a firm's profit and loss account (except if, say, an exempt item is purchased whose price includes an element of VAT incurred in earlier stages), the workings of a VAT can usefully be illustrated by reference to the profit and loss account, which, after all, is the central summary statement of a business firm's activities. Consider the stylised example in Table 4.1, which shows the quarterly profit and loss account of a British trading firm, as well as the items that enter into the VAT base and the corresponding gross and net tax liability. The business sells goods and services that it produces by adding the value of the services of its own labour and capital equipment to its purchases from other firms. The top of the table shows the transactions liable to VAT, namely sales (line B) and purchases (line A). The difference between sales and purchases is the net value added by the firm (line C). Since the tax is levied at a rate of 10 per cent, the net VAT liability is £160 minus £110, or £50 (also line C).

Clearly, the entries in the profit and loss account on purchases cannot be used directly to ascertain net taxable value added. The reason is obvious. Although the profit and loss account and the VAT both record the transactions on an accrual basis, the net consumption type of VAT is also levied on a cash flow basis of accounting. Thus, no correction needs to be made for the change in the value of inventory (which must be made in the profit and loss account to match sales and purchases). Furthermore, the cash flow basis of accounting implies that the tax on the purchase of machinery (which is assumed to be depreciated every four years in the profit and loss account) is credited immediately against the VAT on sales. As a result, as accountants will note, gross profits (£400; not shown in the table) are not the same as net value added (£500).

In the table, the net VAT liability is computed by deducting the tax on purchases (more generally referred to as inputs) from the tax on sales (also referred to as outputs) for each tax period. This method, which is used in all OECD countries, is called the indirect subtraction technique, or tax credit method. Since the tax on sales must be stated on invoices to provide documentary evidence for the credit claimed by registered buyers, the tax credit technique is also referred to as the invoice method.

Obviously, as is evident from the table, the net VAT liability can also be ascertained by deducting the aggregate value of purchases (£1,100) from the aggregate value of sales (£1,600) and taxing the difference (£500) between them. This approach to computing the VAT is called the direct subtraction technique, or accounts method. Under the direct

Table 4.1 Computation of VAT Liability

(In £'s, excluding 10 per cent VAT)

Costs	Profit and loss account	VAT Base	VAT Tax	Proceeds	Profit and loss account	VAT Base	VAT Tax
Transactions liable to VAT							
A. Purchases	1,200	1,100	110	B. Sales	1,600	1,600	160
Goods	950	950	95	Goods	1,200	1,200	120
Inventory - open: 350	200			Services	400	400	40
close: 150							
Services	50	50	5				
Machinery (depreciation - 4 years)	—	100	10				
C. Net value added		500	50				
Sub-total	1,200	1,600	160	Sub-total	1,600	1,600	160
Items not liable to VAT							
D. Factor rewards	800	—	—	E. Investment income	400	—	—
Wages	450			Dividends	125	—	—
Depreciation	25			Interest	275	—	—
Interest	90						
Net profits	235						
F. Total	2,000	1,600	160	F. Total	2,000	1,600	160

subtraction type of VAT, goods and services cannot be identified separately. Hence, rate differentiation, if desired, is not feasible. Also, invoices do not provide documentary evidence on the payment of the VAT (referred to as the 'audit trail') and border tax adjustments are more difficult to implement properly.

Apart from identifying value added through the indirect or direct subtraction technique as the difference between outputs and inputs, value added can also be computed as the sum of factor rewards: wages, depreciation, interest and net profits (line D in Table 4.1). In the literature, this approach is referred to as the addition method. To arrive at net value added, investment income (line E; this income does not represent value added by the firm) and the purchase price of the machinery (£100) must be deducted from factor rewards (line D), while the change in the value of inventory (£200) must be added (or deducted if the value of closing inventory exceeds the value of opening inventory). Clearly, this approach is more complicated than the subtraction method, which does not require inventory accounting. Virtually no country uses the addition method, although Argentina and Israel have applied it to selected economic activities, such as banking and finance, where the value of inputs and outputs is difficult to measure.

What is the Nature of a VAT?

Under a VAT, the sum of purchases (the value added at earlier stages) and the value added by the firm itself equals, by definition, the value of the inputs (which have a full tax credit attached to them) of the next firm in the production–distribution process. As a result, the same value added is never taxed twice; that is, cumulative effects do not occur. Moreover, at the final stage – that is, the retail stage – the sum of all values added throughout the process and, by the same token, the sum of all the differences between sales and purchases, equal the consumer price, excluding tax. In other words, the total tax collected piecemeal under the VAT from all stages of production and distribution is exactly equal to a tax collected on the sale from the retailer to the final consumer or user – that is, an RST.

Since the VAT is partly collected at pre–retail stages, does this mean that firms at early stages of production and distribution advance the tax and, hence, that their working capital requirements are greater than under an RST? Does the piecemeal collection process impose an extra burden on manufacturers and wholesalers in the form of an interest charge that could be avoided if the government only taxed the final stage – that is, imposed an RST? Although some economists and businessmen believe this to be so, it is not true for the simple reason that the purchaser's right to a tax credit (and refund) arises at the same time that the supplier has to account for the tax. After all, the invoice date (closely linked, in turn, to the date of supply) is the date on which the tax on sales becomes due and the tax on purchases becomes eligible as credit. That date is the same for supplier and purchaser.

The multi–stage collection feature of a VAT does not require greater capital outlays than the single–stage collection characteristic of an RST, provided that the period of time for remitting tax and for processing any refunds is synchronised with commercial payment conditions and that bad debts do not arise. Under a VAT, as under an RST, taxable firms will not even bear the cost of financing carrying charges for tax paid on, say, inventory accumulation or capital equipment purchases. Under an RST, such items are exempt from tax – that is, the tax is suspended. Under a VAT, the tax invoiced for such items will be refunded if the tax paid on purchases exceeds the tax payable on sales. This conclusion is not affected if production, sales, or net inventories rise or decline.

But if registered businesses bear no net tax in relation to their own value added, why do they nonetheless remit some tax to the authorities? To understand this apparent paradox, one should look upstream at financial flows rather than downstream at the flow of goods and services. The answer is, then, that the consumer pays in full the tax that is collected by the retailer but that is remitted to the tax authorities by all registered firms in proportion to their share in the total value added embodied in the final product. In essence, any net tax remitted by upstream firms is simply paid to them by downstream firms in the production–distribution process. (Incidentally, this makes it more likely that a VAT, like an RST, will be borne by consumers in relation to their expenditures on taxable goods and services.)

To be sure, cash flow benefits (and costs) arise if a registered firm's collection date (the date on which the tax is collected from customers before being handed over to the tax authorities) does not coincide with the remittance date (the date after the collection date but before the latest day designated for handing over the tax). This will happen under an RST if sales are made against cash but the tax is remitted, say, every three months, or if accounts receivable, inclusive of tax, are settled earlier than the tax is remitted to the tax authorities. If the tax payment conditions are similar, the effect also arises under a VAT, but part of the tax–induced cash flow benefit may be spread upstream to the wholesale and manufacturers' level if retail purchases are also made against cash. Cash flow costs arise with respect to sales on credit if the average length of time that customers defer payment exceeds the average length of time required for remitting the tax to the authorities. The same occurs with zero–rated goods if suppliers are paid before refunds are received.

Without a judgement on the net position of individual taxable firms, it is difficult to say whether a benefit or a cost arises, but there is no reason to assume that the position differs much, if at all, between a VAT and an RST. In the aggregate, the imposition of a VAT or an RST should involve a cash flow benefit for taxable firms for two reasons: (1) as a rule, consumers pay more often in cash than businesses do; and (2) usually, tax payment terms are more generous than commercial payment terms.

What is the Difference between a VAT and an RST?

If a VAT is identical to an RST, why not collect the full tax at the retail stage – that is, impose an RST? A VAT is preferred for four reasons: the potential coverage of the tax, its ability to distinguish producer goods from consumer goods, its ability to effect correct border tax adjustments and its administrative feasibility.

First, RSTs are less effective in taxing services that are rendered primarily by small business establishments. There is no 'tax credit' link with suppliers and no 'automatic' sorting out of taxable and non–taxable customers. Not taxing services means that services are favoured over goods. This distorts the economic choices of both consumers and producers and unnecessarily accentuates the regressive impact of the tax, because the demand for services is generally more income elastic than is the demand for goods. In industrial countries, services comprise up to 50 per cent of national product, too large a portion of economic activity to be ignored by a broadly based consumption tax. Administratively, taxing goods but not services involves complex and inherently arbitrary distinctions when the two are rendered in combination.

Second, RSTs have difficulty distinguishing between producer and consumer goods. How does a registered firm know that a shovel it supplies tax free is used not as an (exempt) input for factory work but rather for (taxable) gardening purposes? Who knows whether sugar is used to sweeten tea at home (taxable) or as an (exempt) ingredient for (taxable) bakery products? Similarly, an RST has difficulty distinguishing between taxable consumer services and exempt services rendered to business. Consider a simple service transaction – the purchase of a train ticket for a business trip. The VAT does not require the ticket office to take the purpose of the trip into consideration. The proper application of the RST, however, would require not only the presentation of an exemption certificate, but also an inquiry into the purpose of the trip. Clearly, the ticket office is not in a position to check that information. A VAT has no such difficulty because the seller is simply told always to charge tax, leaving it to the purchaser to obtain a tax credit if he or she is also a registered taxpayer.

Third, because RSTs are unable to distinguish effectively between producer and consumer goods, in practice many producer goods (fuel, office furniture, computers) are taxed. This discourages capital–intensive production and, hence, economic growth. Also, it means that the tax enters into the cost of exports, with detrimental effects on international competitiveness. Similarly, because the price of domestic goods incorporates an element of tax on producer goods, in addition to the RST itself, while the price of goods imported from countries with a VAT that is rebated in respect of exports does not, domestic goods are discriminated against artificially. (To some extent, these effects are also inherent in a VAT that exempts certain business inputs, such as financial services and insurance. While the EC zero rates direct exports of these services, the element of tax related to the taxable inputs of the exempt services enters into the cost of other goods and services if produced with the aid of exempt services. Similarly, domestic products may have a disadvantage *vis–à–vis* imports, if the VAT in respect of the latter is more fully rebated in the exporting country or if no sales tax is levied.)

Fourth, a VAT is a more robust form of consumption tax. It disperses the collection process over the whole of industry and commerce; it transfers part of the burden of proof with respect to tax liability to taxpayers (who must prove that they are entitled to the tax credit on purchases); and it penalises dishonesty more than an RST does, because every invoice throughout the production–distribution process is a 'public declaration' with respect to the tax liability.

The major point in favour of an RST is that it requires little or no border tax adjustments, since goods are not taxed until sold to final domestic users or consumers. In other words, unlike a VAT, the RST is almost inherently destination based. Unless imported by end users, imports are not taxed and, as a rule, exports do not pass through taxable retail channels. This makes the RST particularly suitable for operation in a federation where each sub–national entity can administer its own version. As will be seen below, the VAT can also be administered in a federation, but the arrangements are more complicated than under an RST. This explains the RST's popularity at the state and provincial level in the United States and Canada.

What is the Aggregate Base of a VAT?

The aggregate base of an EC type of VAT, being equivalent to the base of an RST, equals total private consumption expenditures shown in national accounts, subject to some adjustments. Thus, expenditures on services commonly exempted (see below), such as health care, education, welfare, finance and insurance, as well as rents and imputed rental values, should be deducted from this base, while taxable intermediate goods and fixed assets of exempt sectors, including new housing, should be added back. Government purchases and investment in fixed assets should also be included in the base, as should inputs of the agricultural sector, if government sales and farm produce would not be subject to the VAT, or if the tax on agricultural inputs would not be washed out in some other fashion (see below). Finally, an adjustment would have to be made for the value added attributable to the small–firm exemption. Overall, the VAT base should cover up to 70–80 per cent of total household consumption expenditures.

Obviously, the VAT base can also be computed by taking the figure for GDP as the starting point. To this figure, the value of imports should be added and that of exports deducted to arrive at total expenditures on private consumption, government consumption, fixed capital formation and an increase (algebraically defined) in business inventories. Subsequently, from this amount should be excluded the value of the services of the exempt sectors, government wages and salaries, fixed capital formation and net consumption abroad. Additions would have to be made for the purchases of intermediate goods and fixed assets of exempt sectors, including government and agriculture, which are not eligible for a tax credit. In considering the tax base for revenue purposes, allowance should be made for the double counting of the tax on government purchases, which may involve an equal increase in expenditures.

Social, Economic and Political Considerations

One of the most serious objections to a VAT is that it falls more heavily on the poor than on the rich. Furthermore, anxieties persist about how the introduction of a VAT would affect prices and economic growth. The question of how a VAT can be administered in common markets and by subordinate levels of government in a federal fiscal system also deserves attention.

Should Anything be done about the Regressivity of the VAT?

The most pointed criticism of a VAT is that its burden is distributed regressively with respect to income. Since consumption as a share of income falls as income rises, a VAT levied at a uniform rate falls more heavily on the poor than on the rich. Although the criticism is valid, it is true only if VAT payments are expressed as a percentage of income. If, instead, consumption is used as the denominator, then, by definition, the impact would be proportional. The burden of a VAT levied at a uniform rate would also be largely proportional if the denominator were lifetime income rather than annual income, because many income recipients are only temporarily in lower income brackets. They move into the middle- or upper-income brackets as their earnings increase. A lifetime income concept takes account of this phenomenon.

Whatever the case, in the political arena the burden distribution of the VAT is usually measured against annual income. The question in this context is whether the regressivity issue should be addressed through the VAT itself or through other tax and expenditure measures. The VAT itself can be used to tax essential consumer items that are disproportionately consumed by the poor at a lower-than-standard rate (or even at a zero rate) and, conversely, to tax luxury commodities that are disproportionately consumed by the rich at a higher-than-standard rate. Corrections outside the VAT system might include higher income tax exemptions or lower basic rates, or increases in transfer payments to the poor.

Strong arguments have been advanced against the use of multiple rates under a VAT. To begin with, rate graduation is a very blunt and expensive instrument for mitigating regressivity. As household budget expenditure surveys indicate, the rich generally benefit at least twice as much as the poor in absolute amounts. This is because, for VAT purposes, it is nearly impossible to distinguish, say, expensive higher–quality food products bought by the rich from less expensive ordinary food products bought by the poor. But if such a distinction is not feasible, lower rates become less effective in mitigating the regressivity of the VAT. This is confirmed by the findings of four recent country studies (see OECD 1988, pp.122 ff) which indicate that the impact of a VAT changes less than might be expected when necessities are zero rated (as in the United Kingdom), taxed at a lower rate (as in the Netherlands), or taxed at the standard rate (as in Denmark and Norway).

Furthermore, the costs of administering a VAT are inevitably increased by a differentiated rate structure, because it brings in its train problems of delineating products and interpreting the rules regarding which rate should be applied. Even with careful design, anomalies cannot be avoided. Differentiated rates also involve a significant increase in compliance costs, particularly of small firms. Usually, it is not possible for them to keep separate accounts for the sales of differentially taxed products. The tax liability must then be determined by applying presumptive methods, an approach that increases the difficulty of monitoring the taxpayer's compliance. Also, there is evidence that the increase in compliance costs attributable to differentiated rates is distributed regressively with respect to income. Smaller firms with lower incomes bear proportionately more of the burden than do larger firms.

It should also be emphasised that, given the amount of revenue to be raised, applying a lower or zero rate to essential commodities means that the standard rate must be higher than it would be in the absence of rate differentiation. This higher standard rate would magnify the distortion of consumer and producer choices. This defect should be taken seriously, because, as a rule, the severity of tax distortions increases progressively with the tax rate that causes them. It has also been shown that high *ad valorem* rates have detrimental effects on product quality. The higher the standard rate required to maintain revenue, the more serious these effects are[1].

[1] On the other hand, some would argue that if food were not subject to a VAT, families at the lower end of the income distribution might have more to spend on high-protein foods and consequently be able to work harder. As Shoup (1969, p.592) has pointed out, regressive product taxes may reduce gainful consumption, defined as 'consumption of a type such that, in the event that it decreases, the output of the economy will decrease, either now or later, by more than the decrement in consumption'.

Similarly, increased rates make little sense. To the extent that they cover expenditures on drinking, smoking and motoring, increases in the related excises or user charges are indicated. Also, higher rates are difficult to enforce with respect to small high–value items, such as jewellery, toilet goods and cameras, which can easily be smuggled in from abroad. In practice, the part of the VAT base that can be taxed at a higher rate is extremely small, at most 5 per cent of total consumption expenditures. This is to be expected. As noted above, higher–income groups usually buy varieties of particular commodities that are more expensive than the varieties bought by lower–income groups, but it is nearly always impossible to distinguish between them in a way that is relevant for VAT purposes. The rich also spend proportionately more than the poor on holidays abroad and on education, but these expenditures either cannot be taxed or must be excluded on merit grounds. Overall, higher–than–standard rates impart little progressivity to the VAT burden distribution.

Clearly, it is advisable to keep the application of the VAT as uniform as possible and to help the poor by means of adjustments elsewhere in the fiscal system. Nonetheless, most OECD countries address the regressivity issue within the context of the VAT, as the Appendix indicates. In fact, fourteen of the twenty–one OECD countries with a VAT apply one or more lower rates to essential items, such as food products, medicines, household fuels, public transportation and some other items. Ireland, the United Kingdom and, to a lesser degree, Canada subject these items to a zero rate, which means that all of the tax paid in previous stages and shown on purchase invoices is refunded. Furthermore, seven countries levy higher rates on luxury items. Admittedly, this picture owes much to the situation in the original EC member states, which adopted the VAT in the late 1960s and early 1970s. These countries were concerned with staying as close as possible to the tax burden distribution of the previous turnover tax so as not to jeopardise the acceptance of a completely novel levy.

Although the arguments in favour of a uniform rate are strong, some countries introducing a VAT may find it politically difficult to adopt such a rate. Parliamentarians would probably be inclined to disregard the theoretical arguments and to point to the actual situation in the EC member states. Also, food may occupy a more prominent position in the household basket of the poor than it does in most member states of the EC, and income transfer systems may be more rudimentary.

If a dual rate structure is desired, a lower–than–standard, but positive, rate, as advocated by the EC Commission, is the preferred way to tax essential consumer items. To avoid troublesome delineation issues, it should apply to all food products, including those served in hotels and restaurants. As in the EC, the coverage of the lower rate might be extended to medicines, household fuel, books, newspapers and public transportation, but it should not include electricity and telecommunications. Moderation is the key to deciding which goods and services should be taxed lower. Otherwise, the lower rate degenerates into a standard rate.

A zero rate is the neatest way of ensuring that the poor do not pay any tax on their food. The United Kingdom and Ireland apply a zero rate to food, except when supplied by hotels and restaurants. As well as being a rather ineffective instrument for helping the poor, this procedure is administratively burdensome because it involves collecting tax from thousands of taxpayers, only to refund it to thousands of others. In contrast, the practice in most EC member states, sanctioned by the Commission, is to set lower rates at such a level that, as a rule, there would be no refund. This seems the best advice for countries contemplating a dual rate structure. An important administrative advantage of the EC approach is that a 'bell' starts ringing in the VAT office whenever a refund is requested. This is not the case in Ireland and the United Kingdom, because the extensive use of the zero rate means that refunds must be issued in a routine manner.

Is a VAT Inflationary?

An often–voiced concern in countries without a VAT is that the introduction of the tax would set in motion a spiral in which the tax, prices and wages would feed on each other – that is, a VAT would be inflationary. However, there is no evidence that the inflation spiral occurred in other European countries. To be sure, normally the introduction of a broadly based VAT would be accompanied by a general price increase of some 0.7 per cent for each percentage point of tax if its introduction were accommodated by the monetary authorities, as is ordinarily done. The crucial question, however, is whether this one–time increase would lead to further price escalations.

Alan Tait (1990) collected empirical evidence on this issue by observing the movements in the consumer price index (CPI) in several countries before and after the introduction (or modification) of the VAT.

Tait tested four hypotheses: (1) little or no price effect; (2) shift in the CPI trend line (a one–time price effect); (3) acceleration (inflation); and (4) shift plus acceleration.

The data suggest that in eleven of the thirteen OECD countries surveyed, considering all the circumstances, the introduction of the VAT had little or no effect on retail prices (eight countries) or simply resulted in a one–time shift of the CPI trend line (three countries). The answer to the question raised above, therefore, is almost categorically 'no'. In only two countries, Italy and Norway, could some interaction between the VAT and inflation be discerned. In Italy the rate of inflation accelerated following the introduction of the VAT in 1973, largely on account of uncertainty and widening profit margins. In Norway the tax change fed a sustained price–wage increase. The public anticipated that the VAT would increase prices without sufficient compensation in the form of lower income taxes.

How does a VAT affect Economic Growth?

A VAT should also be judged as regards its effect on saving (and investment). Given the amount of revenue to be raised, the effect should be measured relative to the effect on saving of another broadly based tax, such as an income tax.

Consider an individual who has the choice to consume £100 in year 1 or to postpone consumption by putting the amount into a savings account where it earns interest at 10 per cent until the accumulated amount of £110 is withdrawn for consumption in year 2. Suppose that the individual is subject to a VAT or an income tax, both levied at a rate of 20 per cent. Under the VAT regime, on the one hand, the individual could consume £80 in period 1 (£100 minus 20 per cent tax) or £88 in period 2 (£110 minus 20 per cent VAT) – 10 per cent more than in period 1. Under the income tax regime, on the other hand, the individual would be able to consume £80 in period 1, but only £86.40 in period 2 (£88 minus 20 per cent of £8) – only 8 per cent more than in period 1.

This example (taken from US Department of the Treasury (p.19, 1984)) shows that a VAT is neutral with respect to the choice whether to consume now or to save for future consumption. Although a VAT reduces the absolute return on saving (that is, the amount of future consumption), the tax does not reduce the net rate of return on saving. In contrast, an income tax does affect the net rate of return on saving, because both the amount saved and the interest earned on that amount are subject to tax. In the example, the net rate of return on saving under the income tax regime – 8 per cent – is 20 per cent less than the return under the VAT regime – 10 per cent. Therefore, if it is assumed that saving increases as the net rate of return on saving increases, a VAT is superior to an income tax in promoting economic growth.

Finally, while it is often said that a VAT has a favourable effect on the balance of payments, this argument is unconvincing. Some marginal improvement in the trade balance might occur if the tax on exports is more fully eliminated under a VAT than under the type of sales tax which is replaced. Also, a VAT would not discriminate in favour of imported products. This happens under, say, a turnover tax because product prices incorporate cumulative turnover tax elements that may not be included in the price of imports. Some improvement in the trade balance might also occur if the VAT were substituted for various payroll taxes and if the latter were also shifted to consumers. But this would happen only if the payroll taxes, when reduced or eliminated, were 'unshifted' and, more unrealistically, if exchange rates were fixed. This discussion assumes that the various taxes are reflected in price.

How can a VAT be Administered in Common Markets and Federations?

In recent years, various countries have joined hands in establishing a common market. What implications does this have for their VAT? Also, subordinate levels of government (be they republics, states, regions or provinces) should be interested in the possibilities of administering a VAT independently of or in co–operation with the national government. In both cases, the experience of the EC as it moves from a customs union with border controls towards a single market without border controls should be instructive.

In the EC, as in other countries, the VAT in respect of goods crossing national frontiers has so far been levied on the basis of the destination principle. This principle, implicitly endorsed by the GATT, holds that goods should be taxed in the country where they are consumed, rather than the country where they are produced. Therefore, goods that are exported are 'untaxed', and goods that are imported are taxed on the same footing as domestically produced commodities. The corrections required by the destination principle – so–called border tax adjustments – ensure that manufacturing location decisions are not distorted and that the revenue of the tax accrues to the country of consumption. So far, in the EC the adjustments have been administered by customs officials in conjunction with border controls. Obviously, with the border controls due for abolition in 1992, other mutually acceptable arrangements had to be made.

In thinking through the issues, for federally organised countries as well as for the member states of the EC, one might keep three basic criteria in mind: (1) manufacturing location decisions should not be distorted; (2) whatever is done, the adjustments should not require border controls; and (3) if possible, the subordinate governments (or member states) should be able to administer the VAT themselves and set their own rate(s). In seeking a solution, one should assume that the VAT has a common base and few exemptions. A VAT with many exemptions causes cumulative effects that render its impact indeterminate. Hence, the adjustments that are required when goods enter inter–jurisdictional trade are also unclear.

Currently, two systems of border tax adjustments without border controls but based on the destination principle are under review in the EC. Under the first system, called the tax credit clearing system, proposed by the EC Commission, the destination principle would be administered on a Community–wide basis. Intra–Community exports would be taxed; importers would be permitted a credit for the tax invoiced by exporters of other member states; and the VAT administration of importing states would be able to claim the amount of the tax credit shown on the importer's return from the VAT administration of the exporting states under the aegis of a mutual clearing system. Conventional border tax adjustments would be retained for trade with third countries.

Under the second system, favoured by most member states because it does not require a mutual clearing system, current border tax adjustments (tax rebates on exports and full taxation of imports) would be maintained, but the adjustments would be shifted from the border to the books of account of the first taxable business inland under a so–called deferred payment system or postponed accounting system. Not taxing imports at borders would imply, under the system, that first inland users would not be able to take a tax credit as an offset against the tax on sales; by implication, they would be taxed on the full value of the imports. (Technically, the deferred payment system, which was pioneered in the Benelux countries, taxes imports to the first inland user, but simultaneously allows a tax credit for the same amount. In effect, this means that imports are not taxed until sold, directly or indirectly, by the first inland user. It will be appreciated that this system permits administrative control over imports, particularly when in transit, yet does not involve the payment of tax at an earlier stage than would occur if the goods had been produced domestically.)

Whereas the tax credit clearing system brings a VAT approach to the problem (no breaks in the taxable production–distribution chain), the deferred payment system introduces an RST type of suspension into the system with respect to goods moving from one member state to another. Both systems require agreement on the treatment of cross–border purchases by consumers (particularly of 'big ticket' items) and exempt entities, as well as cross–border sales by mail order firms. For the time being, the Community has opted for the deferred payment system (exports free of VAT). Exporters will have to report on their sales to customers in other member states on a quarterly basis. The system will be evaluated before 1995. Also, it has been decided that the border controls over excisable goods will be shifted from borders to bonded warehouses inland.

Either of the approaches outlined above would be suitable for a federal fiscal system in which subordinate governments would administer their own VAT without border controls. Obviously, rates between adjacent jurisdictions should not be far apart, but uniformity of rates, in contrast to uniformity of the tax base, would not be necessary. Small jurisdictions would not be able to set their VAT rates much higher than the rates in large adjacent jurisdictions. However, they could set them lower if they decided to snatch part of the tax base of adjacent jurisdictions. Luxembourg is an example of the latter phenomenon. The repercussions of tax base snatching would be most serious if one of the jurisdictions decided to opt out of the VAT.

Administratively, the easiest way to levy the VAT in a federation would be to have a national tax in conjunction with a revenue–sharing arrangement with subordinate units of government based on consumption or some other key, as in Austria and Germany. Elsewhere, however, subordinate governments might object to the implied surrender of tax sovereignty. This approach or the arrangements envisaged for the EC are far superior to the idea aired by some economists that the VATs of a federation or common market should be administered on the basis of the origin principle; that is, goods should be taxed where they are produced, not where they are consumed. Whatever its economic equivalence to the destination principle, under a tax–credit VAT, the origin principle would require valuation at export (to catch the value added domestically), as well as at import (to make sure that the value added abroad is not taxed at home). This situation would be far worse than current border controls in the EC. Moreover, the revenue would accrue primarily to the producing states.

Tax Coverage, Base and Rate Issues

Once it has been decided to introduce a VAT, three major structural issues must be addressed: (1) the coverage of the tax: should the VAT extend through the retail stage and how should small traders, farmers and public sector bodies be treated? (2) the base of the VAT: which services should be exempted and, in particular, how should housing services and second–hand goods be treated? and (3) the rate structure of the tax – which has already been considered above.

Should a VAT Extend to the Retail Stage?

All countries with a VAT in the OECD area and most countries elsewhere extend the tax to the retail stage – and for good reasons. As an economy matures, a manufacturers' (or wholesale) VAT is beset by major valuation and trade organisation problems that are difficult to cope with and that draw valuable administrative resources away from audit and compliance control. The term 'manufacturing' is difficult to define properly (should it include such activities as mixing, blending and packaging?); sales at different trade levels (by manufacturers to wholesalers as well as to retailers and consumers) require adjustments of the taxable value; transfers between related parties (from manufacturers to subsidiary wholesalers or to retailers) demand careful scrutiny; and sole distributors, particularly of imported goods, tend to be favoured over other distributors (typically, the latter will undertake more marketing functions, the cost of which is included in the value for tax of the domestic manufacturer).

In addition to these technical problems, a manufacturers' VAT, which does not include distribution margins, distorts producer and consumer choices. Given the same tax rate, luxury products tend to be favoured over essential consumer items because their trading margins are usually greater. Furthermore, producers are induced to push as many trading functions forward as possible so as to keep their cost outside the tax base. Because trading margins are not included in the value for tax and because it is difficult, conceptually as well as administratively, to tax services under a manufacturers' VAT, the rate of such a tax would have to be approximately twice as high as the rate of a retail type of VAT to raise the same amount of revenue. Obviously, this higher rate would aggravate the distortions inherent in a manufacturers' VAT.

There are strong arguments, therefore, to extend the VAT to the retail stage from the beginning. The argument that the retail stage comprises numerous small businesses that keep such inadequate records that it would be wasteful of administrative resources to try to levy the tax on them suggests that the appropriate coverage of a VAT is not a 'stage' problem, but rather a small firm issue. There is no reason why large and medium–sized retailers, which may be assumed to keep adequate accounts, should not be registered. Moreover, the appropriate treatment of small businesses is an issue that concerns all levels of production and distribution – producers, wholesalers, as well as retailers. In other words, the small firm issue is not solved solely by excluding the retail stage. Obviously, therefore, a VAT should extend to the retail stage and the sole criterion for tax coverage should be the size of the business, regardless of the stage at which it is situated. The focus should be on the design of an appropriate small–firm exemption.

How should Small Traders and Artisans be Treated?

Generally, small traders and artisans face relatively higher costs in complying with the obligations imposed under the VAT than do other taxpayers. Similarly, the tax administration has to incur relatively higher costs in enforcing the tax on them. For these and other reasons, most OECD countries with a VAT exclude small–scale traders and producers with an annual turnover below a specified amount, referred to as the registration threshold, from the obligation to register, furnish returns and pay tax, or to keep prescribed records. The VAT paid by small firms is confined to the tax invoiced to them by their registered suppliers.[1]

---

[1] It should be noted that under the Japanese VAT, a tax credit is imputed to purchases by registered firms from exempt firms (although no tax has been paid in respect of the purchases), exempt firms benefit fully from the relief (and the benefit is passed on to registered firms). As a result of these arrangements, however, more tax than actually has been paid is refunded at the point of export and more tax than is actually being paid with respect to similar domestically produced commodities is imposed on imports.

While small firms benefit from not being taxed on their own value added, they suffer from not being able to pass the VAT on inputs explicitly on to their customers, because, as non–registered entities, they are not allowed to issue tax invoices. Nor can they obtain a refund when exporting their output or purchasing expensive machinery. For this reason, the small–firm exemption is generally optional.

In addition, or in lieu of the turnover exemption, several OECD countries with a VAT have alternative schemes for simplifying the calculation of the VAT liability of small firms or reducing that liability.

- Belgium and Spain exempt small traders but require their suppliers to impose an equalisation tax – that is, a higher–than–normal rate of VAT – on purchases. This scheme has the disadvantage of requiring identification of the purchaser, who has no interest in providing particulars of his or her tax status.

- Austria, Germany and the Netherlands, in addition to exempting very small traders, reduce the net VAT liability of other small traders in the form of a percentage of either the turnover or the tax itself. Here, of course, the drawback is that the VAT liability has to be computed before the relief can be provided.

- Belgium, Greece and Spain exempt some small firms by reference to the type of trade they carry on – for example, peddlers and hawkers or low–margin outlets. Problems arise in identifying the type of trader or the type of product eligible for the relief.

- France has an elaborate presumptive assessment (forfait) system, with no registration threshold, which requires the computation of the VAT liability on a case–by–case basis. Similarly, Spain computes the VAT liability of small traders on the basis of various external indicators, such as the size of the business premises, its location and the number of employees.

- Several countries have also introduced simplified assessment schemes for small traders whose turnover is above the registration threshold but who are really too small to comply with regular requirements. Under these schemes, the net VAT liability is computed as a specified percentage of turnover or purchases. Also, such schemes may be necessary when, say, retailers sell goods subject to more than one rate without being able to account for them separately.

It would seem good economic and social policy if initially countries were to adopt a fairly high optional registration threshold. To prevent avoidance, the exemption should apply to the combined turnover of all outlets owned by an individual. Furthermore, optional registration should be allowed but should be mandatory for a minimum period of, say, five years.

As small businesses prosper and as inflation erodes the real value of the small firm exemption, more traders would be covered by the VAT and the tax office would presumably be in a better position to deal with them. At that time, countries might contemplate the introduction of a simplified scheme for specified small businesses, which would provide for the presumptive computation of the tax liability and, if desired, modified administrative concessions to small taxpayers. Such taxpayers might be obliged to furnish returns less often than regular taxpayers, to maintain simplified records and to keep their accounts on a payments, rather than an accrual, basis. Although it would not be advisable to spend excessive administrative resources on presumptive assessment schemes, some arrangement may be necessary, particularly if small firms would not be subject to the income tax.

Should Farmers be Taxed?

The VAT treatment of farmers and other primary producers engaged in agriculture, animal husbandry, horticulture, viticulture, forestry and fishing requires special attention because of their importance to the economy and the essential nature of their products. If taxed, farmers would have to comply with the usual VAT obligations. If they were exempted, however, while they would not incur compliance costs they would still have to pay the element of VAT on their inputs of feed, seed, fertilizer, equipment and machinery for which a deduction cannot be provided. Because farmers are situated at the beginning of the production–distribution process, this element of tax would cascade throughout the process. Clearly, therefore, a straightforward exemption of primary sectors (without compensatory measures) would be neither fair nor good social policy.

In the various OECD countries, farmers are either taxed or exempted (see OECD, 1988, chap. 9). New Zealand, Sweden and the United

Kingdom treat farmers in the same manner as any other producers of taxable products; that is, they have to comply with the same requirements for furnishing returns and making payments. Generally, modifications of these requirements can be obtained only under the small–firm exemption.

Other OECD countries do not require farmers to register and compensate them for the tax borne on their purchases of VAT–liable inputs. These (optional) compensation measures take various forms.

- In Belgium, Ireland, the Netherlands and Spain, purchasers of agricultural products receive a presumptive tax credit approximately equal to the tax borne by farmers on their inputs. Obviously, the purchaser is expected to pass that benefit on to the farmer, who is not otherwise involved in the compensation procedure.

- In Austria, Germany and Luxembourg, primary producers are taxed at a rate (different from the normal VAT rate) approximately equal to the rate of tax (expressed as a percentage of sales) they bear on their inputs. As a result, no tax needs to be paid nor a return furnished, but the farmer is able to invoice the tax to the purchaser of his products, who subsequently can take a deduction for it.

- In France and Spain (exporters only), farmers are compensated directly by the government for the tax borne on their inputs. The amount is calculated as a flat–rate percentage of turnover.

- Portugal exempts farmers without compensation, but applies a lower rate to the main agricultural inputs, such as feed, seed and fertilizer, and machinery and equipment. Portugal also sets a zero rate on inputs for sea–going fishing activities.

The most appropriate approach to the VAT treatment of farmers depends to a large extent on the size of production units. The only sensible VAT treatment of primary sectors, predominantly consisting of large production units, is registration and payment of tax, which would ensure that agricultural products bear a more even VAT burden than they would if they were exempted. The small–firm exemption would then apply to small production units – for example, employees owning plots on the farm and selling part of their output on the market. If most production units are small, an exemption approach might be adopted in conjunction with some flat rate scheme as used in the Benelux countries, Germany and Austria. Optional registration should be allowed.

Does it Make Sense to Tax Public Sector Bodies?

To begin with, public sector bodies should always pay tax on their purchases of taxable supplies, even if this means that they pay tax that is collected simultaneously by another government agency. This approach safeguards the integrity of the VAT, in that taxable suppliers do not have to make a distinction between taxable and non–taxable goods and services and consumers cannot find illegitimate access to untaxed supplies. Thus, in countries with a VAT, supplies of, say, stationery and personal computers are taxed along with roads, bridges and tanks. Obviously, for exempt government agencies, financed out of general revenue, there would be no net effect on the budget, since both VAT receipts and the appropriations to pay for the tax would be higher. Arrangements should be made to compensate subordinate units of government for the increase in the cost of their purchases. Taxable public sector bodies, however, would be able to credit the VAT on purchases against the VAT on sales.

Public sector bodies should register for VAT purposes according to whether they generate goods and services that are used by or benefit businesses and individuals (except, of course, goods and services explicitly exempted by the legislator) and for which a price is charged. Such chargeable services include all public utilities. Exceptionally, on administrative grounds, consideration might be given to exempt government fees and charges for, say, the registration and issuance of various documents, such as passports and drivers' licences.

The Sixth Directive of the EC takes a somewhat narrower view of the taxation of public sector bodies. In principle, it requires public sector activities to be taxed only if their exemption would involve 'significant distortions of competition' *vis-à-vis* the private sector. This is broadly interpreted, however, and, in practice, the result may come close to the situation in New Zealand, for instance, which taxes a wider range of government activities. In the EC public sector bodies must be registered for VAT with respect to telecommunications; the supply of water, gas, electricity and steam; the transportation of goods; port and airport services; passenger transport; warehousing; the activities of travel agencies; the running of staff shops, co–operatives, industrial canteens and similar institutions; and various other activities.

As a minimum, countries should tax all of the above–mentioned activities of public sector bodies. More generally, the distortion–of–competition criterion may be too narrow a concept for judging the VAT status of public sector bodies. If a government agency has a monopoly on the supply of certain services, it cannot be said to compete with private sector firms in a formal sense. The post office, for example, may not compete with other letter carriers, but it does compete with other forms of transportation and communications, such as delivery services and newspapers. Hence, the post office should be registered for VAT purposes.

Broadly, non–profit institutions and government should be treated in a similar fashion; sales of goods and services that would be taxable if supplied by business should also be taxable if supplied against a charge by non–profit institutions – for example, canteens and gift shops. However, the VAT should not be applied to services that are supplied without consideration, for example, by churches and charitable institutions. After all, there would be no basis on which to calculate the tax. Even if non–profit institutions are not taxable on services rendered, their purchases should be taxed on the basis that suppliers should not be required to differentiate their sales according to the end user. Care should be taken that various sports and social welfare organisations, zoos and similar non–profit bodies do not engage in (untaxed) activities (on a scale in excess of, say, the small firm exemption) that compete directly with similar (taxed) activities of the private sector.

Which Goods and Services should be Exempted?

The integrity of a VAT is safeguarded best if it applies to all final goods and services. Taxing one commodity but not another distorts consumer choices and reduces the tax intake at a given rate, although some concessions must be made for social policy considerations or on administrative grounds. Thus, it would be difficult to defend and, in the absence of a charge, to administer the taxation of health, education, social and religious services. In the EC the Sixth Directive exempts these public interest activities, as do other OECD countries. As discussed above, this means that no credit is given for the tax on purchases. Given the nature of the exempt services, which are rendered directly to consumers and which are often subsidised, distortions should be small. It should be noted, however, that if any of the above–mentioned activities are performed on a commercial basis, they should be made taxable. Thus, say, computer courses may be provided for a fee and health spas may operate on a profit basis.

A second group of activities exempted under the EC's Sixth Directive includes financial transactions, insurance, gambling and immovable property, although, with the exception of gambling, the Directive provides the option of taxing them. The exemption of immovable property is a roundabout way of excluding current housing services and transfers of used real estate from the base, but of taxing newly created property (see below). To tax gambling, other more appropriate levies on admissions and payouts are available.

There are various problems in trying to tax financial services. Should the tax be imposed on the full price – the interest – of the financial service, or should the tax be confined to the gross margin of the intermediary as measured by the difference between the revenue from lending and the cost of borrowing? Because of these conceptual difficulties, as well as practical problems in measuring inputs and outputs, all OECD countries have opted for the exemption approach (although EC countries, under the Sixth Directive, tax secondary financial services, such as financial advice, debt collection, keeping securities and the rental of safety deposit boxes. After considerable study, Canada and New Zealand, too, have decided to exempt financial services.[1] OECD countries with a VAT assign a zero rate to such services when they are exported, which means that the tax on inputs must be pro–rated between exempt and zero–rated activities – not an easy task.

For similar reasons, OECD countries exempt all forms of life insurance from the VAT. Non–term life insurance premiums, for instance, have a savings element that is difficult to separate from the portion that is attributable to the costs of administering the insurance scheme. Other forms of insurance are also exempted, except in New Zealand, which taxes fire, general and accident insurance premiums. To confine the tax to the gross margin, insurers are allowed a credit for the tax fraction of any indemnity payments. A number of countries subject

---

[1]The value of financial activities might be computed by the addition method as was done in Argentina and Israel. This method, however, does not permit the use of tax invoices, which enable the recipient of financial services to take credit for the tax. Hence cumulation of tax occurs. Zero rating would achieve neutrality, if desired, but would require registration and refund of tax.

non–life insurance premiums to a separate tax. Nearly all countries assign a zero rate to exported insurance services.

While the taxation of financial services and insurance is theoretically desirable, a practical solution has so far eluded the experts. Probably the best advice for countries introducing a VAT is to adopt the exemption approach of the EC rather than experiment where other countries have failed.

How should Immovable Property be Taxed?

The treatment of immovable property – that is, the construction, lease and sale of land and buildings (real estate) – is one of the more complicated issues under the VAT. In most industrial countries, housing services, comprising rents and rental values of owner–occupied property, constitute 15 per cent or more of total annual consumption expenditures – too large a portion to be ignored under a broadly based VAT. Moreover, once an essential part of the tax base has been excluded, it becomes exceedingly difficult to recoup.

It is probably difficult to improve on the basic approach to the treatment of immovable property found in the Sixth Directive, which, with minor differences, is followed by nearly all OECD countries. Basically, the Sixth Directive exempts the sale of land, used buildings and the leasing and letting of immovable property.[1] In conjunction with optional registration, this is an indirect way of taxing all new housing and, if desired, providing a credit for the tax on new industrial and commercial real estate (subject to conditions prescribed by the tax office). In analysing the issues, one should distinguish construction activities from the lease or sale of immovable property.

As regards construction, nearly all countries in the OECD area tax building materials, as well as repair and maintenance services, at the standard rate. Logically, these materials and services, broadly interpreted as construction activities, add up to a new building. Most

---

[1]Except the letting of hotel and boarding rooms, camping and holiday sites, parking space, berths and storage spaces for boats, which are taxed. Permanently installed equipment and machinery form an exception to the exemption of immovable property. Since, in most EC countries, these items are immovable property by law, their exemption along with land and buildings would imply that the tax credit would have to be denied. Hence, the exception.

countries recognise this and, under their VATs, newly created buildings are subject to the standard rate as well. If the rate on new buildings were different, the effective rate on materials and services embodied in these buildings would, of course, be different from the tax rate applied to materials and services used for maintaining, repairing and renovating the existing housing stock. This would create distortions, raise administrative problems and create a breeding ground for tax evasion and avoidance, as evidenced by the experience in the United Kingdom, which applies a zero rate to new dwellings.

While new buildings are taxed on first sale, subsequent sales are exempt, as noted above. This means that non–registered individuals who buy a new dwelling pay the full VAT on it. In effect, in their case, the VAT on new residential property is viewed as the capitalised value of the tax that would have been payable in respect of current housing services had the VAT been applicable to imputed rental values. Because it is hardly feasible to tax imputed rental values and because it might be considered unfair to tax rents, housing is treated as an exempt sector. (Austria and Japan, however, do tax rents, which may be the better approach if most immovable property in the rental sector is owned by commercial lessors or building societies). Dwellings and business buildings, which can be close substitutes, are accorded the same treatment under the Sixth Directive. Potential cascading effects are eliminated by permitting commercial lessors to apply for registration and payment of VAT. They then obtain a full credit for the tax on purchase, and pay VAT on rents received and on the sale of the building. Usually, this treatment is subject to the condition that lessor and lessee are both registered taxpayers or agree to become so. Thus, the option is not available to lessors of apartments and houses.

Countries that follow this approach also exempt the sale of immovable property other than new buildings. This is logical, although it means that increases in the value of the stock of building services are not taxed, nor is a tax credit provided for decreases in that value. Taxing the transfer of (exempt) real estate would imply that a (presumptive) tax credit would have to be given for the tax, if any, paid on the purchase of the property, a choice that no country has elected. Again, owners of industrial and commercial real estate could become registered taxpayers and receive the usual VAT treatment. The sale of their property would then be taxable, but any subsequent registered owner would be able to claim a tax credit if he or she, in turn, were to lease or sell the property to a registered taxpayer. Although most countries exempt the sale of used real estate, they do levy gross transfer taxes (registration duties) on the sale. If the VAT, as well as the transfer tax applies, usually the VAT is levied in lieu of the transfer tax.

What about Second–hand Goods?

The treatment of second–hand goods, such as motor vehicles, household appliances, works of art, antiques and collector's items, deserves to be mentioned briefly. It might be argued that if these goods were to be taxed on the gross consideration after having been bought and subsequently resold by a registered dealer, the new tax would come on top of the old tax paid at the time of purchase by the user. Thus, the VAT would deter the re–use of goods and would divert the trade in second–hand goods from registered traders to private channels. As a result, specialisation would suffer.

Different solutions to the problem are found in the OECD area. New Zealand and Sweden allow registered traders in second–hand goods a full deduction for the tax that may be assumed to be included in the purchase price of an item bought from an unregistered person. Most Southern European countries, as well as Belgium and the United Kingdom, tax registered traders only on their gross margin by allowing the purchase price as a deduction from the sale price. Unlike the first approach, the credit for tax is not available until the good is re–sold. The Benelux countries tax specified second–hand goods at a lower–than–standard rate. Spain achieves the same effect by applying the standard rate to a proportion of the sale price. Finally, Austria and Germany do not have any special rules for the trade in second–hand goods.

The latter solution appears to be the preferred one. As in Austria and Germany, a large part of the trade in second–hand goods might not be affected if the goods were sold at auction on behalf of non–registered vendors. Only the auctioneer's commission would then be subject to VAT as services rendered. Most of the trade in other second–hand items would probably fall under the small–firm exemption and thus would not be taxed again. Although very neat in theory, the New Zealand and Swedish approach implies that exporters of second–hand goods receive a VAT refund, clearly something that most countries would not want to do.

Basic Requirements for a Good VAT

In this paper, the discussion of an appropriate VAT has proceeded from the widely agreed premise that the tax should be used almost exclusively to generate revenue for the government budget in as neutral and administratively feasible a manner as possible. While the income tax can be employed to achieve distributional objectives and the excises to attain allocative goals, the focus of the VAT should be on revenue.

In summary, the requirements for a properly designed and operated VAT are the following.

- The VAT should be productive of revenue and responsive to changes in revenue needs. This requires that (1) the tax base be broad, covering as many goods and services as possible; and (2) the point of impact of the tax be as close to the consumer as possible, so as to capture the largest value for tax of any single taxable item.

- Under the VAT, unintended distortions of producer choices, with respect to the form and the methods by which business is conducted, and of consumer choices for one good over another should be minimised. This means that (1) the anti–cascading device of the VAT – that is, the tax credit method – should be as comprehensive as possible, applying to all producer goods: raw materials, intermediate goods and capital goods; (2) refunds should be paid quickly; and (3) tax–to–consumer price ratios should be as uniform as possible by extending the tax through to the retail stage.

- The VAT should permit the unequivocal application of the destination principle. In other words, commodities should be taxed in the country where they are consumed (not the country where they are produced), as required under the provisions of the GATT. This means that (1) the tax on imported goods should be the same as the tax on domestically produced goods; and (2) exports should leave the country completely free of tax.

- The VAT should be simple and easy to understand. Thus, (1) the value for tax should be based on the actual selling price of goods and services rather than on presumptive or deemed selling prices; (2) exemptions of goods and services should be limited to those essential for social reasons or those involving administrative complexity; (3) the rate of tax should be uniform or as little differentiated as possible; and (4) the zero rate should be confined to exports.

- Costs of collecting and enforcing the VAT should be kept low. This requires that (1) the tax be fully administered on a self–assessment basis; (2) small shopkeepers, artisans and small service establishments be exempted; (3) part of the tax be collected at the import stage; and (4) tax invoices play a central role in enforcing the tax.

- The VAT should be easy to comply with and should interfere as little as possible with the free functioning of business and trade. This objective implies that (1) the tax should be attuned as closely as possible to actual business transactions and accounting methods; (2) taxable firms should be obliged always to charge tax regardless of whether a purchaser is a consumer, another business, or a government entity; (3) the time when the tax becomes due and payable should be clear and precise; and (4) the tax should be verified primarily through checks on accounting records rather than through physical types of control.

References and Further Reading

Casanegra de Jantscher, M., and C. Silvani, 'Guidelines for Administering a VAT', in *Value–Added Tax: Administrative and Policy Issues,* IMF Occasional Paper 88,   International Monetary Fund, Washington, 1991.

Cnossen, S., 'Harmonization of Indirect Taxes in the EC', in ed. Charles E. McLure, Jr. *Tax Assignment in Federal Countries, ,* Australian National University, Canberra, 1983.

Cnossen, S., 'VAT and RST: A Comparison', *Canadian Tax Journal,* Vol. 35, pp.559–615, May/June 1987.

Cnossen, S., 'What Rate Structure for a Goods and Services Tax - The European Experience', *Canadian Tax Journal,* Vol. 37, pp.1167–81, September/October 1989.

Cnossen, S., 'The Interjurisdictional Co–ordination of Sales Taxes', in eds. M. Gillis, C. S. Shoup and G. P. Sicat, *Value Added Taxation in Developing Countries,* World Bank, Washington, 1990.

Cnossen, S., 'Key Questions in Considering a Value–Added Tax for Central and Eastern European Countries', *IMF Staff Papers,* Vol. 39, pp.211–55, June 1992.

Cnossen, S., and C. S. Shoup, 'Co–ordination of Value–Added Taxes', in ed. S. Cnossen, *Tax Co–ordination in the European Community,* Kluwer Law and Taxation Publishers, Deventer, The Netherlands, 1987.

Due, J. F., 'The Implications for Australia of the Experience in the United States, Canada and Other Countries with Retail Sales Tax', in ed. John G. Head, *Changing the Tax Mix,* Australian Tax Research Foundation, Sydney, 1986.

McLure, C. E., Jr., *The Value–Added Tax: Key to Deficit Reduction?,* American Enterprise Institute of Public Policy Research, Washington, 1987.

Sandford, C. T., M. R. Godwin, P. J. W. Hardwick and M. I. Butterworth, *Costs and Benefits of VAT,* Heinemann Educational Books, London, 1981.

Shoup, C. S., 'Production from Consumption', *Public Finance,* Aldine Publishing Company, Chicago, 1969.

Shoup, C. S., 'Choosing Among Types of VATs', in eds. M. Gillis, C. S. Shoup and Gerardo P. Sicat, *Value Added Taxation in Developing Countries,* World Bank, Washington, 1990.

Tait, A. A., *Value–Added Tax: International Practice and Problems*, International Monetary Fund, Washington, 1988.

Tait, A. A., 'VAT Revenue, Inflation and the Foreign Trade Balance', in eds. M. Gillis, C. S. Shoup and G. P. Sicat, *Value Added Taxation in Developing Countries*, World Bank, Washington, 1990.

OECD, *Taxing Consumption*, OECD, Paris, 1988.

US Department of the Treasury, *Tax Reform for Fairness, Simplicity and Economic Growth, Vol. 3: Value–Added Tax*, Government Printing Office, Washington, 1984.

APPENDIX to Chapter 4   VATs and Other Sales Taxes in OECD Member Countries, 1992

Revenue Contribution[1]

Type of tax and country	Year of introduction	Percent of total tax revenue	Percent of GDP	Rate structure[2] (in percent) lower	standard	higher
Value-added tax (21)		**17.6**	**7.1**		**17.1**	
European Community (12)		(18.0)	(7.1)		(17.4)	
Denmark	1967	19.5	9.7	—[3]	25.0	
France	1968	19.3	8.4	2.1 and 5.5	18.6	22.0[4]
Germany	1968	15.4	5.9	7.0	14.0	
Netherlands	1969	16.3	7.5	6.0	18.5	—
Luxembourg	1970	13.9	5.9	3.0, 6.0 and 12.0	15.0	—
Belgium	1971	16.3	7.2	6.0 and 17.0[3]	19.0	25.0 and 33.0
Ireland	1972	21.6	8.1	0.0, 10.0 and 12.5	21.0	
Italy	1973	14.1	5.3	4.0 and 9.0[3]	19.0	38.0
United Kingdom	1973	16.8	6.2	0.0	17.5	
Spain	1986	16.7	5.8	6.0	13.0	28.0
Portugal	1986	20.1	7.1	5.0	16.0	30.0
Greece	1987	25.8	8.6	4.0 and 8.0	18.0	36.0
Other countries (9)		(17.1)	(6.9)		(16.1)	
Sweden	1969	13.6	7.6	18.0[5]	25.0	
Norway	1970	19.1	8.7	—[6]	20.0	—
Austria	1973	21.1	8.7	10.0[7]	20.0	—
Finland	1976	24.4	9.3		21.0[2]	—
Turkey	1985	17.7	5.1	8.0	12.0	20.0
New Zealand	1986	20.2	8.1		12.5	—
Iceland	1990			—	24.5	—
Japan	1989	3.3	1.0	—	3.0	—
Canada	1991	—	—	0.0	7.0	—

VATs and Other Sales Taxes in OECD Member Countries, 1992 contd.

Type of tax and country	Year of introduction	Revenue Contribution[1]		Rate structure[2] (in percent)		
		Percent of total tax revenue	Percent of GDP	lower	standard	higher
Retail sales tax (3)						
United States (States)	1932-1969	8.4	2.7	—	7.0	
Switzerland	1941	7.4	2.2	—	4.25-8.25[8]	—
Canada (Provinces)	1948-1967	10.0	3.2	—	6.2[9]	—
Other sales taxes (1)		7.7	2.7		5.0-12.0	
Australia[10]	1930	9.0	2.7	10.0	20.0	30.0

[1] Fiscal year 1989; averages are unweighted.

[2] Expressed as a percentage of the tax-exclusive value of taxable sales, which is the practice in most countries. Finland has a tax-inclusive rate. The relationship between the two rates is expressed by $f_e = f_i/1 - f_i$ where f_e is the tax-exclusive rate, and f_i is the tax-inclusive rate. Averages are unweighted.

[3] A zero rate applies to newspapers.

[4] The French Government intends to abolish the higher rate.

[5] A zero rate applies to newspapers and prescription drugs.

[6] A zero rate applies to books, newspapers, certain periodicals, public roads, railways, ferry services and electricity supplied to households in northern Norway.

[7] A zero rate applies to newspapers, live animals, specified wood products and minerals.

[8] Inclusive of RSTs levied by county and city governments in the United States.

[9] A 9.3 percent rate applies to sales by wholesalers to small retailers that are not registered for sales tax purposes. Furthermore, Switzerland taxes construction at an effective rate of 4.65 per cent.

[10] The Australian sales tax is levied at the wholesale level.

Sources: Rates: country legislation; revenue figures: *Revenue Statistics of OECD Countries, 1965-1990*, OECD, Paris, 1991, Tables 28, 29.

CHAPTER 5

LOCAL TAXATION - LESSONS FROM BRITAIN

David King*

Introduction

In 1993 Great Britain replaced the community charge, or poll tax, with a new local tax - the 'council tax'. The poll tax itself was a relatively new tax, having been introduced in Scotland in 1989 and in England and Wales in 1990 as a replacement for the previous local tax, a property tax known as rates. This paper focuses on three key questions. Why were rates abandoned? Why has the poll tax been abandoned? Will the new council tax prove satisfactory? This chapter addresses these three questions in separate sections, though it precedes them with a section that gives a brief historical outline of local government in Great Britain.

As it happens, British practices are unusual. No other OECD country has relied exclusively on a poll tax for local authorities, and no other OECD country, save Ireland, seeks to rely exclusively on a property tax at the subcentral level. Rather, as Table 5.1 shows, almost all OECD countries have more than one subcentral tax. In terms of yield, the most important subcentral taxes in the OECD are taxes on income, followed - at a good distance - by taxes on property. There are good reasons for the popularity of these two subcentral taxes. Property taxes are popular for several reasons: it is clear which authority is entitled to tax any taxed subject; the tax is usually paid by businesses as well as households and so secures some local revenue from businesses who benefit from many local services; the tax rate can vary between authorities without much danger of tax bases migrating from one area to another; the incidence of the tax falls largely on residents; the tax is highly perceptible; and all households have to pay the tax (unless some form of rebates gives complete relief for some households).

*Senior Lecturer in Economics, University of Stirling, Scotland.

108

Table 5.1   The Yields of State and Local Taxes in OECD Countries
as Percentages of GDP, 1990

Country	Income taxes	Property taxes	Sales taxes	Other taxes	Total taxes
Sweden	17.9	—	0.1	—	18.0
Canada	6.8	3.4	4.6	1.9	16.7
Denmark	14.4	1.1	—	—	15.5
Switzerland (West)	10.3	1.9	0.1	0.4	12.7
Germany	7.8	1.2	2.5	0.4	11.9
Finland	10.9	0.1	—	—	11.0
Norway	9.0	0.9	—	0.4	10.3
Austria	4.3	0.4	3.6	1.4	9.7
United States	2.5	3.1	3.4	0.7	9.7
Japan	5.3	1.9	0.7	0.4	8.3
Australia	—	2.7	0.7	2.9	6.3
Spain	0.8	2.0	1.3	0.7	4.8
France	0.5	1.5	0.2	1.9	4.1
Turkey	1.8	0.1	1.5	0.6	4.0
United Kingdom[1]	—	0.6	—	1.7	2.3
New Zealand	—	1.9	—	0.1	2.0
Portugal	0.4	0.8	0.6	0.1	1.9
Belgium	1.6	—	—	0.2	1.8
Italy	0.7	—	0.2	0.4	1.3
Netherlands	—	0.8	—	0.3	1.1
Ireland	—	1.0	—	—	1.0
Greece	—	—	0.1	0.4	0.5
Unweighted mean	4.3	1.2	0.9	0.7	7.0

[1]1990 is a transitional year with the rates still yielding some income, but most coming from the community charge.

Source: Derived from OECD (1992).

Income taxes also have their virtues: they can produce high yields; they are hard to fault on fairness or ability-to-pay grounds; their incidence falls largely on residents; and they can be used to secure some tax from businesses that benefit from local services. Also, with a local income tax, tax rates can vary from area to area without causing much relocation of the tax base, though rich households may avoid living in areas where rates are very high while poor tax-exempt households may be attracted to high service level areas despite the high local tax rates; these factors provide a good reason for not having a local income tax on its own, and none of the countries covered by Table 5.1 does.

The following sections indicate that, on their own, neither rates, nor the poll tax, nor the council tax seem very satisfactory when used as the sole local tax. So it would seem wise for Britain to contemplate following the general OECD practice of adopting a local income tax in conjunction with one or more other local taxes. Certainly Britain has much to learn from a study of the rest of the OECD. However, the aim of this paper is to see what others can learn from Britain, not vice versa, and there are some lessons to be learned from Britain, mostly of a cautionary nature. The lessons noted in the text are summarized in a short concluding section.

Local Government in Great Britain

Both Scotland and England were divided into counties around a thousand years ago. However, these counties were not local authorities. Rather they were administrative units of central government, each being overseen by a shire reeve whose main function was the maintenance of law and order. The earliest local authorities were not established until the thirteenth century. These were boroughs, that is large towns which were allowed to 'opt out' of the control of the sheriffs and run their own affairs. Their financial needs were modest.

Financial needs grew in the sixteenth century when boroughs and, elsewhere, parishes were required to cater for the needs of the poor and were allowed to raise a property tax - rates - to finance their outlays. The financial problems of local authorities in the twentieth century stem largely from the fact that they were not given access to any extra taxes even though their financial needs rose greatly over the years. Today these needs cover almost all school education, most roads, refuse services, fire and police services, various social services and numerous minor services. By 1980, total local expenditure on current account was some 10 per cent of GDP, and despite all the pressures of the Thatcher years, it was still around 10 per cent in 1990.

Governments accepted that there was a problem with local finance and numerous Green Papers were published. The most important enquiry was that of the Layfield Committee (HMSO, 1976) which reported in 1976. Their chief conclusion was that the government should decide between two quite different approaches to local government - the localist and centralist approaches - for these have very different financial implications.

The localist approach regards local authorities as democratic bodies providing certain services in line with local preferences. The central government may lay down a few rules, especially in situations where one area's actions affect people elsewhere, but wherever possible it leaves local authorities alone. In contrast, the centralist approach regards local authorities as agents of the central government, implementing centrally determined policies. However, local authorities may be allowed some marginal freedom - and local elections concern only these marginal areas of independence.

When a country adopts the centralist approach, there are two reasons for arguing that most of the finance should come from central government grants. First, this strategy makes the government aware of the cost of its policies. Secondly, it seems wrong for local authorities to have to raise money for purposes chosen by the central government.

When a country adopts the localist approach, there are three reasons for arguing that most local revenue should come from local taxes. First, this strategy means that local spending levels can vary in line with local wishes. Secondly, local politicians, officials and voters will probably act more responsibly over local money than over grants. Thirdly, central grant payments will almost certainly lead to central control - certainly they should do so since the central government is responsible to its own tax payers for what it does with the money it raises from them.

Arguably, the main reason there has been no satisfactory reform in British local government finance since 1976 is that no government has been prepared to make the simple choice outlined by the Layfield Committee. The issue was considered only in the 1977 Green Paper (HMSO, 1977) which was prepared as a response to the Layfield Committee's report. This paper rejected both approaches and advocated a 'middle way' in which there would be joint central and local responsibility for local services, and in which local spending would continue to be financed with local taxes and grants each contributing roughly equal shares. Broadly speaking, such an approach has also been followed by successive British governments.

A middle way with joint responsibilities may sound attractive, but it is liable to cause conflict between central and local government. Two classic British examples are the controversies which surrounded the imposition of comprehensive schools and the forcible selling of council homes. Some local authorities claimed their voters had given them a mandate to retain selective schools and some claimed their voters had given them a mandate not to sell council homes. Yet the relevant central governments claimed their voters had given them mandates to force local authorities to have comprehensive schools and to force them to sell council homes. A situation where two levels of government can each claim opposing mandates on the same issue is a recipe for conflict. It seems wiser to lay down clear demarcation lines for local authority discretion, and this can best be done by following the Layfield Committee's advice and choosing either the centralist approach or the localist approach.

But instead of adopting one of these approaches and its appropriate system of finance, governments have struggled on with the middle way. And, as far as finance is concerned, they have simply reacted in an *ad hoc* fashion to any difficulties which arose. The next section focuses on the problems with rates. It was these problems which led to the 1989-90 reforms of local government finance and the introduction of the poll tax.

Rates

To understand the problems with the rating system, it is necessary to explain some of its details. Each property was given a rateable value based on its annual rental value at the time of valuation. In principle governments accepted that revaluations should occur every few years, but in practice revaluations were infrequent. The last one in England and Wales took place in 1973. In Scotland, a revaluation in 1978 led to a sharp fall in the domestic share of the total tax base, a fall which was substantially reversed by the 1985 revaluation. The subsequent rise in domestic tax bills caused an outcry which encouraged the government to look for an alternative tax rather than undertake a revaluation in England and Wales. Even if there had been regular revaluations, rates would still have been unpopular. One problem was their unfairness - that is a poor relationship between individual payments and abilities-to-pay. The reasons why rates were unfair need explaining carefully, but before noting them it should perhaps be stressed that a high yielding unfair tax must be less acceptable than a low yielding one. Thus a poll tax, for example, with an annual rate of £1 per head would be less of a problem than a poll tax with an annual rate of £1000 per head. Likewise, a property tax which extracted 0.04 per cent of GDP would be less of a problem than one which extracted 4.0 per cent. Yet Britain's property tax actually had a yield of around 4 per cent of GDP in 1989, and was by far the highest yielding property tax in the OECD. This high yield aggravated the problem of its unfairness. It may be added that the OECD country with the third highest property taxes is the United States, and there, too, the property tax has at times come under fire, on one occasion leading to the famous 1978 Proposition 13 in California (see Brazer, 1981) which prompted massive cuts in state and local spending.

A potential equity problem with any property tax is that it may cause hardship for the poor. This hardship can arise whether the legal incidence falls on occupiers - as applied in Britain - or on owners, since the effective incidence is the same in either case. In Britain, this particular problem was eased by a system of rate rebates whereby low income ratepayers received help with their payments. For those on the lowest incomes, this help equalled 100 per cent of their rate bills. People on rebates actually received their help in cash from local authorities who recouped virtually all of their rebate outlays from the central government.

While the problem of the poor was mitigated, there were two other alleged unfairnesses with rates. One is inherent in any normal property tax, namely that a single adult - unless he or she is entitled to a rebate - has to pay as much as, say, four adults living in a similar house next door. It is very difficult to argue that this situation is fair.

The second unfairness arose as a result of a quite separate problem. The total rateable value per head varied considerably from area to area. Consequently, two local authorities wanting to spend equal amounts per head would be likely to require very different tax rates. This in itself would be unfair because it would mean that people would pay different tax rates for similar services according to where they lived. However, the government tackled this problem with the help a general grant called the rate support. The basic philosophy of this grant was that any areas which set a certain standard tax rate should be given enough grant to ensure that their total tax income plus grant income would enable them to provide their services at certain standard levels. To operate the grant, the government had to work out how much each local authority would raise from rates if it set the specified tax rate. It also had to estimate - as it still does - how much each area would have to spend to provide its services at the standard levels.

The result of this system was that large sums of grant were channelled to areas where property values were low while few grants were channelled to areas where property values were high. Consequently, the situation arose where a rich person living in a large £100,000 house in an area where property values were low would often pay the same tax rate, and hence the same tax, as a poor person living in a small £100,000 house in an area where property values were high. People in high property value areas felt doubly aggrieved: they had to pay more to acquire a home, and having acquired it they were deemed to be in a rich area which needed little grant.

It might appear that equity would have been served better with a grant system that ignored variations in rateable values per head. Thus the government could have said that each area wishing to provide its services at the standard levels was expected to raise a standard tax revenue per head and would be given enough grant to bridge the gap between that revenue and the sum it needed to spend to provide its services at the standard levels. On this approach, an area with high property values could set a low tax rate, and vice versa.

This solution would be defensible if the only reason that per capita tax bases varied between areas was that property values for similar types of property varied between areas. For then people who happened to live in a high tax base area, where housing costs were high, would find their high individual tax bases offset by a low tax rate. Likewise, people who lived in a low tax base area would find their low tax individual tax bases offset by a high tax rate. However, there are other reasons why property tax bases per head vary. For instance, some areas have very little non-domestic property and some areas are dominated by small domestic properties. If such areas had to compensate their low tax bases with high tax rates, people in them would be disadvantaged compared with people elsewhere.

It is clear that there is a case for addressing varying property tax bases with equalization grants, and clear that doing so causes an equity problem insofar as varying tax bases arise because property values for similar types of property vary from area to area. This problem seems incapable of a wholly satisfactory solution; a partial solution is to be attempted with the new council tax, as outlined later.

Quite aside from its equity problems, Britain's rating system created difficulties in terms of what the government referred to as 'accountability'. Essentially, the government believed that the rating system did not promote optimal levels of local spending. For spending to be optimal, the last £1 worth of spending by any local authority must provide benefits that local citizens value at £1. The government believed that as roughly half the rate payments in any area came from non-domestic properties, the domestic citizens might vote for spending to be raised until the last £1 was devoted to services whose benefits were valued at only £0.50. The point is that the cost to the voters would be only £0.50 and they would expand spending until the marginal benefit equalled the marginal cost to them, even if the true marginal cost was well in excess of the benefits.

This problem was partially mitigated by the grant system, for the grants actually paid to authorities depended on their tax rates. In broad terms, their grants were adjusted so that each time they raised their spending by £1 per head, they had to raise their tax rates by a specified amount. An average authority would find that if it raised its tax rate by the specified amount, its tax revenue rose by around £1.60 per head. So such an authority would then be given £0.60 less grant than it previously received. Consequently, the cost to the authority's taxpayers of an extra £1 spending was around £1.60. But of this £1.60, only about £0.80 fell on local domestic taxpayers, so, arguably, they were still tempted to vote for excessive spending.

The situation was much worse in a few areas with very high tax bases. These areas did not warrant grants at all, since they could fully finance the spending needed for services at standard levels with rates levied at a tax rate below the standard tax rate. These areas were generally those with high amounts of non-domestic property, and consequently the cost to domestic tax payers of an extra £1 local authority spending was often well below £1. Overspending was typically highest in these areas.

The government argued that there was a further incentive for excessive spending, namely that domestic tax bills were sent only to one person in each household. It was argued that people who did not receive bills might regard local services as 'free' and vote for excessive spending. There was little evidence to support this hypothesis, which is not surprising since the incidence of rate bills was probably shared between all the adults in most multi-adult households. In any event, if the hypothesis was correct, a corollary of it would be that the people who did receive the rate bills would vote for sub-optimal spending since they were given an inflated idea of local service costs. Since a majority of the population received bills - one person in all two-adult households and every adult in one-adult households - the most likely outcome would seem to be that most people voted for too little spending. But this corollary was never spotted by the government which seemed convinced that introducing a poll tax on all adults would lead to lower local spending.

The Community Charge

The foreword to the Green Paper that presaged the introduction of the poll tax (HMSO, 1986) leaves little doubt that the main reason the government introduced that tax was a hope that it would reduce local authority spending. The government was committed to cutting public spending, but it is arguable that it should not have tried to cut local spending on the grounds that local authorities are democratically elected and should spend however much local voters want. However, this argument might be contested on three grounds.

First, it might be feared that local spending increases would raise aggregate demand and hence disturb the government's macroeconomic policies. However, the effects are likely to be trivial. If local spending rises, so do local taxes; consequently consumer spending falls, perhaps by almost as much as local taxes rise. So there is little net effect on total spending. Suppose that local tax- and grant-financed spending in a country is 10 per cent of GDP, as in Britain, and suppose that local authorities raise this spending by a tenth. Then their spending would rise by 1.0 per cent of GDP. But they would have to finance this by raising their taxes which would, typically, reduce consumers' disposable incomes by a similar amount. With a marginal propensity to consume of, say, 0.9, consumer spending would fall by 0.9 per cent of GDP. So the overall increase in demand would amount to 0.1 per cent of GDP which is about one part in 1000. This is a tiny impact for a large rise in local spending. (Admittedly there would be more reason for concern if a rise in local spending were financed by borrowing, for then there would be no necessary fall in consumer spending, but this concern can be met with controls over local borrowing levels, and in Britain these levels have long been directly or indirectly controlled.)

Secondly, it might seem that there could be supply-side effects if local taxes deterred effort. This is scarcely a problem in Britain which has so far relied only on property and poll taxes where payments are not affected by income rises - except for people on rebates. But in any case, it must be doubtful if people can be encouraged to work harder by reducing their freedom to devote some of their extra income to local authority services.

Thirdly, and more plausibly, the government might argue that the system of local finance failed to promote accountability or optimal spending levels. The poll tax system was intended to correct the three main accountability problems of the rates system. First, non-domestic rates became a central government tax, albeit one used to finance larger grants to local authorities. Secondly, the grant system was revised to be one of lump-sum grants. Taken together, these changes meant that all increases in local spending fell on households. Moreover, the possibility that some voters would regard local services as 'free' was removed by replacing domestic rates by a poll tax which fell on all adults, that is all people of 18 or over save for a few special categories - chiefly those who were severely mentally handicapped, those who were living in homes and hostels (which continued to pay rates), those who were convicted prisoners and those who were still at school.

The main worry with the poll tax was its unfairness. It seemed difficult to imagine that it would have anything but a looser relationship with ability-to-pay than rates. And it was intended to have precisely the same gross yield as domestic rates. The unfairness was somewhat eased by the use of rebates which, for something like the poorest 20 per cent of the population, met up to 80 per cent of their poll tax liability. Nevertheless, for all remaining adults there was a flat charge, the sum depending only on where they lived. The grants system operated so that all areas could charge the same standard poll tax for standard spending levels, and would have to finance the whole of any increased spending from higher poll taxes.

Surprisingly, perhaps, the poll tax didn't seem too bad on equity grounds compared with the rates, as shown in Table 5.2. Column (1) shows for 1988-89 the average payments of rates, net of rebates, as a percentage of net household incomes (that is incomes net of central taxes and transfers) for households in various income groups. Column (2) shows the tax payment figures which would have applied if the poll tax had then been in operation. It can be seen that the average level of household payments overall would have fallen, a result of the poll tax being accompanied by slightly more rebates. It can also be seen that the only groups to be much affected would be very rich households and very poor households. The former would gain from the ending of a property tax on their large homes. The latter would gain because they tended to have only one adult, and single adult households typically gain when a tax on property is replaced by a tax on people. Of course there is something a little spurious about the claim that the poorest households gain, since one-adult households on low incomes may be better off than two-adult households on slightly higher incomes. Nevertheless, two-adult households can usually survive on far less than double the income of a one-adult household, and there is no doubt that many of the people who are truly poor are single pensioners and single mothers who stood to gain from the change in the local tax.

**Table 5.2 Net Domestic Rates and
Net Community Charge Payments Compared**

Range of net household income (£ per week)	Net rates (% of net income) (1)	Net community charge (% of net income) (2)
Under 50	4.1	3.4
50 -75	4.4	3.7
75 -100	4.6	4.4
100-150	4.7	4.6
150-200	4.0	4.0
200-250	3.4	3.4
250-300	3.0	3.0
300-350	2.7	2.7
350-400	2.6	2.5
400-500	2.3	2.2
Over 500	2.1	1.7
All households	3.3	3.2

Source: Department of the Environment (1988).

The reason that the new tax was so close in its incidence to rates was that under rates many rich households - those living in low property value areas - paid little, so that average payments by the rich were less than might be expected. Equally, many poor households - those living in high property value areas - paid much, so that average payments by the poor were more than might be expected.

It must be appreciated that the picture presented in Table 5.2 overlooks the fact that there were large changes in the bills paid by many households when rates were replaced by the poll tax. The Department of the Environment (1988) estimated that a quarter of a million households stood to lose over 5 per cent of their net incomes as a result of the change. The actual figure was probably lower than this as the government subsequently paid extra grants to areas where the total domestic tax bill was likely to rise substantially so that these areas could reduce their poll tax rates. But this policy was of limited use because it offered no help to those losing households who happened to live in areas that were, as a whole, gaining. And, perversely, it actually helped those gaining households who lived in areas that were, as a whole, losing! As local authorities knew the total tax demands sent to each household both before and after the change, it would have been much better to channel help to the individual households most affected.

In practice there was a substantial increase in local spending as soon as the new system came in. Some authorities chose the opportunity to raise their spending and blame their high taxes on 'the new system'. Also, the government recalculated each area's need to spend, and areas who were told they now needed to spend less might have wanted to respond by spending less, but cuts in spending usually take place only slowly; in contrast, areas told they needed to spend more were likely to respond with rapid increases. Perhaps, too, some authorities opposed in principle to a poll tax raised their spending to set high poll taxes and so discredit the new tax. It would have been wise to restrict rises in local spending in the first year of the new system.

The poll tax found few friends, partly because it was on average so high and partly because it was felt to be much less fair than rates, despite its help to one-adult households. Also, its supporters conceded that administering it was costly, partly because bills had to be sent to every adult and partly because many adults move each year which makes it hard to maintain up-to-date registers; a poll tax would be much easier to operate in a country whose citizens were all registered under an identity card system. Opponents of the tax organised widespread non-payment campaigns, especially in Scotland. The tax was a political albatross to the Conservatives, and its death-knell was sounded when all those seeking to replace Mrs Margaret Thatcher as party leader in 1990 declared that they would oppose it.

The anti-poll tax campaign might have been weakened if the government had used the poll tax along with another local tax, for then it would not have been true to say that all adults (save those on rebates) had to make equal local tax payments. Also, the outcry might have been less if the level of the tax had been lower. The level was actually reduced in 1991 when extra grants were paid to local authorities, financed by a rise in VAT rates. From then on, local taxes contributed only about 15 per cent to local spending. This aggravated the problem already inherent in the poll tax in that an area seeking to raise its spending above the level estimated by the government as necessary to provide its services at the standard levels must substantially increase its poll tax. Thus, from 1991, an authority raising its expenditure to, say, 15 per cent above the standard spending level must typically double its poll tax rate. In accountability terms, the huge changes in poll tax needed to secure modest rises in local spending can only bewilder the electorate. Moreover, the fact that the government now finances 85 per cent of local spending means that the centralist approach to local finance has virtually arrived by default with no real discussion.

One postscript to the poll tax is that while it was intended to cut local spending, its failure to do so has seen an extension of capping, a system introduced under the rates system whereby local authorities deemed under various criteria to be planning to spend too much can be forced to revise their plans downwards by capping - or limiting - their tax rates.

The Council Tax

The council tax proposals were first outlined in a Department of the Environment discussion paper (1991). This argued that the recent reforms had successfully addressed the key problems of accountability under rates by ensuring that all changes in local spending fell on local voters - a result of introducing lump-sum grants and ending non-domestic rates as a local tax. The reforms had also addressed the accountability problem caused by many voters not directly paying local taxes by having a tax on everyone. And the poll tax had ended the unfairness of rates whereby a one-adult household paid the same as a multi-adult household living in an identical home. However, it added that 'the public have not been persuaded that the scheme is fair'.

This appraisal suggested that the only problem with the new system was the domestic tax element. An obvious improvement would have been to introduce a second domestic tax, possibly a local income tax, and combine this with the poll tax. In that way, it would no longer be the case that all citizens in an area had equal local tax liabilities irrespective of their incomes, yet it would still be true that through the poll tax all voters would have to make a direct contribution. This solution would have had the further merit that a local income tax could raise a high yield and so move local finance away from the centralist approach which has almost been reached. This solution would also have had much in common with the arrangements in other OECD countries which, as shown in Table 5.1, mostly have more than one local tax and which, overall, rely for subcentral tax yields on income taxes more than any other tax.

However, British governments are apparently so keen to restrain local spending that they are convinced that local authorities should not have more than one tax and should certainly not have a buoyant local income tax - though any tendency for excessive spending could readily be tackled by capping local income tax rates. Since the government was reluctant to introduce a local income tax, and since it had political reasons for scrapping the poll tax, it decided to replace the poll tax with a new type of property tax. It doubtless felt that opponents of the poll tax could hardly object to a return to something akin to rates, and it doubtless felt that any form of property tax on the domestic sector alone would be levied in moderation by local authorities. Notwithstanding any hopes of moderation, capping will continue under the new scheme.

The government could not return to the old rates for two reasons. First, it accepted the criticism of rates that tax payments were not related to the number of adults in households. Secondly, it accepted that the old rating system had unfairly penalised people living in areas where property values were high. The new council tax is a modified property tax which seeks to overcome these two difficulties.

Under the council tax scheme, a mean capital value for domestic properties is established - there are separate means for England, Wales and Scotland. In each country, each property is placed in one of eight bands according to its capital value in relation to the mean, as shown in column (1) of Table 5.3. Column (2) shows the forecast likely values for England. Under the council tax scheme, each local authority will determine a tax bill for properties in band D; the bills for properties in the other bands will then be determined as shown in column (3). The variations in tax payments will be much smaller than the variations in property values. Thus within any area the most valuable properties will pay only three times as much as the least valuable (their bills will be in the ratio of 2:0.67). Incidentally, the tax bill for each household will be sent to a single adult, and poor householders will be eligible for rebates of up to 100 per cent of their tax bills.

Table 5.3 The Council Tax Banding Arrangements

Band	Range of property values (% of mean)	Range of property values[1] (£)	Tax bills (as a ratio of the bill for a property in Band D)
	(1)	(2)	(3)
Band A	Under 50	Under 40,000	0.67
Band B	50-65	40,000 -52,000	0.78
Band C	65-85	52,000 -68,000	0.89
Band D	85-110	68,000 -88,000	1.00
Band E	110-150	88,000 -120,000	1.22
Band F	150-200	120,000-160,000	1.44
Band G	200-400	160,000-320,000	1.67
Band H	Over 400	Over 320,000	2.00

[1] The mean values for properties in Scotland and Wales are likely to be £54,000 and £60,000 respectively instead of the forecast £80,000 for England.

The new grant scheme will ensure that, within each country, all areas spending the amount which the government estimates they need to spend to provide their services at standard levels will be able to set a common bill for properties in Band D - say £400. The fact that tax bills will vary much less than property values will ease the burdens on people in areas where property values are high. Suppose that areas X and Y each set spending at the government level for standard services so that each sets a bill of £400 for a house in Band D. If X is an area of low property values, a three bedroom detached house might be worth just £55,000, while if Y has high property values such a house may be worth £110,000. But the occupiers of such a house in Y will not have to pay twice as much as their counterparts in X. The house in X will be in band C and will be sent a bill of 0.89 times £400 which is £356. The house in Y will be in band E and will be sent a bill of 1.22 times £400 which is £488. £488 is just 37 per cent higher than £356.

To deal with the problem of varying numbers of adults per household, some properties will have a discounted bill. Properties where there is only one adult - or only one adult who is not a full-time student - will be deemed 'one-adult households' and will attract a 25 per cent discount. But there will be a 50 discount for any one-adult households where the adult is in a 'discount category' - chiefly people who are severely mentally impaired or members of visiting forces.

Some households with more than one adult will be also be liable for discounts. Thus households with two or more adults will get a 25 per cent discount if they have only one adult who is outside the discount categories, and they will get a 50 per cent discount if they contain no adults who are outside the specified discount categories. And properties where there are no adults other than full-time students will be deemed 'empty properties' and will attract a 100 per cent discount.

The council tax is ingenious, but it has some potential troubles. One problem is that of ensuring that a household which claims a discount will receive one only if it is entitled to do so. The government argues that there will be no need to maintain costly registers of adults, like those needed with the poll tax, but the exercise is bound to be costly. Another problem is that when properties are put in bands, there will surely be complaints from households at the lower ends of each band.

A further potential trouble spot, though not an inherent one, is that the government is not committed to any revaluations after the scheme is first introduced. A plausible sounding case could be that, effectively, all properties are given only one of eight values, and a revaluation might not affect the band that most properties were in - though it would obviously have to affect the values attached to each band. However, given how much relative values can vary from area to area, this argument seems a little shaky. Without revaluations, clear cases of unfairness will soon occur. This point can be illustrated with an example of relative price changes. Between 1952 and 1975, average prices in the South-East region of England fell from being 50 per cent higher than those in East Anglia to a mere 17 per cent higher.

Aside from the characteristics of the new tax, perhaps the most worrying aspect of the new scheme is that local authorities will still, on average, rely on grants to cover some 85 per cent of their current revenue. For a typical authority, raising spending by 15 per cent will still require a 100 per cent rise in its tax rate. The exact figure will vary from area to area. Dependence on grants will be high in areas with high needs, low property values and many discounted properties. Thus in Tower Hamlets a rise in spending of 15 per cent above the level for standard service levels is expected to raise local taxes by 170 per cent.

At the other extreme, the rise needed in South Bucks is expected to be a mere 33 per cent.

There are two crucial implications of this gearing problem. First, the tax rates needed to secure services that are genuinely at the levels envisaged in the government's calculations of areas' needs will be very sensitive to errors in the calculations. Thus a 1 per cent underestimate in the estimate for Tower Hamlets will force the tax rate up there by 11.3 per cent - say from £400 to £445 - if this area actually wants services at the approved levels. This seems a substantial rise for a trivial error.

The second worry is that the gearing problem, combined with capping, will make it very hard for local authorities to raise local spending when local citizens want them to. Sooner or later, the government will have either to admit that it is imposing the centralist approach and is entitled to determine local spending levels, or it will have to find extra local taxes. Aside from the obvious possibility of a local income tax, some modest local tax on businesses seems reasonable since businesses generally get some benefit from improvements in local services. Thus it seems unlikely that the new system will remain unaltered unless the government persuades people to accept the centralist approach.

Conclusions

Twelve key lessons emerge from this discussion of events in Britain.

• Governments are unlikely to devise a satisfactory system of local finance if they are not clear whether they wish to adopt the centralist or localist approach to local government.

• Any attempt at a 'middle way' is more likely to lead to conflict than to cooperation.

• Governments which allege that it is hard to find high-yielding local taxes may effectively impose a centralist solution by default.

• Governments which allow local authorities to operate a property tax need to provide for regular revaluations, partly to keep the tax payments fairly related to property values and partly to protect people from the sudden large changes in individual tax bills that arise with occasional revaluations.

- Governments need to be very wary of having local property taxes if the tax base per head varies considerably from area to area. The problem may be eased if tax payments rise less than proportionately with property values.

- Governments should be careful not to have a local domestic property tax that it is at 'too high' a level - the unfairness of the tax will probably become unacceptable when the yield rises much above one per cent of GDP.

- Local overspending may be encouraged if a large slice of a property tax falls on non-domestic properties. Equally it seems important to have some form of local non-domestic tax.

- When one system of local taxation is replaced by another, it is better to concentrate any transitional relief on the individual households most hurt by the change, not to give it to the areas where households in aggregate are most hurt.

- When changing the system of local taxation, it might be wise to prohibit - or at least strictly control - any rises in local spending in the first year of the new system.

- Poll taxes should probably not be used in countries where citizens are not already registered under an identity card system.

- In order not to seem too unfair, poll taxes should raise even less than property taxes, perhaps well under 1 per cent of GDP, and they should not be used as the sole local tax.

- With a property tax, a system of discounts for single-adult households - and perhaps for other categories - may help reduce unfairness, but may also be administratively difficult.

- If governments truly want to adopt the localist approach, a local income tax seems virtually essential unless local spending in its country is under, say, 4 per cent of GDP.

References and Further Reading

Brazer, H.E., 'On tax limitation' in eds. N. Walzer and D.L. Chicoine, *Financing State and Local Government in the 1980s: Issues and Trends*, Oelgeschlager, Gumm and Hain, pp. 19-34, Cambridge, Mass., 1981.

Foster, C., R. Jackman and M. Perlman, *Local Government Finance in a Unitary State*, Allen & Unwin, London, 1980.

Gibson, J., *The Politics and Economics of the Poll Tax: Mrs Thatcher's Downfall*, EMAS, Warley (West Midlands), 1990.

Gibson, J., *Fiscal Tiers: the Economics of Multi-Level Government*, Allen & Unwin, London, 1984 (Spanish edition published in 1988).

King, D. (ed), *Local Government Economics in Theory and Practice*, Routledge, London, 1992.

Owens, J. and G. Panella (eds), *Local Government: an International Perspective*, North–Holland, Amsterdam, 1991.

Paddison, R. and S. Bailey (eds), *Local Government Finance: International Perspectives*, Routledge, London, 1988.

Department of the Environment, *News Release*, London: Department of the Environment, 13 January 1988.

Department of the Environment, *Local Government Review: A New Tax for Local Government*, Consultation Paper, London, Department of the Environment, 1991.

HMSO, *Local Government Finance*, Report of the Committee of Enquiry, (Chairman F. Layfield), Cmnd. 6453, London, HMSO, 1976.

HMSO, *Local Government Finance*, Green Paper, Cmnd. 6813, London, HMSO, 1977.

HMSO, *Paying for Local Government*, Green Paper, Cmnd. 9714, London, HMSO 1986.

OECD, *Taxes on Immovable Property*, OECD, Paris, 1983.

OECD, *Revenue Statistics of OECD Member Countries 1965–91*, OECD, Paris, 1992.

KEY ISSUES IN TAX REFORM

PART II
TAX REFORM - ADMINISTRATION

CHAPTER 6

MINIMISING EVASION AND AVOIDANCE - LESSONS FROM AUSTRALIA

Ian Wallschutzky*

Introduction

Minimisation usually occurs within given constraints. This is true of evasion and avoidance. Many constraints can operate, not the least of which are the quantity and quality of resources that governments consider should be devoted to the cause and the degree of control or intrusion that citizens of a particular country are likely to tolerate. Another issue is the time period considered for minimisation. In the short run, very tight controls over taxpayers might minimise evasion and avoidance. However, in the long term, systems which rely on less controls and greater co-operation of taxpayers might be more effective. This chapter proposes to discuss a number of policy options which can be considered if governments want to reduce evasion and avoidance.

Australia is chosen as the main source of reference, not only because the author is familiar with its experience, but also because successive Australian governments and tax administrations have had to deal with evasion and avoidance on a large scale. This has meant a number of options have been considered or tried and in some instances a number of unique solutions have been found. Both the roles of the legislature and the tax administration will be discussed as both have important roles to play. First, some attempt should be made to define the terms 'evasion' and 'avoidance'.

*Associate Professor of Taxation at the University of Newcastle, NSW, Australia.

What is 'Evasion' and 'Avoidance'?

In the absence of any statutory definition to the contrary, tax evasion usually refers to acts in contravention of the law, whereby taxpayers pay less tax than they are legally bound to pay. Evasion presupposes that liabilities have already fallen on taxpayers who then take steps to avoid payment. The methods by which this is achieved include omitting income, over-claiming deductions, rebates, credits or exemptions and failing to lodge a return.

While this definition can apply to all countries, it does not mean that specific acts by taxpayers will be evasion in all countries. For an act to be against the law, the law must first be stated. As laws vary from country to country, so will the characterisation of particular acts. For example, failure to include capital gains in a tax return will only be evasion if the law requires it to be included. Similarly, claiming deductions for private expenditure, such as home mortgage costs, will not be evasion if the law specifically permits such claims.

Like evasion, avoidance results in less tax being paid. However, this is achieved by means which are within the law because steps are taken before tax liabilities actually accrue. If tax legislation provides deductions for gifts to charities, then taxpayers who on the last day of the tax year make such gifts will avoid tax, but in ways contemplated, in fact encouraged, by the law. On the other hand, consider the position of taxpayers who on the last day of the tax year enter into pre-paid interest schemes. Assuming the law does not prohibit such schemes, they also avoid tax. However, in these cases, by means which the law most likely would not want to permit. Herein lies the problem of defining avoidance. There are at least two types. One type, which is contemplated, is acceptable and should be encouraged and another type, which is not contemplated, is not acceptable and should be discouraged. Further, the dividing line between the two is neither clear nor fixed.

Government enquiries in different countries have sought to distinguish them but have taken a variety of approaches.

- In the United Kingdom, the Radcliffe Commission (1955, para. 1019) considered that unintended tax avoidance included situations where persons without being the owners of income had in effect the power to enjoy it or to control its disposal for their own benefit.

- In Canada, the Carter Commission (1965, p.538) considered that unintended avoidance included arrangements which took advantage of some provision or lack of provision. Further, that this was more likely to be the case where a taxpayer chose a particular course of action primarily for tax purposes and not for business or personal reasons.

- In Australia, the Asprey Committee (1975, para. 11-14) considered that unintended avoidance consisted of arrangements entered into solely for the purpose of tax avoidance and not for ordinary business or family transactions and that such transactions ought to be prevented.

Where a legislature acts to outlaw particular avoidance arrangements, it is possible to say, ex post, that those arrangements were of a type which were unintended or unacceptable. In the absence of such legislation there will be some difficulty in making this judgement. Some guidance will be available by reviewing the way arrangements were entered into or carried out. The greater the degree of artifice, the greater the degree of secrecy, or the more dominant the motive of obtaining the tax benefit, then the more likely is it that they involved tax avoidance of a type that was not intended.

Paying or not paying taxes are examples of taxpayer behaviour. If behaviour is a function of opportunity and orientation, then it might be helpful to consider evasion and avoidance in terms of the same framework. The next two sections will look at ways to minimise opportunities for evasion and avoidance. The following section will then consider ways of reducing taxpayers' orientation to evade or avoid tax.

Minimising Opportunities for Evasion

If evasion occurs mainly through omitting income, over-claiming deductions and not lodging returns, then measures to minimise evasion must address these activities. Each of these activities will be considered in this section, together with lessons, mainly drawn from Australia, indicating how they might be reduced.

Minimising Opportunity to Omit Income

Compliance rates for income depend on a number of factors, not the least of which is whether tax is required to be deducted at source. Table 6.1 shows that, in the United States, compliance has been highest for wages and salary. This type of income has been subject to deduction at source. Interest income experienced the next highest rate of compliance. This class of income was not subject to deduction at source but was subject to information reporting. Compliance was least for informal supplier income. This category was not subject to either deduction at source or information reporting.

Table 6.1 Compliance Rates for Different Classes of Income for the United States 1981 and 1987 - percentages

	1981	1987
Wages and salaries	94	97
Interest	86	80
Capital gains	58	85
Informal supplier income	20	11

Source: *Income Tax Compliance Research: Estimates for 1973-81*, Internal Revenue Service, US Government Publishing Service, Washington, Table III, July 1983; and *Income Tax Compliance Research: Supporting Appendices to Publication 7285*, Publication 1415, US Government Publishing Service,Washington, Table D 16, July 1988.

Prescribed Payments System. In many tax systems it is common for tax to be deducted at source for wages and salary, though it is not common in respect of other types of income. Since 1980 there have been changes to the Australian tax system which, through increased source deduction, have reduced the opportunity to omit income. The first was the prescribed payments system and the other was imputation.

The prescribed payments system, which has operated since September 1, 1983, requires tax to be deducted at source from 'prescribed payments', i.e. payments for labour and services in the following industries:
• building and construction;
• joinery and cabinet-making services;
• architectural services;

- engineering services;
- surveying services;
- motor vehicle repair;
- cleaning.

Tax is required to be deducted from intra-industry payments, irrespective of whether the payee is an individual, partnership or company. Domestic transactions (e.g. those between a householder and a builder) generally do not fall within the scope of the system.

Initially, and in the absence of exemption certificates or variation certificates, payers were required to deduct tax at the rate of 10 per cent from prescribed payments. This basic rate has since been increased and is now 20 per cent. Tax deducted at source is not payees' final liability to tax. Liability is determined at the end of the year, once payees' taxable income is determined. Credit is given for prescribed payments tax which has been deducted during the year.

The industries covered by the prescribed payments system were those where compliance had been low. Based on the number of payees who registered and the amount of tax collected, the system has been highly successful. Table 6.2 shows the results since 1983-84.

Table 6.2 Tax Collected by the Prescribed Payments System

	Number of payees	A$ mill.	Percent of total tax collected
1983-84	289,091	251[1]	0.7
1984-85	311,405	412	1.0
1985-86	318.185	515	1.1
1986-87	357,220	765	1.5
1987-88	457,830	958	1.6
1988-89	580,123	1308	1.9
1989-90	747,000	1734	2.3
1990-91	631,000	1358	1.8

[1]This sum is for a part year (17/24)
Source: Commissioner of Taxation Annual Report, 1983-84 to 1990-91.

The system identified some 30,000 taxpayers who had not been lodging returns. Payees were required to quote their tax file number. Non-lodgers generally did not have a file number and could not quote file numbers. They had the option of obtaining file numbers (and subsequently lodging returns) or having tax deductions at a higher rate (initially at 25 per cent, but subsequently at 48.25 per cent). The reduction in collections in 1990-91 may be an aberration due to the recession.

Imputation. Since 1 July 1987, Australia has had a full imputation system for company tax. This system, introduced for equity reasons, has had implications for evasion because personal tax on dividends has, in effect, been collected at source. The imputation system is compared below with its predecessor which was a classical system.

	Classical System (pre 1 July 1987) $	Imputation System (in 1987-88) $
Company Profit	100	100
Company Tax	(46)	(49)
Amount left for Dividends	54	51
Max Dividend Paid	54	51
Amount Assessable	54	100[1]
Maximum personal tax	32.4	49
Credit for company tax	—	49
Net tax payable by shareholders	$32.4	NIL

[1]$51 dividend plus $49 imputed tax)

Since the introduction of imputation the corporate tax rate has been reduced from 49 per cent to 39 per cent. Whilst this means shareholders with marginal rates in excess of 39 per cent still have to pay some tax (a maximum of 9.25 per cent) on dividends, those with lower marginal rates have surplus credits which can be used to offset tax liability on other income.

Imputation has improved equity and has alleviated the need to collect from shareholders much of the tax on dividends. It has also streamlined the withholding tax system applicable to non-residents because fully franked dividends paid to them are exempt from withholding tax. There is now less opportunity and less incentive for dividend income to be omitted from tax returns.

Non-cash Employment Benefits. One type of income which is often omitted, or not fully taxed, is non-cash benefits conferred on employees.

Prior to 1 July 1986, in Australia, such benefits were to be included in employees' assessable income. The relevant provision required employees to include in their assessable income 'the value to them' of the benefit given. The question of valuation was difficult and often led to the omission of these benefits. Effective policing would have required a large investment in resources. Instead it was decided to introduce a tax on employers in respect of the fringe benefits provided to employees or to their associates.

Employers self-assess the tax according to specific valuation rules. The rate of tax has been equal to the maximum marginal rate imposed on individuals. Fringe benefits tax paid by employers has not been a tax deductible expense.

If other countries have problems in taxing non-cash fringe benefits, they could consider introducing a fringe benefits tax similar to that introduced in Australia.[1] Alternatively, they could strengthen provisions assessing employees, though these might be more costly to police, or they could deny employers a deduction for amounts paid to employees as fringe benefits.

Cash Transactions Legislation. In Australia, the Cash Transactions Reports Act 1988 has helped reduce the opportunity to omit income, as it requires cash dealers to:

- check the identity of those who open and operate certain accounts;
- report to a government agency any significant[2] or any suspicious cash transactions. (The agency then refers matters, as appropriate, to the revenue authorities or the National Crime Authority).

This legislation has also made it a criminal offence to open or operate an account in a false name.

Minimising Opportunities for Over-claiming Deductions

The previous section showed how a tax system could be changed to reduce the opportunity for omitting income. This part concentrates on reducing the opportunity for over-claiming deductions. There are

---

[1]For a consideration of fringe benefit taxes on employers, see Chapter 2. For a full account of the Australian tax, see B. Marks, *Understanding Fringe Benefits Tax*, 2nd ed., CCH Australia Ltd., 1989.

[2]Transactions are significant if they are in excess of A$10,000 or if, being in a foreign currency, they are in excess of A$5,000.

several ways a tax system can do this. Some of these are discussed
below.

Penalties. The imposition of, or at least the threat of, penalties is one
means by which taxpayers are discouraged from over-claiming
deductions (as it is also a means of discouraging under-statement or
omission of income). However, if penalties are to be effective, they
must be perceived as penalties. Where the level of penalties is low or
where the penalty rate for late payment is less than the rate of inflation, it
may be an overall advantage for taxpayers to be penalised. Prior to
1984, one of the problems with the penalty structure of the Australian
tax system was that many penalties were expressed in fixed dollar terms.
Over time these lost their effectiveness. If penalties are to be effective,
the following principles need to apply. Where possible penalties should
be expressed as a percentage of tax which taxpayers sought to evade and
the penalty for late payment should at least equal 'market rates' of
interest.

Care should also be taken in drafting the wording of the applicable
provisions. Prior to 1984, the operative provision in the Australian
legislation was s226(2) which provided, *inter alia*, that penalties applied
where taxpayers omitted income or where they *claimed deductions in
excess of amounts actually incurred*. The italicised words proved
defective in respect of taxpayers who claimed amounts which had
actually been incurred but which were not allowable deductions. The
provisions were replaced by a schema the relevant provisions of which
was to penalise taxpayers for:

• making a statement which is false or misleading in a material
  particular, or
• omitting matters without which statements are false or misleading in
  a material particular.

These words also proved to be defective. The lesson remains. Care
must be taken in drafting the provisions used to penalise taxpayers for
committing particular offences. Failure to state the offence clearly might
see the Courts refusing to resolve ambiguity in favour of the Revenue.

Record Keeping Requirements. Where taxpayers fail to keep
adequate records, it is difficult to establish their proper tax liability. Tax
systems should encourage good record-keeping and discourage poor
record-keeping. Good record-keeping might be encouraged by advising
taxpayers that if they keep good records, they are less likely to be
audited or that audits are likely to be less intrusive. Poor record-keeping

might be discouraged by threat of greater chance of being audited or by more intrusive audits. Other penalties for poor record-keeping could include fines or even denial of deductions.

Since 1 July 1986, the Australian tax system has contained substantiation requirements for work related expenses and for car expenses. In essence these require taxpayers, who want to claim deductions for these items, to keep receipts for such expenses and to keep log books in respect of car travel. Failure to keep receipts or log books can mean denial of the relevant deduction, even though the expenses may actually have been incurred.

These provisions were introduced to correct a deficiency in the law which, while specifying the type of expense which qualified for deduction, failed to specify what level of proof was required to substantiate those claims. The substantiation provisions are not popular among taxpayers but the provisions might serve as a model for other countries which experience problems with taxpayers over-claiming deductions. They are appropriate where taxpayers abuse existing provisions.

Denial of Deductions. Where taxpayers exploit or are likely to exploit particular provisions, tax systems can deny deductions for particular types of expenditure. Since 19 September 1985, the Australian tax system has denied deductions for entertainment expenses. This includes expenditure on business lunches, cocktail parties, tickets to sporting and theatrical events, sightseeing, etc., even though taxpayers may be able to demonstrate that the primary purpose of such expenditures was to promote business.

In other circumstances, governments might decide to limit the amount of expenses which are deductible. For example, expenses might be deductible up to a specified amount. In Australia, a limit of A$1,000 applies in respect of expenditure incurred by candidates contesting local government elections.

Minimising Opportunity for Non-Lodgement of Returns

Taxpayer Identification. Tax systems may not be successful unless taxpayers can be identified. Identification systems often allocate unique numbers to taxpayers who are then required to use these numbers when lodging returns or participating in transactions involving income. Tax file numbers are important where large numbers of taxpayers have the same or similar names. In Australia, since 1989, there has been a greater incentive for taxpayers to obtain and quote their tax file numbers. Table 6.3 shows the range of circumstances where taxpayers are rewarded for having and quoting tax file numbers.

Table 6.3 Consequence of Failure to Quote a Tax File Number

	Tax file number	No tax file number
Recipient of a Prescribed Payment (from 1/7/89)	Tax deducted at 20%	Tax deducted at 48.25%[1]
Employees (from 1/1/90)	Tax deducted at varying marginal rates ranging from 20% to approx. 48.25% when 'salary or wages' reaches approx. A$700 per week	Tax deducted on all 'salary or wages' at 48.25%[1]
Unemployment and sickness beneficiaries (from 8/1/90)	Entitled to benefits	Not entitled to benefits
Age and invalid pension (from 1/1/91)	Entitled to benefits	May not be entitled to benefits
Investors' interest-bearing accounts[2] (from 1/7/91)	No tax deducted	Tax deducted at 48.25%[1]
unfranked dividends	No tax deducted	Tax deducted at 48.25%[1]

Notes:
[1] Or at prevailing maximum marginal rate of tax (including Medicare levy).
[2] Subject to a *de minimis* rule, set initially at interest of A$120 per annum.

The benefit to the revenue of the introduction of tax file number (TFN) quotation for interest bearing deposits was noted in 'Compliance: Taxpayers Go Like Lambs', *Taxation in Australia*, (April 1992, at p.470):

'A dramatic increase in the amount of interest income declared - $12 billion during 1990-91 compared with $8.7 billion the previous year - powerfully demonstrates the impact of enhanced tax file numbering on the taxation system. The TFN net dragged in 5.2 million people declaring income in the period: up 200,000 from the year before.'

The lessons for other countries are twofold. First, the integrity of the tax file numbering system requires to be enhanced. This can be done by requiring taxpayers to produce source documents (such as birth certificates) to identify themselves. Unique numbers can then be allocated to them. Second, taxpayers should be encouraged to use their tax file numbers in various situations. This allows information reports given to the revenue authorities to identify the taxpayers accurately, which leads to more efficient information matching and checking by those authorities. *Amnesties.* Sometimes taxpayers are reluctant to come forward and register for a tax file number because they have a history of delinquent returns. In Australia, just prior to the new penalties for not having a tax file number, the Commissioner of Taxation offered a Tax Amnesty. According to his Annual Reports the amnesty was a great success. More than 75 per cent of the estimated 360,000 taxpayers not lodging returns came forward. In the long run this should enable the Taxation Office to collect more tax because more taxpayers will be lodging returns.

Other countries which consider offering an amnesty should do so on the basis that it is a once-in-a-lifetime opportunity for taxpayers. If taxpayers come to expect amnesties then they will not have the desired impact. *The Report of the Taxation Commission 1990* (Sri Lanka) considered the results of six amnesties offered in Sri Lanka over a period of twenty-five years to 1989 and recommended against continued use of tax amnesties. At paragraph 30.13 the report stated that:

'Tax amnesties may work well once. But when offered with regular frequency they undermine the equity objective in taxation and lower the society's respect for the tax administration.   The Taxation Inquiry Commission of 1966 disapproved amnesties, stating that "an amnesty, though its results may be impressive, discriminates against honest taxpayers and in the long run affects taxpayer morale".   It would not be incorrect to say that the regular amnesties have made non-compliance look less immoral than it would otherwise be.   It is unlikely that an environment of co-operative taxpayer attitudes could be built if amnesties continue to be granted to tax evaders.'

Tax Administration.   The quality of tax administration is important in almost all matters with which this chapter deals, but specific mention is made here.   The extent to which a tax system is computerised and the quality of its data base and systems is important in ensuring non-filers lodge returns.   What is required is a national data base which is updated each night and which has the capacity to transfer information from one branch to another.

Experience in the United States has shown that care needs to be taken when designing information reporting systems.[1]   To be effective, systems should:

- require to be reported the name and tax file number of the person beneficially entitled to the income;
- ensure that reports relate to the same fiscal year. (Problems usually arise where reporters have substituted accounting periods);
- impose penalties on reporters who do not properly screen information before it is reported;
- clearly specify the accounting method (cash or accruals) which underlies the reports.

Audit quality can be improved by employing higher qualified staff or improving staff training.   In the United States, the *mentor system*[2] has proved useful in transmitting audit skills to new recruits.

---

[1]'The Next Step in Information Matching: Business Returns', *Tax Notes*, pp.1236-7, 19 September 1988 .
[2]Under the *mentor system*, newly recruited auditors work with experienced auditors so as to obtain on the job skills, much like an apprentice learning from a master.

Steps can also be taken to develop *expert systems*[1] which can be used by auditors during audits to probe unusual items. Use of standard questionnaires often overlooks these leads.

Minimising Opportunities to Avoid Tax

Earlier in this chapter it was emphasised that tax avoidance could be intended or unintended, acceptable or unacceptable and often it was only after remedial legislation that it was clear what the legislature intended. This section reviews, in essence, such remedial legislation in the last decade in Australia to determine how its tax systems have been redesigned to minimise opportunities for avoidance. This might then offer lessons to others.

Opportunity to Convert Income into Capital

Structural features, or lack thereof, often provide opportunity for tax avoidance. In Australia prior to 20 September 1985 capital gains, as a general category, was not part of the tax base[2]. This allowed taxpayers to avoid tax by converting income into capital (or more correctly, to ensure that when an amount was received it was characterised as capital and not as income).The decision in Stanton v FCT 92 CLR 630 provides an example of how this was done. The taxpayers, who were graziers, were to receive money from a saw miller for timber situated on their land. If the payment was based on the quantity of timber taken, it would have been assessable as a royalty. If payment related to the graziers' ordinary business activities, it would have been income under ordinary concepts. Instead, the taxpayers received payment for granting the saw miller the right to enter their land and cut timber. According to the Court, this was a receipt of a capital nature. In the absence of a general capital gains provision, the payment was not assessable.

Dividend stripping schemes were also successful because capital gains were not assessable. Under these schemes shareholders in companies pregnant with dividends would sell their shares for a capital

---

[1]*Expert systems* are decision support systems developed from information and decision criteria used by the best auditors.
[2]Profit from the sale of property acquired for the purpose of resale at a profit was assessable under s26(a) and its predecessors. This proved to be an extremely narrow capital gains provision.

sum which included an approximate value of the dividends, rather than receive dividend income. Where shareholders had not acquired their shares for resale at a profit, the amounts they received were not taxed. Such amounts would have been taxed had a general capital gains provision existed.

Further, in the absence of capital gains legislation, other taxpayers could purchase, with virtual immunity from tax, shares which had little or no dividend yield but larger returns by way of increase in share prices. If capital gains were assessable then shareholders would be taxed on the profit made on the sale of shares. Few developed countries exempt capital gains from tax. Some, though, treat capital gains on better terms than ordinary income. Failure to tax income and capital gains on the same footing leaves open opportunities for tax avoidance.

Opportunity to Split Income

The existence of high rates of tax together with a progressive rate scale provides taxpayers with an incentive to split income with others. Design features of tax systems can either provide or limit opportunities for income splitting, for instance, if:
- the corporate rate of tax is less than the top marginal rate of tax individuals will prefer to operate through a company;
- partnerships and trusts are not taxed on the same basis as companies then, on tax grounds alone, there will be reason to choose one structure over another.

In fact, with the four structures, sole trader, partnership, company and trust, significant tax differentials can arise. Particularly in the case of trusts, taxpayers in Australia have obtained benefits which probably were not intended. This has been particularly so where trust income has been distributed to infant and/or non-resident beneficiaries. The legislative response to this was to reduce the tax-free threshold for these groups ($416 and $0 respectively) and for infants, to apply the maximum marginal rate of tax (presently 47 per cent) to income in excess of the $416 threshold.

An alternative would have been to tax partnerships and trusts on the same basis as companies; that is, to assess partnerships and trusts for primary tax and give partners/beneficiaries tax credits for distributed income.

Other tax systems should consider carefully:
* how different structures are to be taxed;
* what tax free thresholds should apply;
* what is the appropriate taxable entity, the individual or the family.

Once tax free thresholds exist and progressive marginal rates of tax apply, then, in the absence of anti-avoidance provisions to the contrary, taxpayers will find ways to avoid tax.

Exploitation of Specific Provisions

Specific provisions are sometimes introduced to provide incentives or relief for particular expenditure or classes of taxpayers. However, some taxpayers always seem to take advantage of these provisions in ways that were not intended. Court cases in Australia provide many examples, for instance, Enquire Nominees Ltd v FCT 73 ATC 4114 shows how Australian residents took advantage of exemptions intended only for residents of certain external territories. Mullens v FCT 76 ATC 4288 shows how taxpayers temporarily become shareholders in mining and exploration companies to take advantage of deductions for money paid on calls on those shares.

What is needed is some general anti-avoidance provision which can be invoked when taxpayers try to take advantage of the legislation. Such general provisions can be difficult to draft. Not only are there difficulties in deciding what type of provisions should be enacted, there can be difficulties in settling on the words that should be used. In terms of types of provisions the options include those:
* vesting administrative discretion in someone to approve or veto particular arrangements, or
* which try to define what type of arrangements are permitted and what are not.

Generally the latter are to be preferred. However, problems can arise finding the right words. Prior to 1981 the Australian legislation relied on s260 which, in essence, rendered 'absolutely void' any arrangements which had the purpose or effect of 'avoiding tax'. Unfortunately, there were many problems with the wording of this provision. Two of the general problems are mentioned here. First, it was clear that the section was not intended to have a literal application. That is, not all tax avoidance was to be attacked, only some. However, the section failed to discriminate between the types that were to be permitted and the types that were to be struck down. Second, in respect of those schemes that were to be struck down (if identified) it was not clear what effect the section had. The section was, according to its terms, an annihilating provision only. It did not provide anyone with authority to reconstruct taxable situations.

Since 27 May 1981 a new provision, Part IVA, has operated. It has attempted to overcome the defects perceived to exist in s260. In particular it:

- defines when it applies, namely where it would be concluded (having regard to eight matters) that the dominant purpose was to obtain a 'tax benefit' (a term which is specifically defined);
- provides a mechanism of raising assessments once a scheme has been struck down *viz*, it allows the Commissioner to cancel the tax benefits and raise assessments on such grounds as he considers necessary.

It should be noted that the Commissioner does **not** have a discretion in determining whether Part IVA applies. His discretion only relates to how assessments are to be raised once, presumably on objective criteria, it is determined whether Part IVA applies.

Where general anti-avoidance provisions fail to prevent tax avoidance, the legislature must continually amend the law. This is unsatisfactory as it diverts legislators from their primary tasks.

Other design features to reduce avoidance include the following:

- keeping to a minimum the number of provisions which offer incentives/exemptions, the theory being that the fewer the provisions the less the opportunity for avoidance;
- considering the introduction of retrospective legislation for blatant schemes. (In Australia the Taxation (Unpaid Company Tax) Assessment Act 1982 is an example of such legislation. It had effect from 1 January 1972 yet received Royal Assent on 13 December 1982. It sought to recover tax where taxable entities had been stripped of their capacity to pay tax).

Attitude of the Courts

An important factor which will determine how successful a tax administration is in preventing tax avoidance is the approach or attitude of the courts. The extent to which they look at form over substance will be important. Similarly, the extent to which they require the legislation to be clear and unambiguous, before they decide it applies to extract tax from taxpayers, will be important. The courts' attitude is important in several other key areas including determining whether:

- arrangements are shams;
- taxpayers should be entitled to take advantage of loopholes in the law;
- general anti-avoidance provisions apply in respect of specific arrangements.

Ethical Requirements of Accounting and Law Professions

To engage in tax avoidance, taxpayers usually require help from bankers, lawyers or accountants. The extent to which professional bodies for accountants and lawyers have ethical rules prohibiting members from assisting taxpayers to undertake tax avoidance arrangements can have an important impact on the proliferation of avoidance schemes. If necessary, governments can encourage professional bodies to adopt ethical standards. Alternatively, governments might make it a statutory offence to promote certain types of schemes or to aid or abet taxpayers entering into such schemes.

Use of Extrinsic Material

In judicial proceedings the range of material that can be submitted as evidence is governed by rules of evidence. These rules are usually developed by common law though they can be enhanced by statute. Governments can therefore give consideration to enhancing the chances of success of its revenue authorities by enacting legislation permitting in certain circumstances particular material to be considered. This could be as simple as amendments to an Act Interpretation Act, or it could be more interventionist. In Australia the Act Interpretation Act has been amended in two respects which could enhance the revenue authorities' chances of success in certain types of tax avoidance cases. Section 15AA directs that in certain circumstances the purpose or objects underlying an Act be considered. Section 15AB, on the other hand, permits extrinsic material to be considered. This could allow Parliamentary Speeches and Explanatory Memoranda which accompany legislation to be considered.

Controlled Foreign Corporation

Unless legislation exists to tax profits derived by controlled foreign companies or trusts, it will be possible for residents to defer or avoid paying tax on such profits. Domestic tax legislation usually requires some territorial nexus before tax can be levied. This nexus is usually source or residence. This is the case in Australia. Prior to 1 July 1990, it was possible for Australian residents to set up non-resident entities to derive, free of Australian tax, ex Australian source income, even though they could control or benefit from that income. For instance, a trust established in a tax haven could invest spare funds in interest bearing deposits and accumulate the income without being liable for Australian tax.

Since 1 July 1990 legislation exists to attribute to Australian residents income derived by controlled foreign entities. Such legislation is not unique to Australia. In fact, Australia lags behind most of its OECD partners in this respect. There are two features of the Australian schema which deserve mention here. First is that when the new legislation was introduced, those involved in non-resident trusts were offered an incentive to wind up such trusts by a particular date. The incentive was that distributions from such trusts were taxed at 10 per cent.

The second feature, probably taken from US legislation, is the power vested in the Commissioner of Taxation to issue offshore information notices. These notices help the revenue authority gain access to information and documents located in foreign countries. Under these notices taxpayers are requested to provide information needed for the operation of the legislation. While taxpayers are not compelled to produce the information, failure to do so will stop taxpayers from producing the documents in proceedings disputing taxpayers' assessments.

Transfer Pricing

Transfer prices are set for many reasons, not the least of which is to transfer profits from one tax jurisdiction to another. Where transfer prices on exports are set at rates above the market rate, then the revenue authority in the exporting country will gain and the revenue authority in the importing country will lose revenue. Domestic tax legislation usually contains provisions permitting revenue authorities to substitute arm's length prices if such prices have not been used in related party transactions. International Agreements usually reinforce this approach by permitting taxation of permanent establishments on business profits that 'might reasonably be expected to have been made'.

Australian tax legislation follows these two approaches. Experience has shown that the way revenue authorities administer the law can be as important as the legislation itself. In Australia tax audits have been used to help regulate transfer pricing practices. These, however, can only be successful if a revenue authority knows who to audit; that is, it needs to know which taxpayers have engaged in international transactions. Here the Australian Tax Office seeks to establish a data base of potential auditees by requiring such taxpayers to complete an information report (Schedule 25A) indicating involvement in international transactions.

In 1991, another initiative commenced, designed to regulate transfer prices through taxpayer co-operation. The revenue authorities of Australia and the United States have signed an agreement which allows taxpayers who transfer goods or services between the two countries to obtain advance determinations for transfer prices. These would allow taxpayers who transferred goods or services to related parties to be taxed by their revenue authority on prices approved by the advance determinations. In the future, further co-operation could see joint audits of multinationals. Transfer pricing remains a complex issue and is likely to require close monitoring of entities involved.

Minimising Orientation to Evade or Avoid

The behaviour component of evasion and avoidance is as important as any other component. Much research has been conducted on why taxpayers might want to evade or avoid.[1] The reasons can vary from time to time and from country to country. No particular policy prescriptions will be advocated here. Rather some of the general hypotheses will be mentioned, together with comment on what might be done in a particular country.

Perhaps it should be noted that evasion and avoidance are being dealt with together. This is for convenience only. In fact, what causes some

---

[1]For a comprehensive summary, see in particular Roth, J. A. *et al, Taxpayer Compliance*, Vol. I and II, University of Pennsylvania Press, Philadelphia, 1989 and Elffers, H., *Income Tax Evasion: Theory and Measurement*, Kluwer, Deventer, 1991.

taxpayers to evade might be quite different from what causes others to avoid. Some even argue that the poor evade because the rich avoid (or is it that the rich avoid because the poor evade?). It should also be noted that while it might be possible to identify what causes some people to evade or avoid, it does not mean that by ameliorating that cause we get a reduction in evasion or avoidance. For example, if it is found that because of high tax rates some people avoid tax, a reduction in tax rates might not reduce the desire to avoid. Similarly, an increase in tax rates might not increase the desire for more avoidance. Perception that tax rates are high might motivate initial avoidance or evasion. However, subsequent avoidance or evasion might occur simply because taxpayers repeat previous behaviour. Taxpayers might therefore attribute their avoidance or evasion to high tax rates but not respond to reductions in tax rates. In short, the behavioural dimension is a very complex matter.

Those wanting to find out what causes taxpayers to evade or avoid could consider the effects of:

- taxpayers' perceptions about:
  - tax rates;
  - equity or fairness of the tax system;
  - how wisely governments spend taxpayers' money;
- individuals' basic predisposition to the State and to the law generally;
- group influence on individuals' behaviour;
- tax audits, information reporting, withholding;
- tax administration styles;
- tax practitioners;
- probability of detection and level of penalties;
- taxpayer services.

Another matter related to what causes taxpayers to evade or avoid is what will help them to comply voluntarily. It is in this area that tax administrations can have an impact and that Australia might have some lessons for others. Over recent years, the Australian Tax Office has undergone a fundamental change in approach, from one of trying to detect and penalise non-compliance to one of encouraging or improving voluntary compliance. One of the present themes of the Australian Tax Office is helping taxpayers to 'get it right the first time'.

The Australian Tax Office now organises itself around its clients (taxpayers) and tries to promote ways it can help them. The centrepiece of this is self assessment: a system whereby tax returns are accepted on their face value and integrity is achieved by subsequent audit. Previously, all returns were reviewed by assessors. Self assessment either facilitated or made possible the Electronic Lodgement System. Under this system, returns are lodged electronically and individuals can expect their tax refunds within fourteen days of their returns being lodged.

There are other initiatives designed to promote voluntary compliance. These include:

- simplification of tax forms;
- production of plain English tax guides and information brochures;
- establishment of Advising Groups;
- establishment of Problem Resolution Groups;
- establishment of targets for resolution of objections and appeals;
- co-ordination of volunteer helper groups;
- production of an increased volume of tax literature;
- increased interaction with community groups;
- increased service for tax agents.

The real significance of these measures is that they recognise that the long run success of a tax system depends on the co-operation of taxpayers rather than the enforcement of tax laws. No better example of this can be given than the Tax Office policy in relation to penalties. Formerly, penalties were imposed at about 40 per cent, irrespective of the reason for non-compliance. Through IT 2517 released in February 1989, there was a range of penalties from zero to 45 per cent. For example, deliberate evasion, 45%; carelessness, 15-30%; taxpayer did not know and could not be expected to know, Nil.

The underlying purpose is to promote long run voluntary compliance. Previously, it was found that penalties imposed without regard to taxpayers' circumstances often alienated those penalised. This did not elicit their long run co-operation.

Summary and Conclusion

The purpose of this chapter was to indicate how a tax system could be designed and administered to minimise evasion and avoidance. Lessons were drawn mainly from Australia. Some of these lessons might be useful for other countries. Each country should determine where to start according to its own particular circumstances. For instance, if paper avoidance schemes are rife, then they should be addressed first. On the other hand, if the cash economy is the major problem, then the first measures taken might address it. If no one area demands priority, then the following desiderata can be considered in turn.

- Tax legislation should clearly define what is assessable and what is deductible; what is permitted and what is not permitted.

- Deduction at source and/or information reporting should be extended beyond mere salary and wages.

- Record-keeping requirements and penalty structure should be regularly reviewed to determine if they are adequate.

- Systematic checks need to be undertaken to ensure that all who should are lodging returns. Those who are not, need to be encouraged to commence lodging. In this regard, amnesties may help break a non-lodgement cycle.

- Systemic defects in a tax system need to be remedied: in particular, the opportunity to change the character of receipts (to give them a non-taxable or preferred taxable character), the opportunity to split income with others and the opportunity to exploit specific provisions of an Act.

- International transactions and use by residents' off-shore entities should be regularly monitored and additional specialised legislation introduced as required.

- Attention should also be directed towards those factors which motivate taxpayers to evade or avoid. (This is likely to be a complex and changing matter in which both government and tax administrators have roles to play).

- In the longer term, it is important that tax administration be seen as serving taxpayers rather than as existing to correct non-compliance.

    Tax evasion and avoidance are likely to remain a part of any tax system. Thus, efforts to reduce evasion and avoidance will continue to be required.

References and Further Reading

Dubin, J. A., M. J. Graetz and L. L. Wilde, 'The Effect of Tax and Audit Rates on Compliance with the Federal Income Tax, 1977-85', *Social Science Working Paper 638*, California Institute of Technology, April 1978.

Elffers, H., *Income Tax Evasion: Theory and Measurement*, Kluwer, Deventer, 1991.

Jackson, B. R. and V. C. Milliron, 'Tax Compliance Research: Findings, Problems and Prospects', Vol. 5 *Journal of Accounting Literature* pp.125-165, 1986.

Kinsey, K. A., 'Survey Data on Tax Compliance: A Compendium and Review', *American Bar Foundation*, Chicago, 1984.

Marks, B., *Understanding Fringe Benefits Tax*, 2nd ed., CCH Australia Ltd., 1989.

Milliron, V. C. and D. R. Toy, 'Tax Compliance: An Investigation of Key Features', *Journal of the American Taxation Association*, pp.54-104, Spring 1988.

Roth, J. A., *et al*, *Taxpayer Compliance: Volume 1: an Agenda for Research* and *Volume 2: Social Science Perspectives*, Philadelphia, University of Pennsylvania Press, 1989.

Wallschutzky, I. G., 'Australia: Revenue Authority Options in Achieving Taxpayer Compliance', Vol. 6 *Asian-Pacific Tax and Investment Bulletin*, pp.347-355, 1988.

Witte, A. D. and D. F. Woodbury, 'What We Know About the Factors Affecting Compliance with the Tax Laws', in ed., P. Sawicki *Income Tax Compliance: A Report of the ABA Section of Taxation Invitational Conference on Income Tax Compliance*, pp.133-148, American Bar Association, Chicago, 1983.

Report of the Royal Commission on Taxation (The Carter Commission), Queens Printer and Controller of Stationery, Ottawa, Canada, 1966.

Report of the Taxation Commission 1990, Department of Government Printing, Colombo, Sri Lanka, 1991.

Royal Commission on the Taxation of Profits and Income, Final Report, The Radcliffe Commission, Cmnd 9474, HMSO, London, 1955.

Taxation in Australia, 'Compliance: Taxpayers Go Like Lambs', *Taxation in Australia*, Vol. 26, No. 9, pp.470-1, April 1992.

Taxation Review Committee - Full Report, The Asprey Committee, Australia Government Publishing Service, Canberra, 1975.

CHAPTER 7

SELF ASSESSMENT AND ADMINISTRATIVE TAX REFORM IN IRELAND

Frank Cassells and Don Thornhill*

Introduction

Between 1988 and 1992 the system of assessing tax liabilities for the direct taxes in the Irish tax code underwent fundamental change. With the exception of the withholding tax on employee incomes (PAYE), the assessment of all the other direct taxes – taxes on self–employment and capital income, corporate income tax (corporation tax), capital gains tax and the taxation of inheritances and gifts – was changed from a Revenue direct assessment system to taxpayer self assessment. Section 7.1 of the paper describes the underlying policy considerations which led to this major change and discusses its results and implications with particular reference to income tax. Section 7.2 describes, as a 'micro' case study, the implementation of self assessment for the taxation of gifts and inheritances (capital acquisitions tax – CAT). Although CAT accounts for only 0.6 per cent of total tax revenue in Ireland, this case study provides a good illustration of why self assessment was introduced as well as its benefits. The case study also describes some of the strategic and organisational issues which had to be addressed in bringing about the change to self assessment.

Self Assessment – A Necessary Precursor to Tax Reform?

Ireland, in keeping with many other countries, has gone through a period of tax reform beginning in the late 'eighties and still continuing.

*Frank Cassells is a Revenue Commissioner and Don Thornhill is Assistant Secretary in the Office of the Irish Revenue Commissioners.

The initial phase of tax reform in Ireland paid particular attention to the administrative systems and structures. This contrasts with the radical alteration of the tax structure itself through reduction of rates and removal of tax shelters that happened in many other countries. The process of reform is now being more directed to reducing rates and removing tax shelters. Why did Ireland go against the general trend and choose to amend the administration of the tax system first before adopting what was then the prevailing tax reform direction?

The Reasons

There were essentially two reasons. First the serious imbalances in the Irish public finances in the middle and late 'eighties, as illustrated by a government debt/GDP ratio of 117 per cent in 1987, were perceived as precluding any radical programme of reform of tax rates and structures. The first public finance priority of government was the restoration of balance in the public finances. Success in achieving this objective – by 1992 the debt/GDP ratio had been reduced to 91 per cent – would in turn open the way to reform of tax rates and structures.

The second reason was that, throughout the 1980s, Ireland faced a considerable tax compliance and collection problem relating particularly to the self–employed. For example, the report of the Irish Comptroller and Auditor General showed total tax arrears of IR£1,318m for the self–employed sector as at 31 May 1988. This figure was roughly five times the expected annual tax yield from this sector! While an arrears problem in this area was recognised it could not possibly have been of this magnitude. The notional figure was more an illustration of how far the traditional assessment and collection system had deteriorated than a measure of the real arrears problem.

However, the annual publication of this large arrears figure created a strong sense of grievance in the minds of other taxpayers and gave rise to unfounded beliefs that the serious imbalances in the Irish public finances could be greatly ameliorated if this figure could only be collected. More seriously for the administration of the tax system, this largely notional figure had a tendency to gum up the works of collection of the real arrears; and the attempts by the tax authorities to explain the figure away, however accurate and laudable, tended to reflect badly on the credibility of the Finance and Revenue authorities.

Previous Study and Action

This sorry state of the Irish tax system for the self–employed had been recognised for many years and various attempts had been tried to improve it, usually by placing increased penalties on the statute books. With some justification this procedure has been pejoratively described as 'administration by conjuring', i.e. based on the belief that if the right words can be found and put on the statute books, the non–complying taxpayers will be spellbound into benign behaviour and the system will suddenly start working again. Regrettably this approach to tax non–compliance does not work, at least in the Irish context, and more direct action is required.

In 1980 a Commission was set up by the Irish Government to examine the Irish tax system and suggest reforms. The Fifth Report of the Commission, published in October 1985, dealt specifically with tax compliance and administration. In addition, in 1987, the Irish Government requested the assistance of the International Monetary Fund (IMF) to advise on tax administration. The IMF report led to a discussion paper prepared by the Irish Department of Finance and the Revenue Commissioners which was endorsed by the then Minister for Finance. This paper attempted, among other things, to summarise the essentials of the IMF proposals. However, its primary purpose was to focus public attention on the difficulties being faced by the tax administration and to stimulate official and public discussion on a possible solution – the introduction of a system of self assessment. In other words, it was recognised that the existing system was simply not working; more radical measures – including the introduction of a new assessment system – were required.

The Changing View of the Tax System

However, most important of all was the emerging awareness in the political and official mind that large–scale tax compliance cannot be achieved solely by threats and penalties. There also arose an awareness that a tax system of itself, if badly structured, could contribute to poor tax compliance simply by its own inefficiencies, whether perceived or real. In other words, an efficient tax system requires the co–operation of the tax paying public. It appeared also that, while lower rates ease tax collection problems, there is still the need to have an efficient tax system if maximum collection and equity is to be achieved.

By coincidence the Revenue Commissioners also became aware at this time of some academic research on fostering voluntary tax compliance (see references), in particular the work by a former employee of the United States Internal Revenue Service, Professor Kevin McCrohan, then Marketing Professor at George Mason University, Virginia. His researches (McCrohan, 1988) and our own analysis of the problems, seemed to indicate that compliance with the tax system bore a direct relationship to the taxpayer's perception of the efficiency, image and openness of the Revenue organisation and to his or her sense of the personal and social rewards to be obtained from dealing honestly with it. In promoting tax compliance, McCrohan's and our own conclusions argue for a marketing approach to tax compliance. Without straining the analogy too far, in essence tax compliance is a 'product' which can, and perhaps must, be sold to the public.

The Key Indicators for Arriving at a Successful Tax System

The following key points were identified as central to any approach to securing the degree of voluntary compliance necessary to drive an effective tax system.

(1) A tax system which is difficult to understand or to respond to, enables taxpayers to rationalise and justify their non-compliance. (By 'tax system' it is meant not only the rates and structures of the taxes but also the method of administration.)

(2) Compliance with the tax system is a largely voluntary act; it is not possible directly to force everybody into compliance. (There is a body of 'taxpayers' who will only comply in response to direct confrontation and enforcement, but this body is not a large percentage of the taxpayer base; and the percentage of potential tax collectible attributable to these 'taxpayers' is probably less than their percentage of the potential taxpayer base. In essence the hard core of non-complying population represents only marginal tax revenue but requires exceptional levels of Revenue resources to confront. However, if equity is to be achieved and taxpayer confidence maintained, it must be confronted.)

(3) Compliance is a function of the perceived efficiency of the tax system and its administration.

(4) It is necessary to concentrate on strategic planning which stresses systems development and persuasion and to put less emphasis on coercion, threat and fear.

(5) Compliance must be reinforced and rewarded.

(6) The benefits of compliance to the taxpayer must be clear.

(7) Taxpayers must be educated to facilitate compliance.

(8) Communications promoting compliance must be effected.

The Deficiencies in the Existing Direct Assessment System

Of equal importance was our acknowledgement that the existing tax system in Ireland may have been encouraging tax evasion or, at very least, delay in tax payment. Three factors supported this hypothesis:

(1) In reality a self–employed taxpayer did not have to respond to the tax system until actually served with an official tax form by the appropriate tax inspector.

(2) Except in unusual circumstances, interest and penalties on tax default only began to run from the time the inspector had actually made an official assessment to tax, estimated or otherwise, following the serving of a formal return of income on the taxpayer.

(3) The vast bulk of returns did not come in on time and most assessments were estimated by the Revenue. This greatly complicated and placed massive demands on the tax appeal system, which helped the taxpayer to delay tax payments and absorbed extensive Revenue resources which could be better employed in confronting tax evasion.

Such a system had a built–in bias in favour of non–compliance. Even when eventually identified and served with assessments, non–compliers were no worse off than if they had declared themselves. So tax evaders could lie low and make no returns to the Revenue authorities in the knowledge that even if they were ultimately caught they would not be exposed to any greater level of penalty than if they had made timely tax returns. However, the major problems in the then Irish tax system were not tax evaders but the 'tax delayers', i.e. taxpayers, known to the Revenue authorities, who would eventually pay up but only after considerable delay and much bureaucratic effort. There was also the risk that the 'tax delayer' behaviour could lead to 'full' evasion.

The Problems to be Faced

Essentially, needs were seen as being:

(1) to promote voluntary compliance by improving taxpayer understanding of and confidence in the tax system and by providing a better service to the taxpayer, ultimately leading to a more positive view of the tax system;

(2) to confront the non–complying and delaying taxpayer more effectively and within a quicker response time;

(3) to restructure the internal organisation of the Irish Revenue Service so as to devote a greater share of increasingly scarce resources to dealing with non–compliers – thereby leading to a more effective use of resources and an increase in the morale of tax officials and complying taxpayers.

Removing the Bias

Initially, the 'evader/delayer' bias had to be taken out of the system. Two initiatives were devised to this end (from which the whole concept of the broad application of self assessment grew and took off):

(1) the introduction of a stipulation that all income tax payers, other than those subject to PAYE, were required to make a tax return by a specific date, irrespective of whether or not they had been served with an official tax form; and

(2) the formulation of a requirement that all taxpayers had to pay their due tax, or a significant proportion of it, on their incomes for a particular tax year on a specific date, irrespective of whether or not they had received a tax assessment. Failure to do this would result

in the total ultimate tax for the year being deemed to be payable on that date.

Accordingly, when the evader was caught, all interest and penalties would run from these set dates and the evader would get no benefit from non–disclosure.

Preliminary Studies before Moving to Self Assessment

While there had been previous explorations of self assessment for capital acquisitions tax (see below), the decision to apply self assessment to one of the major tax heads was an important departure. However, the existing administrative system was considered so bad that something had to be done before moving to tax reform proper. It was no use merely reducing tax rates and tidying up the structure of reliefs and allowances if the existing administrative system was not effective.

One consequence of the 'product' model for tax compliance was the need to develop a more professional and business–like approach to tax administration. While the authors would not support the view that private sector business structures represent a complete model for the structuring of the activities of government departments, they thought that much could be learned from, and adapted from, the private sector's approach to management. To this end, senior staff in the Revenue Commissioners held a number of intensive discussions with top managers in the private sector – with particular emphasis on the management of long–term organisational change – a process which proved extremely fruitful.

Its most important consequence was to convince the Revenue participants of the need to break out of their at times somewhat organisationally xenophobic shell and be prepared to employ the talents of external experts in improving the structure and approach to the 'customers'. Whilst many tax officials, tax practitioners and taxpayers may gag at the notion of taxpayers as 'customers' of the Revenue authorities, the concept is a useful one.

What is a Revenue Organisation?

Revenue authorities have an identity crisis: are they police forces or service organisations? Thy must police the tax system and confront tax evaders and avoiders. But, in practice, the vast bulk of the transactions between the Revenue authorities and taxpayers or their agents (perhaps up to 90 per cent or more in the authors' view) are non–confrontational. The answer to the question, 'What type of organisation are we?' tends accordingly to be more in the direction of a service organisation and only marginally a policing force. The basic structure of the relationship between the Revenue authorities and the taxpayer/agent is one involving information and money flows. Information or money flows into the Revenue authorities and assessments to tax and requests for information flow out from the Revenue authorities. The procedure operates through a number of conduits and anything which blocks or restricts these conduits affects the efficiency of tax collection. The collection of the correct amount of tax with the minimum of administrative burden should be the objective of all tax systems. The psychological factors which influence tax compliance (discussed above) must be put into practice.

Some of the Practical Difficulties of Tax Compliance

Some of the practical difficulties identified as contributing to impeding the flows of information and money, quite apart from a poor administrative tax structure, included, *inter alia*:

- poor staff attitudes in some cases;
- bad form design;
- fear and uncertainty in the minds of the public as to therequirements of the tax system;
- lack of confidence in the system and a belief that the wealthy influential sector was not paying its fair share.

In other words, there is no room for complacency in administering a tax system and the administration must be continuously monitored to ensure that it is not contributing to its own failures. There is also the delusion that tax systems are not in competition with other sectors of the economy. A tax bill is just another demand on a taxpayer's cash flow and must compete with other such demands from organisations such as banks, suppliers and utilities who often have more immediate methods for enforcing their demands.

Progress Towards Reform

In the Irish Revenue we attempted to address these problems in a number of ways.

(1) The introduction of enhanced and revised training courses for staff, some given by Revenue's own training staff and some by outside professionals, aimed at altering the internal attitudes to the tax administration system and at promoting a more dynamic and innovative approach to the administrative system as well as improving taxpayer related attitudes.

(2) The employment of professionals to help improve form design.

(3) The employment of external public relations experts to help improve the means of communicating with, and relationship to, the tax–paying public.

(4) The employment of professional advertising and design consultants to ensure that the message was getting across properly.

The Tax Practitioner

Another area in which a changed and more dynamic approach had to be adopted was in the relationship with tax practitioners. No tax system can work without the help and co–operation of tax practitioners, particularly a self assessment system. A self assessment system is, to all intents and purposes, a privatisation of the process of tax calculation. Old methods allowed material of variable quality to be submitted to tax inspectors who then calculated the tax or sought further information. In all too many cases the inspectors had no information and resorted to estimated assessments. In Ireland the vast bulk of assessments on the self–employed were estimated and up to 90 per cent of these estimates were ultimately appealed, creating the huge administrative burden which diverted resources to processing procedures in respect of taxpayers who were largely complying. With self assessment the onus of getting the information and the tax correct first time is transferred to the taxpayer with only selective *post hoc* review by the Revenue authorities to ensure compliance is maintained.

Of course, for most self–employed taxpayers the task of return filing and tax computation is the responsibility of his paid tax adviser. He or she is most likely to be an accountant, lawyer or member of the Institute of Taxation (the educational and professional body representing many Irish tax practitioners). If the tax adviser makes an incorrect computation or provides wrong information to the Revenue the client may insist that the adviser rather than the taxpayer suffers the monetary consequences. Accordingly, it was specifically decided to target the tax practitioners and advise them in advance of the new system. Seminars were set up around the country for practitioners and their active support for the new system was sought and obtained. A special Tax Administration Liaison Committee, consisting of representatives of the Revenue Commissioners and the main organisations representing tax practitioners, was set up and meets regularly to discuss difficulties in tax administration.

Overall Summary

To summarise, the strategy of moving to a self assessment system was recognised as effecting a fundamental change in the relationship between the Revenue and taxpayers. Under the direct tax system, the Revenue is responsible for identifying and calculating tax liabilities – and furthermore, for notifying these to individual taxpayers. The taxpayers' responsibilities consist essentially of providing information and completing tax returns (and in general, only when requested to do so by the Revenue) and of paying tax which had been correctly assessed by the due dates. A self assessment system on the other hand, leaves to taxpayers the responsibility for notifying the Revenue of potential tax liabilities and, indeed, of computing them. The potential benefits are lower compliance and administrative costs, as well as more efficient targeting of resources by the tax administration.

The latter is particularly important. One major criticism of the direct assessment approach was that it diverted Revenue resources and attention from non–compliance to processing the affairs of compliant taxpayers. In theory this should not happen. In an ideal world the completion by the taxpayer of a return form providing detailed information relevant to the assessment of a tax liability should be followed quickly and without the expenditure of significant resources, by the issue of an assessment by the tax authorities. Furthermore, it can be plausibly argued that, compared with self assessment, there should be an efficiency and compliance cost gain by having the assessment prepared by specialised and experienced tax officials rather than by the taxpayer or by his or her agent.

The Irish experience did not bear this out – with the exception of the income tax PAYE withholding tax system which operates in respect of employees' incomes. In most non–PAYE cases, the difference between practice and theory was that taxpayers tended to challenge the Revenue assessments – which in the great majority of instances were issued on the basis of inadequate information about taxpayers' affairs, because of the reluctance of many taxpayers to provide full information until faced with the inevitability of a tax assessment or demand. The outcome included extensive and protracted rounds of correspondence and extensive recourse to the statutory appeals system.

These inefficiencies affected both taxpayers and the Revenue, increasing both compliance and administration costs. The direct assessment system also created a further efficiency cost for the Revenue by reducing the ability of Revenue management to target resources in an optimal way. As long as the dynamics of the system required the administration to compute and issue high volumes of tax assessments, it was very difficult to allocate staff and other resources to produce an optimal incremental return.

One serious disadvantage was that the direct assessment system created a perverse incentive for an individual faced with a choice of being compliant or not. For this individual, the costs of compliance would consist not just of payment of any due tax, but often additional compliance costs. In contrast, non–compliance would involve savings under both headings with a decreasing risk of detection.

A move to self assessment therefore requires a fundamental behavioural change on the part of both taxpayers and the Revenue authorities. For the taxpayer, disclosing and assessing his own liabilities, rather than waiting for enquiries and assessments from the tax authorities, marks a fundamental shift in responsibilities. For the tax administration it entails an obvious shift in focus away from the examination of returns and the computation of tax liabilities to checking, screening, auditing and investigation work. It also requires the administration to devote considerably more resources to taxpayer information and advisory programmes – ranging from technical briefing for practitioners to media advertising on compliance issues, such as return filing dates.

The Move to Self Assessment

Self assessment for income tax for the self–employed was eventually launched in the Finance Act 1988. Two particular features should be emphasised about introduction of self assessment in Ireland.

(1) Although many people thought it impossible, self assessment was introduced in stages. This was to reduce the shock to the existing system and to keep sufficient control over and monitoring of the new system to ensure that flows of revenue to the Exchequer were maintained.

(2) For the seemingly perverse reason that it was the most difficult tax to apply it to, the first major tax to which self assessment was applied was income tax for the self–employed. The Revenue did not want any false successes to lead to over–confidence in applying the system generally and in any event, it was the income tax system for the self–employed which was most in need of remedial treatment.

Perhaps the most significant 'non–change' which accompanied the introduction of self assessment for the self–employed was that the practice of assessing most sources of income on a preceding year basis was unaltered. It was also decided not to make it mandatory for taxpayers or their agents to calculate tax liabilities, although a calculation form was provided with the return of income and taxpayers and their professional agents were encouraged to use it.

Success or Failure?

While the authors would not claim spectacular success for the new system, the following comparative figures show a significant improvement.

(1) The anticipated tax yield from the first payment in 1988 of the tax liability for the 1988/89 tax year under the old basis was IR£100m to IR£110m – the actual yield under the new system was IR£174m.

(2) The number of tax returns received on time for the previous year under the old basis was 92,803 – the number received on time under the new basis was 134,344.

(3) The number of outstanding tax appeals for the previous year under the old basis was 105,603 – the number outstanding for the year of introduction of the new system was 9,669.

Further Developments

In the year 1989 the system was allowed to bed down; however, in 1990 two substantial further moves were made. The preceding year basis of assessment for income tax was got rid of so all income became taxed on the actual income of the year, save that business income is charged to tax on the basis of the accounts made up to a date within the year; and the system was extended to corporation tax. In 1991 the system was extended to capital gains tax.

Are the Revenue Commissioners Now Satisfied with the System?

There remain gaps in the system compared to a full–blown self assessment system, but closing them may be either difficult or unnecessary. The following aspects require further thought.

(1) The calculation of the tax with the tax return remains voluntary, although an increasing number of taxpayers (ultimately expected to include all persons with professional tax advisers) are making the calculation. The difficulty of dealing with those persons whose incomes are insufficient to employ a tax adviser is likely to inhibit a move to a mandatory requirement to self assess the tax calculation until either the system can be further simplified to help these persons or until a network of 'return filers' emerges, providing a low cost compliance service for people with less complex income tax problems.

(2) While the percentage of persons who file returns on time is increasing to the point where it is now about 75 per cent, it is still below the standard that should be expected from the system, particularly in the corporate sector. Percentages in the 'nineties are the ultimate goal.

(3) The dates for final tax payment and return filing are still separate and, if anything, have tended to drift further apart. Some thought may have to be given to bringing the dates into line, although it is recognised it will not be easy. Taxpayers are required to make a substantial payment of tax (100 per cent of last year's tax or 90 per cent of the current year's tax) in advance of the return.

(4) Because of this situation, a system whereby payment of the full tax due accompanies the return cannot be introduced. Assessments are still required and this involves both administrative expense and cash flow loss. However, there are procedural and security problems also involved in the movement to such a system.

Audits and Policing the System

Finally, even though we have stressed the need for a vigorous marketing approach to encouraging voluntary compliance, a word or two must be said about enforcement! There is always a danger, although it tends to be exaggerated, of self assessment systems becoming 'write your own ticket' systems unless they are adequately policed. This means more emphasis on auditing as well as random checking on the accuracy of the returns filed. For inspectors of taxes this means a significant cultural change. Auditing requires tax officials to leave their desks and to visit taxpayers' premises in order to check directly the accuracy of the taxpayers' records. New skills are required and audit techniques and methods of handling interpersonal relationships between inspectors, taxpayers and practitioners have to be developed. At present in Ireland, the needs to deal with the transitional problems of handling the detritus of the old system while moving to the new system has limited the resources available to develop a comprehensive audit structure. However, the resources are now becoming available and the process of moving to a full audit programme is well in hand. However, there will always be problems about how cases should be picked for audit. As audits are expensive and time–consuming, it would be ideal if only those cases likely to involve default could be targeted, but in practice a certain degree of random auditing is needed to ensure compliance and also to check that the audit selection programme is optimally focused.

A vexed question is the percentage of audits which should be carried out annually. Audits are expensive and also disruptive and create compliance costs for taxpayers. Accordingly, only the minimum number necessary to ensure continuing compliance should be undertaken. The optimal number or proportion for Irish circumstances cannot yet be estimated. Further experience and empirical evidence are necessary before reliable estimates can be produced. It may even be that a larger percentage of audits is required in the early stages to convince taxpayers that self assessment is not a 'write your own ticket' system, with a possibility of reducing this proportion as the message gets across. It is likely that the ultimate percentage will be quite small. This has been the experience in some other self assessment jurisdictions. To date, the comparatively limited audit procedures introduced are proving effective and there is reason to believe that the fully developed system will be far more effective in confronting evasion than the old system.

Conclusion

So far in Ireland, there is reason to be confident that the decision to move to a sel assessment system was correct. But there is no room for complacency. The world is becoming more fiscally complex and the individual taxpayers are becoming more fiscally adept. The notion that a tax administration can develop to a point where it needs no further change or development is no longer viable, if it ever was, and the process and procedures of organic change and development will have to become part of all tax administrative procedures.

Self Assessment: Capital Acquisitions Tax

Capital Acquisitions Tax (CAT)

CAT is a tax on gifts and inheritances. Since 1984 CAT has been a full accessions tax, involving aggregation of all benefits taken by any beneficiary from all disponers. Details of the structure of the tax and its place in the Irish tax system are summarised in the Appendix to this chapter.

Administration

Until 1989 CAT was administered as a direct assessment tax. Potential tax liabilities came to the notice of the Revenue through the operation of the probate system (in the case of taxation of inheritances) and through voluntary declarations and the operation of stamp duty procedures (in the case of gifts of land and company shares). Taxpayers or their agents were asked to complete returns which provided the basis for Revenue assessments. The only element of self assessment in the system was a statutory requirement on beneficiaries to lodge returns where they received a benefit greater than 80 per cent of the relevant tax–free threshold.

Direct Assessment – A Candidate for Reform

Despite improvements in revenue yield and staff productivity in the early and mid–1980s (see Table 7.3 in the Appendix), the direct assessment system exhibited a number of serious shortcomings – two of which were particularly striking:
*   about 30 per cent of the returns submitted resulted in the issue of nil assessments;
*   almost 60 per cent of assessments required subsequent revision.

Other unsatisfactory features of the system included the following:
*   long delays (in some cases, as long as two years) in processing relatively routine and simple cases from the date of initial submission of returns to the issue of a final assessment; (a sample survey carried out in 1986 showed that it could take up to ten rounds of correspondence to finalise taxable cases;
*   significant delays in receiving payment following the issue of assessments.

The high figure of 30 per cent for nil assessments arose because the presence or extent of tax liabilities were not always apparent from the initial examination of cases. The first assessments in many taxable cases were issued on the basis of information provided during the probate process. At that stage, factors such as the effects of possible reliefs and credits would quite often not have been known and, in many instances, they eliminated the originally assessed tax liability.

There were two main reasons for the high re–assessment figure. The provision of further information by a taxpayer – usually in response to the issue of tax assessment by the Revenue – required a re–assessment. In addition, there was a great deal of impressionistic and anecdotal evidence to the effect that many tax practitioners did not complete returns adequately, as they knew that the Revenue would check the material and issue queries in respect of any short–comings. Indeed, for the taxpayer there was a powerful incentive to delay the issue of a formal assessment through inadequate form completion, as interest on due tax was not charged during periods when documentation was being processed or was awaiting processing by the Revenue.

From the perspective of efficient management and resource allocation, or indeed the quality of service provision to taxpayers, there appeared to be little by way of increased value–added or productivity which could be squeezed out of the system by making incremental changes. Significant procedural and administrative changes had already been introduced in 1982 – which included the issue of guidelines to staff on the selective and critical examination of cases. These changes contributed to the increase in yield which was achieved in 1982 and sustained in subsequent years.

Why Self Assessment?

The statutory scheme for direct assessment was not efficient. Furthermore, it appeared unlikely that any improvements to the system would result in significant productivity or yield gains. One of the powerful attractions of a statutory self assessment scheme was that by changing the relationship between taxpayers and the Revenue, resources could be transferred from the preparation of assessments to examination and investigation activity – thus achieving significant benefits in the form of reduced compliance costs for the general body of taxpayers and more selective (and more productive) allocation of Revenue resources.

A move to self assessment for CAT was also consistent with the conclusions of the general policy review undertaken in the Revenue in the late 1980s, described earlier in this chapter.

The Case Against

The arguments against self assessment revolved around the perceived complexity of CAT and its unusual administrative and practitioner profile. The tax was widely perceived to be very complex – in part because of the life–time aggregation provisions but also because of the interaction of the tax law with the general law of property. As a result, virtually all taxpayers used a practitioner (generally a solicitor) to handle their CAT affairs. To some extent, the perception of complexity is reinforced by the administrative arrangements on the Revenue side. In contrast with the other direct taxes (income tax, corporation tax and capital gains tax) which are administered on a decentralised, tax district, basis, the administration of CAT is centralised in the Capital Taxes Branch at Revenue Headquarters in Dublin – where the 'office culture' places a very high premium on technical expertise and excellence.

In contrast, there were, and still are, relatively few CAT specialists on the practitioner side. Although only a very small number of CAT cases are handled by the taxpayers themselves, cases are handled by solicitors who are not tax specialists – many are sole practitioners or work in small practices and taxation work represents only a small part of their professional practice. This contrasts with the other direct taxes where the practitioners tend to be taxation specialists.

The complexity of the tax code and the lack of specialisation among practitioners did lead to expressions of concern about the feasibility of introducing a self assessment system for CAT. For this reason it was decided to experiment by introducing a pilot scheme of self assessment on a voluntary basis. This scheme, which was administered side–by–side with the then existing statutory direct assessment scheme, was launched with the formal support of the professional tax practitioner bodies (most notably the Law Society, the regulatory and representative body for solicitors). The central compliance requirement was that within four months of the valuation date (in general, the date on which the beneficiary took beneficial ownership of a taxable gift or inheritance), the taxpayer would file, or have filed on his or her behalf, a tax return setting out details of the benefit taken, as well as other information relevant to the assessment of the tax liability (e.g. relationship between the disponer and the beneficiary, and details of any previous gifts or inheritances), accompanied by a computation of the tax due and a payment (cheque or banker's draft).

Results of the Pilot Study

After a particularly slow start, the pilot study quickly gathered momentum. Within nine months of inception, a significant number of cases were being self assessed. By the end of 1988, almost 50 per cent of the relevant yield from CAT was being paid through self assessment.

This was obviously a very encouraging response, particularly as there had been some misgivings, not just about the feasibility of self assessment for CAT, but also concern about the willingness of solicitors to participate in a voluntary scheme involving the earlier payment of tax by their clients. Indeed, there was a view that any solicitor participating in the scheme would conceivably be exposed to legal action from a dissatisfied client, for computing assessments under a voluntary, as opposed to a statutory scheme. First, because under the self assessment scheme, a client might end up paying due tax at an earlier date than would otherwise be the case – because of the delays and backlog in dealing with the direct assessment cases and, in particular, because of the loss of the 'interest holiday' which applied to cases which were awaiting processing by the Revenue. Secondly, because of the possibility that, as a result of a computational error made by a solicitor, a taxpayer might make a significant overpayment to the Revenue. As a result of this concern, the Revenue undertook, during the duration of the voluntary self assessment period, to check carefully all self assessment returns for computational errors. The results were very encouraging – errors made by practitioners were insignificant, accounting for a net 0.6 per cent of the yield.

Key Success Factors

The following were the key reasons for success.

(1) *Viability of the project.* For the practitioner, self assessment was a better 'product' than its predecessor. In contrast to the tedious and costly rounds of correspondence required to complete direct assessment cases, most self assessment cases were settled immediately. Revenue receipt of an assessed return and payment was followed within a short period (generally a week), by the issue of a certificate of discharge from tax. For practitioners the initial investment of time in preparing self assessment returns more than paid off in terms of faster completion of cases.

(2) *Marketing.* The Capital Taxes Branch undertook a programme of tax practitioner education and training. Teams of officials presented a country–wide series of seminars on CAT self assessment. The objective was to encourage participation in the scheme by practitioners as well as increasing practitioner knowledge and expertise. The seminars involved a 'learning by doing' approach through a series of graduated exercises as well as formal lectures on the tax. The response of practitioners to the seminars was very enthusiastic and by the end of 1989 attendance had reached almost 2,000. The seminar programme was later supplemented by a series of workshops which took the form of one–to–one meetings between practitioners and tax officials in respect of difficult cases which the practitioner was unable to complete or where he was uncertain about the result. The purpose of the meeting was to complete the self assessment and pay the tax due. This outcome was achieved in virtually all cases.

The seminar and workshop programme was probably the most critical success factor. It fulfilled the stated objectives of increasing practitioner knowledge and expertise in relation to CAT and of promoting the self assessment pilot programme. It also achieved the very valuable result of improving relationships between practitioners and Revenue personnel which has contributed considerably to the subsequent positive compliance climate. The success of the seminars, which reflected directly on the members of the seminar team, also had a very positive effect on staff morale in the Capital Taxes Branch – an important benefit at a time when work procedures and organisation were undergoing considerable change.

(3) *Design and preparation of the relevant documentation.* A new self assessment form and a set of operating instructions for taxpayers/practitioners were prepared. The new self assessment return form followed a flow–chart design. Before completing each section of the return, the attention of the taxpayer or practitioner was drawn to systematic checklists of items – such as credits, deductions, etc., which reduced the possibility of errors and omissions. This was supported by a comprehensive 55 page manual of 'operating' instructions which included worked examples. In designing both the return form and the accompanying manual, considerable effort was made to ensure that a person carrying out a self assessment could do so accurately and confidently without having a detailed knowledge of the principles or complexities of the CAT legislation.

(4) *Staff improvement and participation.* From its inception, a conscious policy was pursued of ensuring as widespread as possible involvement of Capital Taxes Branch staff. The initial staff reaction to the self assessment proposal varied from enthusiasm to concern about possible adverse consequences for staffing levels, for income from overtime and for work procedures and organisation. Much of the criticism or scepticism reflected a predictable reaction to proposals for change. There was also concern and scepticism about the technical ability of many practitioners to carry out self assessments as well as fears that self assessment would create new opportunities for evasion.

The design of the new compliance documentation – the assessment form and the instruction booklet – and the organisation of new work procedures and organisation was undertaken by broadly–based project teams. Considerable use was made of brainstorming sessions and a conscious effort was made to encourage an experimental approach to working methods and procedures. This approach, which contrasted with the traditional hierarchical culture in the Branch, succeeded in ensuring a sufficient level of commitment and enthusiasm for the project.

(5) *Support of the organisations representing practitioners.* Both the Law Society and the Institute of Taxation supported the project. This support and particularly their involvement in the organisation of seminars, made a major contribution to success.

Self assessment for CAT became mandatory with effect from January 1, 1989. In contrast with income tax, the new CAT regime requires taxpayers or their agents to compute tax liabilities. Following the introduction of mandatory self assessment the seminar programme was maintained for a further two year period, to maintain the goodwill and commitment of the practitioners and to build on the high level of correct return completion achieved during the pilot scheme. A reduced seminar programme is still in operation. In addition, a programme of lectures by Capital Taxes Branch personnel to Law Society students has been put in place to assist the transmission of technical knowledge to new practitioners. A taxpayer advisory service is provided which allows practitioners and taxpayers to obtain assistance with form completion and in computing assessments.

Following the enactment of the statutory self assessment scheme in 1989, there have been further significant developments.

Amnesty for Unpaid CAT, 1991

In order that all available resources could be devoted to servicing the new self assessment regime, it was necessary to 'clear the decks' of residual direct assessment cases. Many of these cases, which pre–dated the self assessment system, involved disputes on legal and valuation questions and absorbed excessive resources. The introduction of self assessment for income tax and corporation tax had been accompanied by an amnesty in 1988 which allowed taxpayers then in arrears to bring their affairs up to date without interest charge. The thinking behind that amnesty was to allow taxpayers a final opportunity to pay arrears in advance of a strengthened audit and enforcement regime. In fact, the 1988 amnesty was very successful, yielding some I£500m in additional revenue. CAT was not included in the 1988 amnesty and the 1990 Finance Act put in place an amnesty specifically for this tax.

Essentially the CAT amnesty allowed a period of some six months for payment of arrears. If payment was forthcoming within that period then interest charges (15 per cent per annum) and penalties would be waived. The 'stick' was the promise of new audit and enforcement procedures to tackle those taxpayers remaining in arrears after the amnesty deadline.

The CAT amnesty was very effective. Two thousand cases were removed from the backlog of direct assessment cases. The additional yield amounted to IR£13m (or 35 per cent of the baseline yield). The CAT amnesty removed, once and for all, the 'drag effect' created by the residual direct assessment cases and paved the way for the new audit and enforcement regime.

Audit

Effective audit is the corner–stone of any self assessment system. To ensure the maintenance of compliance in the medium to long term, it is critically important that taxpayers perceive that self assessment is much more than an ability to 'write their own cheque'. On the contrary, the effective policing of compliance requires that each and every taxpayer (and of course, the practitioner acting on his behalf) feels that, in completing his self assessment return, the prospect of audit, in the event of under declaration, is very real.

In putting in place an effective audit regime, it is necessary to balance the need to provide a speedy and efficient service to the compliant taxpayer against the requirement to provide a visible deterrent to non–compliance. In striking this balance the screening approach is critical. This approach must not be so intrusive as to cause large scale administrative and processing delays and, in effect, mirror the old direct assessment system. On the other hand, the screening operation must protect the Revenue's interest by detecting those cases which warrant audit.

The CAT screening operation embraces two phases. The first is basically an arithmetic check which verifies rates, thresholds, etc. The second phase focuses on the return in its entirety and judges factors such as the disponer's level of assets in the light of his previous income and occupation. Emphasis is also placed on critical aspects such as valuation of assets and reliefs claimed which can materially influence the tax liabilities. The screening operation is applied to all returns and results in the selection of a proportion for audit. In addition a limited number of randomly selected cases are audited.

The audit operation embraces both a desk and field dimension. The services of the professionally staffed Government Valuation Office are also used for the valuation of real property.

The CAT audit programme has been in place since early 1992 and has to date addressed in excess of 200 cases (approximately 4 per cent of taxable cases). Of this number, some 100 have been finalised, resulting in an additional yield of IR£0.5m in the period up to end June 1992. This represents an additional 3.5 per cent of the yield during the same period.

Enforcement

Until 1990, the CAT collection operation was underpinned by the court judgement procedure and penalty action. This contrasted with the other taxes such as VAT, income tax, corporation tax and capital gains tax, where powers of sheriff enforcement and attachment had been operational for some years. As with audit, effective well–targeted enforcement is an essential support for a self assessment system. Indeed, the underlying measure of the effectiveness of any enforcement system is its deterrent value. Thus, one would expect that an effective enforcement regime should ultimately be applied only to a small proportion of cases.

By its nature, CAT is a high compliance tax. The need to secure title to assets following the death of a disponer prompts disclosures. Furthermore, the CAT liability attaches as a charge to houses and land, thus impeding a future sale in the event that it remains outstanding.

Despite the high compliance profile, there are inevitably cases of entrenched default. In the post amnesty period, the new enforcement powers are being directed against these cases. It is anticipated that the 'demonstration factor' which is very much a feature of well–targeted enforcement action will progressively diminish the incidence of default under the CAT self assessment system.

Conclusion

The introduction of self assessment into CAT has been an unqualified success. The service to taxpayers and to their agents has improved significantly. Furthermore, the sustainable annual yield has increased by about 30 per cent through the combined effect of more efficient administration and an improved compliance climate.

References and Further Reading

Allingham, M. G. and A. Sandmo, 'Income Tax Evasion: A Theoretical Analysis', *Journal of Public Economics*, pp.323–338, 1972.

Lewis, A., 'An Empirical Assessment of Tax Mentality', *Public Finance*, Vol. XXXIV (2), pp.245–257, 1979.

McCrohan, K., 'Can Income Tax be Marketed?', Paper presented at the Foundation for Fiscal Studies, Dublin, Ireland, April 27, 1988.

Scott, W. J. and H. G. Grasmick, 'Deterrence and Income Tax Cheating: Testing Interaction Hypotheses in Utilitarian Theories', *The Journal of Applied Behavioural Science*, Vol. 17 (3), pp.395–408, 1981.

Spicer, M. W. and S. B. Lundstedt, 'Understanding Tax Evasion', *Public Finance*, Col. XXXI (2), pp.295–305, 1976.

APPENDIX to Chapter 7

Capital Acquisitions Tax (CAT)

CAT is a tax on gifts and inheritances. The current tax–free thresholds and tables of rates are shown in Tables 7.1 and 7.2.

Table 7.1 CAT – Tax–free Thresholds

Relationship of the beneficiary to the disponer	Threshold (IR£s)
Child of the disponer	166,350
Parent, grandchild, brother, sister, nephew or niece of the disponer	22,180
All other relationships and strangers	11,090

Notes: In certain exceptional circumstances, provided for in the legislation, some categories of beneficiaries, (e.g. grandchildren, parents, nephews, nieces) may be entitled to higher thresholds than those listed in the table. The thresholds have been indexed to the Consumer Price Index since 1990.
IR£1 = US$1.7935, Stg£0.9352, 1.3071 ECU as at August 1992

Table 7.2 CAT – Tax Rates

Slice	Cumulative slice	Rate of tax percent
Threshold Amount	Threshold Amount +	NIL
IR£10,000	IR£ 10,000	20
IR£40,000	IR£ 50,000	30
IR£50,000	IR£100,000	35
Balance		40

Notes: The aggregation system and the progressive rate structure can mean that a later benefit is taxed at a higher rate than an earlier benefit when both benefits have been aggregated.

The tax was introduced in 1976 following the abolition of estate duty. At the time of its abolition, estate duty accounted for an annual yield of some IR£13m (about IR£63m in 1992 prices).

Capital acquisitions tax (CAT) comprises an inheritance tax, gift tax and a tax on discretionary trusts. The inheritance tax accounts for some 80 per cent of the total CAT yield, with gift tax and discretionary trust tax each yielding some 10 per cent of the yield. Gift tax is levied at 75 per cent of the inheritance tax rate. Discretionary trust tax (DTT) is in effect an anti–avoidance measure to deter the use of the discretionary trust mechanism as a means of postponing a CAT liability indefinitely. It is levied as an annual charge (an initial 3 per cent followed by 1 per cent per annum thereafter) on the value of the trust fund.

Table 7.3 sets out the CAT yield since 1980 and Table 7.4 gives the CAT yield in the context of the overall tax yield. The yield increased significantly (by 30 per cent) in 1990 which was the first full year of mandatory self assessment. The 1991 yield which includes a once–off amnesty figure of IR£13m, indicates a capacity to sustain this enhanced yield. While the CAT yield by its very nature can be heavily influenced by a few very large gifts/inheritances, the efficiencies inherent in the self assessment system have brought real and sustainable benefits in terms of timeliness of payment and Exchequer cash flow advantage.

Table 7.3 CAT Yield

Year	IR£m
1981	9
1982	13
1983	15
1984	18
1985	20
1986	21
1987	25
1988	27
1989	29
1990	38
1991	50

Table 7.4 CAT Yield and Total Tax Revenue

	1989	1990	1991
Total tax revenue (IR£m)	7,164	7,616	8,028
CAT (IR£m)	29	38	50
CAT as % of total tax revenue	0.4	0.5	0.6

CHAPTER 8

FORMS DESIGN AND COMPREHENSIBILITY

Michael Foers*

Introduction

Improvements in the design and comprehensibility of tax forms and other tax literature themselves constitute tax reform on the broadest definition. Additionally, attention to form design and comprehensibility is especially necessary at a time of major structural changes in the tax system.

In the 1980s simplification was one of the stated objectives of tax reform in a number of countries, for example, the United States of America and Australia. But in both those countries and in others, for example, New Zealand, tax reform has been recognised as increasing rather than reducing the complication of the system. In both Australia and New Zealand special committees were set up to recommend ways of simplifying the system. Whilst simplification comprehends much more than the language and design of tax forms, if it is to get very far it must include a programme which looks to providing assistance to the taxpayer. This can be achieved through forms and literature that are easier to understand and simpler to use. In this chapter we look at how the tax administration can develop design frameworks to try to ensure that forms are user-friendly.

The Organisation for Economic Co-operation and Development in a document (OECD, 1988), examined tax reform and citizen initiatives. This study makes the distinction between initiatives which are a direct response to changes in the tax system and those which are part of a broader concern to improve the quality of communication with taxpayers. The authors recognise that many countries are now focusing their attention on tax forms.

*The author was, from 1980 to 1985, head of the United Kingdom Inland Revenue forms design section.

Forms Control

Forms control is perhaps one of the most critical areas in any administration and it is often the most neglected.

It is critical because it represents the largest single point of contact between an organisation and its customers - whether this is a customer in the usual commercial sense or, for our purposes, a taxpayer. It is neglected because some managers know little of the use of forms as an aid to good management of the operation. Indeed many of those managers believe forms design to be a simple process; one that in a crisis, given a piece of paper, they can quickly resolve by designing the form themselves.

Forms control means the continuous and systematic review of all forms and paperwork which originates from an organisation. It consists of dealing with requests for new or revised forms, seeking to reduce the number of forms, recommending improvements to those that remain by simplifying them, designing them so that they are easier to use and standardising them.

The savings from eliminating unnecessary forms are self-evident and simpler forms will be welcomed by most recipients. But the users of forms are less likely to be confused if they receive forms that follow similar structures in design and are expressed in consistently clear language. For then people will begin to develop a sense of what they are required to do when they receive a form.

In the 1960s and '70s there was evidence to suggest that governments, despite being the largest producers and users of forms, were inherently opposed to change. Forms were for the benefit of the organisation and the user was expected to be able to deal with the legitimate requests for information quickly and accurately. The needs of the taxpayer were seldom taken into account.

In some countries it was justifiably claimed that the burden on the public of administrative paperwork was the largest tax - a hidden tax - imposed on the taxpayer.

As non-governmental organisations became more and more concerned with costs and cost efficiency and their own needs to obtain information, so attention was focused on forms. Customers' needs and abilities were considered for the first time by the forms' designers as market forces began to influence service. Plain language concepts were actively promoted. Customer service became a key competitive issue and so there was some motivation from within organisations for change.

Much of the early work was inspired by the achievements of Citibank in New York. Concerned about the costs of litigation when borrowers failed to meet their obligations under loan agreements, the bank engaged designers and linguists to look at its documents. The bank recognised that perhaps people did not really understand what arrangements they were entering into when they signed a loan agreement. This work resulted in a radically different loan agreement form, greatly increased customer awareness and satisfaction and led to cost savings and international acclaim.

As a result, the mid-1970s saw the first plain language laws enacted in the United States. The question, 'How do we say it so that people understand what we are talking about?' was asked in the boardrooms of banks and insurance companies across America. In the ABA Banking Journal, the BankAmerica president said, 'It is essential for us to communicate in clear and concise written form. Confusion is eliminated by using plain language and avoiding jargon. We service our customers' needs when we provide understandable easy-to-read forms.' Soon the message began to spread around the world.

There were also dramatic developments in printing technology. Colour printing was not new but as more and more printers were investing in new equipment, so colour printing became more accessible and cheaper. Commercial organisations began to demonstrate how innovative forms design could be.

Gradually governments began to realise that their bureaucracies could operate on open market principles and various initiatives were promoted to try to make administrative forms easier to use.

What is an Administrative Form?

The General Service Administration in Washington describes a form as 'A fixed arrangement of captioned spaces designed for entering and extracting prescribed information'. In France, it is, 'A medium bearing printed notes, some of which are intended for completion. It is a means of collecting, exchanging and retaining information'. But, put quite simply, an administrative form is the means by which the citizen and government talk to each other over a wide range of business. And talking to each other is the most important aspect, for this clearly implies a two-way communication.

The differences between these definitions is revealing. The first reflects, all too clearly, that forms were designed for the benefit of the organisation. The second still dwells on the collection of information. But do so many aspects of our daily life have to be one-sided; where one party understands and the other is left in the dark? The third definition begins to recognise that there are people involved on both sides of the information collection process. Forms, and administrative forms in particular, must become a two-way process. Everyone will benefit from well designed forms.

There is a wide gap between the ordinary citizens' powers of understanding and the language in which they are addressed by government. Many people are bewildered by the letters and forms they receive. Yet everyone is entitled to receive communications that are in the simplest and clearest language possible. Administrative forms designers, however, make certain assumptions about the abilities of their audience. They anticipate a level of understanding, expect the reader to have a certain amount of knowledge and assume a certain level of literacy. To be literate is not an absolute state but covers a whole range of ability; it is more than just the opposite of illiterate.

The skill of the effective forms designer is the ability to recognise the needs of the audience for a particular form. And each form must be seen as a new challenge with different problems to face.

Income tax forms almost always appear high on any list of forms that cause people concern and worry. The ability to read and comprehend decreases under stress and it varies inversely with the reader's willingness to approach certain material. Who can remain calm when faced with completing a tax form?

In 1980 a report on the German tax return found 'a comparatively high external resistance to being read'. The report went on to say:

'Apart from the linguistic complexity, the main criticism is the form's incomprehensibility of content, insufficient explanation, poor structure and the length.'

Work in Holland identified similar problems and the press there gave much publicity to the public's complaints about unclear and formal language.

But it is not only tax forms that pose problems. In the United States research concluded that the 1980 census form evoked 'unnecessary anger, hostility and resistance'. And in discussion groups, during research in 1984 into the Department of Health and Social Security forms in the United Kingdom, participants became anxious at the prospect of form filling.

So, how do we set about creating a document that meets the requirements of the administration and satisfies the needs of the reader? How do we ensure that forms enable people to talk to each other? Such a project needs a number of people - each one with their own separate skills but working together as a team. And each function or role must be considered, for it is when one is sacrificed - usually for the sake of expediency - that errors creep in. The outcome is often a disaster of major significance for someone - usually the taxpayer.

The process must involve a writer, an editor, a designer and where resources permit, or circumstances demand, a researcher. The writer takes responsibility for establishing the facts and preparing a brief. The writer and editor then, together, look at the logic and the language. The designer and the editor consider the structure and specification before the designer takes the project through to production.

Even without areas of difficulty the compliance costs attributable to administrative forms are high. In the United States, the Executive Office of the President, Office of Management and Budget, monitors the Information Collection Budget, or 'paperwork budget'. In 1986 two billion hours of the public's time was spent complying with federal requests for information (*Information Collection Budget*, 1986). Over 45 per cent of that was attributable to ten requirements and top of the list, with 12.5 per cent of the total time cost, was the Individual Income Tax Return, form 1040. This represented a slight improvement on 1981 when the form 1040 topped the list with 13.5 per cent, although the total hours needed to complete the form in 1986 had in fact increased. In 1981 there were eleven tax forms in the top twenty most burdensome administrative forms issued in the United States.

In 1984 an official study was commissioned of the paperwork burden imposed on taxpayers by the federal tax system (Arthur D. Little Corporation, 1988). The exercise took the form of a diary study and a mail survey of individual taxpayers and a mail survey of partnerships and corporations. It concluded that the average individual burden was 26.4 hours (with fees to advisers and tax preparers being converted to hours) and the aggregate burden for the country was 1.59 billion hours. Evidence suggests that the Tax Reform Act of 1986, although reducing the paperwork burden on taxpayers in some ways, overall increased it.

Currently the United States Internal Revenue Service invites the public to indicate, on their income tax form, how long it took to complete.

The Royal Commission on Government Organisation (Ottawa, 1962) estimated the clerical costs of processing forms at roughly twenty times the origination costs, but in some cases it could be as high as fifty times the costs.

So it is clear that a little more time spent in creating a form can have a huge pay-off for the administration as well as the public.

Forms Analysis

Before any design or re-design work starts, there is much preliminary work to do. The purpose of the form must be clearly established by an in-depth **investigation** looking into all aspects of using the form. Who uses it? How is it used? How is it issued? Who completes it? What information is it asking for? And so on. Each of these points should in turn be questioned - why is it so? For example, can it be sent out by other means? Can the information be obtained by some other method?

These findings are then **analysed** so that a clear picture is available to the designer.

The **design** of the document is not a matter for imagination or flamboyance. It must all be neat, orderly, logical and practical and, above all, the language must be clear and easy to understand. The designer must consider, amongst other things, the size of the form; how many lines are needed for making entries; is it to be printed on both sides; will colour be used in the design; will people be expected, or able, to complete the document on a typewriter; what type and size of envelope is proposed or available? These and many other questions need to be answered.

At the design stage variations on a theme will begin to emerge and they must all be tested. Testing at this stage need not be a complex task. A simple design given to a junior clerk, typist or cleaner for an initial reaction can soon pick out any weaknesses - or strengths - in the concept. And soon the form begins to take shape and quantitative and qualitative **testing** can be considered. This means a short print run - but this is a cost that can produce striking results and avoid expensive mistakes.

The final step in a comprehensive forms design programme is **evaluation**. How did the form behave under test, both inside and outside the organisation?

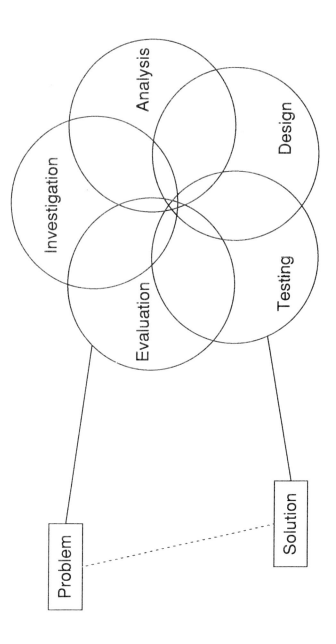

Fig. 8.1 Forms Analysis and Design

But that is not the end of the matter, for no doubt in all but the simplest of forms some omission, ambiguity or unexpected result will have been identified. And so the process must start again. The design this time will incorporate any changes deemed necessary to rectify the problem areas identified during testing.

Investigation, analysis, design, testing and evaluation will lead to a solution and eventually to a form that is effective and efficient.

Language is an important ingredient in any document: how questions are asked or information requested is crucial to the operation. Sadly, bureaucratic forms frequently show all the worst sides of an organisation. Government departments are geared to routines. This is not really surprising for a department must treat each member of the public fairly - not only with regard to the law but also with regard to other customers. Forms reflect that underlying philosophy, where orderliness and consistency are sacrosanct. And so we have language that covers every eventuality, however small the likely incidence. Verbosity, tautology and legal language are claimed to be necessary for the avoidance of doubt.

However, greater attention to customer service has added impetus to the need to change. Forms are now more often seen as essential communication tools which, if designed so that they function well, will not only project a different image of the organisation but in turn save money. Information, and moreover the correct information, will be obtained first time. The organisation can function more efficiently and the costs of monitoring and policing non-compliance due to ignorance or innocent mistakes will fall. The goal must be to have fewer and better forms, but simplicity and clarity demand much more thought by writers and designers.

Plain Language

Forms and leaflets are not literature - there are no Nobel prizes for elegant government writing.

Research into literacy suggests that something in excess of 10 per cent of the population of the United States, Australia and Great Britain are unable to read and write. Described variously as 'functionally illiterate', 'marginally illiterate' or simply people with low reading ability, such people are represented in many walks of life.

A literate person as defined by UNESCO is someone who 'can with understanding both read and write a short, simple statement of his everyday life'. Not a very demanding standard.

Clearly, language must play an important part in any form of communication. In speech we can usually get some immediate response or reaction from facial expression or the demeanour of our audience. With forms and written communication we get no such feedback.

In a discussion paper prepared for the Canadian Law Information Council in 1986, Gail Dykstra, the Director of the Council's Public Legal Education Branch, defined plain language as the marrying of 'content and format to create documents that can be understood by anybody. It is an approach to writing that is more successful in helping readers understand what they are reading than is a more formal and traditional style of writing.'

She goes on to claim that plain language has been used to translate technical and complex ideas into explanations that ordinary people can understand.

There are five simple rules for writing in plain language: use

*   active verbs;
*   familiar words;
*   short sentences;
*   personal pronouns;
*   simple sentences.

Active verbs. Text should contain about 90 per cent active verbs and 10 per cent passive verbs. Administrative language usually results in a reversal of these proportions for it is much easier for the writer to avoid responsibility and be vague by using passive verbs.

Familiar words. Use the words that people use in everyday conversation; the words learned in early life. Using such words does not show a lack of education on the part of the writer but a sympathetic awareness that not everybody has a wide reading vocabulary.

Short sentences. Any sentence longer than 25 words is probably a poor sentence - a sentence containing too many ideas. Most people will not get through to the end of a sentence of 40 words - they stop at the second 'and'. Long sentences are hard labour.

Personal pronouns. Personal pronouns make sentences active. They identify the writer and involve the reader.

Simple sentences. Try to keep sentences to one main idea with perhaps one secondary idea: too many embedded clauses will certainly confuse the reader.

Active, simple sentences with fewer words - unless two or three short, familiar words can replace a less comprehensible long one - should be the aim.

The plain English movement has been promoting plain language since the early 1970s, although the concept of plain language is not new. The United States, Australia, Sweden and the United Kingdom have been among the front runners. Other countries have been quick to see the advantages too.

Take these two extracts - the first in traditional language, the second in plain English:

'State the total amount of rent or other payment and/or other consideration paid to your landlord, including any rent charged therefore, or any sum charged for the use of furniture, fixtures, fittings and other furnishings therein, or for the maintenance of the property and the grounds thereof, or for services provided in connection with the property.'
(IR Department Singapore. Form 204 1/83)

'Please state
(a)   Duration of lease, tenancy or license
(b)   Rent of premises per month
(c)   Rent of furniture and fittings per month
(d)   Service charge/maintenance fee per month
(e)   Others (please specify).'
(Form 204 1/85)

Not only is the rewritten version clearer, but it is also much shorter.

Reading Ability

Reading skills are developed so that people may acquire information from the material they read. If people are unable to understand forms and instructions then the fault must rest with the forms designer or the author of the document.

Research in Denmark identified certain characteristics in school children and how they choose the material they read (Jansen *et al*, 1978). The findings are useful to people engaged in forms design. The research found that above average ability children were influenced by the content of what they read. The average ability readers were influenced primarily by the style of language but children with below average ability were most influenced by visual appeal.

These findings are supported by other research (for example, Gilliland, 1972). In choosing books, readers are influenced not only by their range of interests but also by the way in which the book has been written. For example, books which look 'wordy' or complicated may be avoided even though the content and style might be acceptable on closer examination.

The significance of these relationships emerges when the characteristics are viewed in the context of forms creation. Writers, who are familiar with their subject, compose text for forms or notes or leaflets. They are experts in their particular field, but not in communications; they concentrate only on content. As a result, their style fails to capture the attention of the less able reader. A barrier is introduced, effectively denying such people access to information or help that they may need. A sentence of 30 words will pose no problems for the person who is reasonably well educated. An average reader, however, will need two or three attempts at a long sentence before reaching the end. Similarly, long, unfamiliar, technical words cause problems.

This communications breakdown has been recognised for some time now and simpler language - shorter sentences, familiar words - as well as other techniques - have been introduced. Many forms rely on graphic cues - particularly some of the simpler forms. There is every reason to believe that this approach is successful. But we are now beginning to stray away from the concept of reading ability to that of readability.

There is plenty of research data available on the problems of readability; it can be measured and formulae used to assess textual difficulties. It is, therefore, possible to find out where problems are likely to arise and take some steps towards correcting them.

The first readability formulae were produced in the 1920s. Their purpose was to try to assess objectively the difficulty of text in an attempt to match written material with the reading/ understanding level of the reader. Some of the early tests used a complicated mathematical formula, but more modern tests involve counting a few features and making a simple calculation. From a sample of text, taking information about sentence length and long words, the level of reading difficulty can be assessed.

But the implication that these two features alone define difficulty is leading to the abuse of readability tests in the assessment of administrative documents. This in turn is tending to discredit the results of such tests.

The tests were devised for assessing material and matching it to children's needs. But research shows that material classified in this way does not always match the appropriate age level. This must mean that other factors are involved. Davison (1984) of the Centre for the Study of Reading at the University of Illinois, writes:

'Concealed within these early simple formulas are several assumptions that need to be examined more closely.
For example, it is assumed... that it is sufficient to measure the factors that reflect difficulty rather than directly measure the factors that cause difficulty in reading.'

She argues that the factors that cause difficulty are those which may vary: the background, experience and the motivation of the reader.

Perhaps sentence length and difficult words dominate most assessment tests because these are the factors most easily quantified. And this highlights the weakness with readability formulae in that they give no indication of what makes a passage of text difficult to read; they give no hint of the degree of comprehensibility.

In *Plain Words*, Gowers writes that the only purpose of writing must be 'to make the reader take his meaning readily and precisely'. It is important to distinguish between testing after writing and writing to satisfy an arbitrary test. The writing process can be manipulated to satisfy a formula but this does not guarantee clarity. A formula should be used only when the writing has been completed. For it is only if clarity is the aim that a formula can say whether a certain level of ease of reading has been achieved. Formulae are an indirect method of assessing difficulty; they do not tell you how to write, or rewrite, a passage of text.

It is important, therefore, for writers to understand the limitations of readability formulae and to place any analysis in its proper perspective. It is only one part of the equation. The other part is the reader's attitude, motivation, interest and background knowledge. These are the aspects which readability formulae cannot measure.

Various other techniques are now being used to try to motivate the reader and offer access to information to those people with less than average reading ability. Colour is used frequently to make forms and leaflets look more attractive. Many organisations use illustrations in leaflets; but why not also use them in forms?

In Sweden, the application form for Housing Benefit caused problems for applicants and had a very high error rate. Claimants were drawn mainly from the poorer sections of the community; (it seems reasonable to assume that this also means that they were from a lower ability group - but this may not have been so). Consultants were engaged to investigate the problem and they recommended that the application form should be redesigned and that the new form should include illustrations. In 1977 a new form was introduced and small cartoon-like figures were used to emphasise instructions at all the points in the document that had previously caused difficulties for claimants. The new form had a markedly better performance with a failure rate of less than 2 per cent compared with the earlier version when the failure rate was 35 per cent. The design concept remains in use - although the style of the illustrations changes.

In Holland, consultants working with the Ministry of Finance recommended the use of 'graphic algorithms' to improve the 'language, design and logic' of some of the Revenue's forms. Linguistic difficulties are only part of the reason why people have difficulty following complicated instructions. Their solution is the 'instructional algorithm' which sets out what the options are and leads the reader through the complexity of the instructions. In this way, any guess-work is removed and people are less frustrated.

Such moves are aimed at making the material more appealing to all readers. A sentiment very much in the minds of the committee on the re-designing of forms in Sri Lanka (Colombo, 1990): 'Every aspect of the design should attract the user. This quality is indispensable in a form used by the public where simplicity of language, readability and reduction of writing are *sine qua non*'.

Legal Language

The complexity of the underlying legislation is often a barrier to simple, effective forms. It is also frequently used as an excuse for delaying, or avoiding, any action to revise forms. The Organisation for Economic Co-operation and Development, in a document, *Administration as Service; The Public as Client*, looks at this problem:

'Language is driven by the needs of law, especially when it is in the form of written communication. The 'small print' of private sector advertising must, in the public interest, be made prominent in official communication. Laws and regulations have to correspond to legal criteria and be adjudicable in legal fora.' (OECD, 1988)

Government departments have to administer these complicated laws and try to explain their meaning. This task will be pointless and the efforts worthless if writers of forms and leaflets use legal jargon when translating the legislation. The success of a good form rests on achieving the correct balance between the comprehensive and the comprehensible. Use of jargon may impress the reader, but it also confuses. And it may lead to the supply of incorrect information if the reader does not understand the questions that are asked. If the department has to begin follow-up action to get the correct information, time and money is wasted.

But bureaucratic language is not confined to legal jargon. It includes pompous, officious, impersonal words that are reflected in much official writing. One must begin to question the reasons for this kind of approach. The Plain English Campaign describes this form of writing as gobbledegook and defines this as:

'The methodology employed by governmental bureaucracies specifically designed to ensure that the simplest instructions are encased in a plethora of treacherous sub-clauses, adverbial phrases and cross-references with the result that the recipient is left baffled, bemused and confused.'

Graphic Forms

We can now turn our attention to the document itself and look at some aspects of design. First we must consider typography - the art of arranging print on a page. Even the most enthusiastic do-it-yourself forms designer feels obliged to consult a printer at this stage. But here are a few tips.

There are five points to consider:
* type size;
* typeface;
* line length;
* justification;
* space.

Type size. Printed text of between 9 point and 12 point (in typography one point is roughly equal to 1/72 of an inch) is legible and easy to read. Smaller type sizes pose problems for the less able reader and even good readers are tempted to skip text where the type size is too small. Type that is too large slows down reading speed.

Typeface. There are two groups of typeface *viz* serif and sans serif. (A serif is the small line, or tail, at the ends of the main strokes in a typed character). Many people prefer a seriffed typeface because it represents a style with which they are familiar. A seriffed face may also have advantages in continuous text for the serifs help the eye to follow more easily the flow of letters along the line. There is, however, little difference between the legibility or a seriffed typeface and sans serif type, but for document design the clearer, open nature of a sans serif type may be preferable.

Within these two groups, typefaces to consider are:
* sans serif - Helvetica or Univer;
* with a serif - Times Roman;
but there are many other suitable typefaces available.

It is a common misconception that text in capital letters adds emphasis and is easier to read. In fact, long lines of capital letters are difficult to read and greatly reduce the speed of reading (Tinker, 1963).

Most words in lower case letters have a distinctive outline shape. All words in capital letters have the same shape:

This word form is an important factor in word recognition and underlining words for emphasis should therefore be avoided since this alters the word form. Words when typeset in capital letters occupy about 40 per cent more space. This, in turn, means that the eye of the reader can see fewer letters along a line of type - and therefore fewer words - and reading is accordingly much slower.

Highlighting text is a visual way of drawing attention to passages of text and bold face or italics are common techniques. They help to make a document look better and help to improve the visual presentation of what might otherwise be a dull page of text. For emphasis words can be printed in **bold**. Research has shown that readers associate emphasis with bold text. Text can also be printed in *italics* but the impact that this has on the reader is different. With **bold text** the eye of the reader is drawn to those words of phrases; with italicised text the reading flow is interrupted when the reader reaches the relevant spot.

Line length. Lines of print of more than 60 character spaces are more difficult to read than shorter lines. However, it is perhaps easier to think in terms of between 10 and 12 words per line. Shorter lines do not make use of peripheral vision and may reduce reading speed. But with questions on forms we may wish to slow down the reader. Longer lines pose difficulties for the less able reader, for they inhibit an accurate tracking of the eyes from the end of one line to the beginning of the next. This results in re-reading lines or sometimes the reader missing lines altogether.

Justification. When lines of text are the same length, that is, they all begin and end at the same position and the margins are even, then text is justified. With typeset text the typesetter can achieve that justification - familiar to most people in books and newspapers - by varying the space between the letters in a word or, more commonly, between words in a line. This irregularity in spacing can inhibit the less able reader. The uneven word spacing can become even more distorted when the lines of text are short. Sometimes the justified line end is achieved by keeping the spacing constant and hyphenating words. This too can cause problems and can result in some peculiar word breaks. Thus, for example, confusion may be caused by splitting the word *mans - laughter*. Research suggests that text which is not justified on the right helps both reading and understanding.

Space. Text with small margins, little space between lines of type, between sections or between paragraphs can produce hostility in the reader and make reading difficult.

An Overview of what Government Departments are Doing

Most government departments around the world have now moved away from the concept that forms were designed for their convenience only. They accept that two-way communication is essential. Customer service and the need to help voluntary compliance are now the main driving forces.

In 1944, after many millions more citizens had become taxpayers as a result of wartime economic measures, the Inland Revenue in the United Kingdom recognised the need for a simple income tax return form. The intervening years saw that form become more and more complicated until in 1983, a major redesign exercise resulted in a fresh start. The designers of this form, the form P1, adopted the plain language guidelines, with a mix of active and passive verbs, personal pronouns, familiar words and short, simple sentences.

In 1982, the United States introduced a simple return, the 1040A, and began work on an even simpler one page form, the 1040EZ. This set the pattern for similar work in Canada, where the province of Quebec followed suit with a one page return. In Sweden, Norway and France, similar developments resulted in short, simple tax returns. Most of these documents relied little on the explanatory notes or booklets which were necessary for the more complex return forms.

In Australia, a simplified return, the form S, appeared in 1985 but this needed a complex set of notes. Further research there showed that taxpayers generally disregard the notes and further work led to the development of a work book - the Taxpack. With this work book the taxpayer completes the return as a result of carefully working through the instructions.

Conclusions

Some significant characteristics emerge from all the recent work. The first is the visual impact achieved from the use of colour. Traditionally, most government forms were printed in black ink on white paper. Coloured paper was sometimes used if, for example, colour was needed to identify the form by relating it to a year or to a procedure. But colour printing was rare and the use of a second colour was always rejected on grounds of cost. Changes in print technology mean that costs are not now so great a factor.

More and more forms are being produced using colour as part of the design as administrations recognise the impact this has on the perceptions and motivation of the public. Colour is used for screening to provide white response areas for the form filler. Forms do not need to be multicoloured; the use of only one colour applied in various percentages can give the appearance of being in more than one colour and produce a very attractive form. The use of a second colour can add variety, impact and interest.

Some unpublished work in Denmark suggests that the use of white response areas highlighted against a coloured background can result in time savings for the user of the document of up to 40 per cent.

How might people react to the greater use of illustrations on forms? The only cited example is that of the Housing Ministry in Sweden. Although the use of illustrations offended some people, the majority seemed to find them helpful. And the improved performance of the new form meant not only less work for the administration but also fewer referrals back to claimants and fewer delays for them in receiving their benefits.

The use of plain language is perhaps the most significant development and this features in many government forms. But do taxpayers react more favourably to being addressed as 'you' with the revenue department referred to as 'we'? Is there a danger that using familiar words will result in some loss of meaning?

The reality is that plain language saves time and money and there is no evidence to suggest that it leads to any loss of accuracy. In 1983, the then Secretary of State for Commerce in the United States, the late Malcolm Baldrige, addressed a Forum on *The Productivity of Plain English*. He said, 'We are, believe me, talking about productivity. When people write letters... that are clear enough and simple enough and accurate enough and short enough, the time it saves the reader is immense. And that is productivity.'

In 1984, the Department published details of twelve case studies describing how some businesses have scored successes by simplifying consumer documents. The report claims that when a company simplifies its language it builds business and saves time and money. That may be the commercial justification for improving forms. But there ought to be another motive - service to the public.

References and Further Reading

Bentley, D., *How and Why of Readability*, The Centre for the Teaching of Reading, Reading, 1985.

Burgess, J. H., *Human Factors in Forms Design*, Nelson Hall,Chicago, 1984

Davison, A., 'Readability Formulas and Comprehension', *Comprehension Instruction: Perspectives and Suggestions*, Duffy, Roehler and Mason!, Longman, New York, 1984.

Felker, Pickering, Charrow, Holland and Redish, *Guidelines for Document Designers*, American Institutes for Research, Washington, 1981.

Gilliland, J., *Readability*, University of London Press, 1972.

Gowers, E., *The Complete Plain Words*, Revised S. Greenbaum and J. Whitcut, HMSO, London, 1986.

Gowers, E., *Plain Words*, HMSO, London, 1948.

Jansen, Jacobsen and Jensen, *The Teaching of Reading without Really any Method,* Munksgaard, Copenhagen, 1978, Humanities Press, New Jersey, 1978.

Landa, L. N., *Algorithmization in Learning and Instruction*, Educational Technology Publication, Englewood Cliffs, New Jersey, 1974.

Nowak and Sorgel , *Investigation into the Emotional Acceptance and the Comprehensibility of the Content of Tax Forms*, Institute of Social Science Gmbh, Report to the Federal Finance Ministry, Heidelberg, 1980.

Strunk and White, *The Elements of Style*, McMillan, New York, 1979.

Tinker, M., *Legibility of Print*, Iowa State University Press, 1963.

Twyman, M., Using Pictorial Language: a Discussion of the Dimensions of the Problem, *Designing Usable Texts*, Academic Press, Orlando, 1985.

Arthur D. Little Corporation, *Development of Methodology for Estimating Taxpayer Paper-work Burden*, Final Report to Department of the Treasury, IRS, Washington, 1988.

OECD, *Administration as Service. The Public as Client*, Paris, 1987.

OECD, *Administrative Responsiveness and the Taxpayer*, Paris, 1988.

US Department of Commerce, *How Plain English Works for Business*, Office of Consumer Affairs, Washington, 1984.

KEY ISSUES IN TAX REFORM

PART III
TAX REFORM - SOME WIDER ISSUES

UK H20
H21   H24

CHAPTER 9

TAX REFORM AND INCENTIVES: A CASE STUDY FROM THE UNITED KINGDOM

Chuck Brown and Cedric Sandford*

Introduction

The major feature of the world-wide tax reform movement, which began in the late 1970s, was the reduction in top rates of personal income tax, typically associated with a broadening of the tax base. Thus, to take some examples: at the beginning of 1979, the top income tax rate on earned income in the United Kingdom was 83 per cent with a 15 per cent surcharge on investment income, making an absurd maximum marginal rate of 98 per cent; after the 1988 Budget the top rate was down to 40 per cent on both earned and investment income. Over the same period in the United States the top federal income tax rate was cut from 70 per cent to a nominal 28 per cent (or 33 per cent over the income band where allowances were phased out). In Canada the top federal rate came down from 43 per cent to 29 per cent. In Australia the

* Chuck Brown was Professor of Economics at the University of Stirling. Cedric Sandford is Professor Emeritus of Political Economy, University of Bath. Sadly, Chuck Brown died in July 1991 after a sudden and short illness. He was the initiator and director of the research study, undertaken with Cedric Sandford, described in this chapter and the effect of taxation on labour supply was his specialist area. Before his illness he had agreed to write the chapter and had discussed its contents with the editor. In the event it has had to be written by Cedric Sandford, drawing heavily on Chuck's work. Chuck's contribution was such that to acknowledge him as joint author seemed only right. The research on which the chapter is based was financed by the Economic and Social Research Council (grant no: ROOO 23 1577) whose support is gratefully acknowledged, as is the contribution of the interviewees who gave generously of their time and answered the interviewer's questions so freely.

reduction was from 60 per cent to 47 per cent over the decade of the 'eighties and in New Zealand from 66 per cent to 33 per cent. Japan, in a series of steps, cut its top rate from 88 per cent to 50 per cent and the Swedish central government rate was brought down at one stroke from 50 to 20 per cent.

The main motive behind these, often dramatic, tax reductions was the desire to make the tax system as neutral as possible, to minimise the effect of tax on economic decision-making. The tax reform movement was part of the outcome of the philosophy of freeing markets; the expectation was that tax reform would generate economic efficiency - the efficient allocation of the factors of production in the economy - which, in turn, would promote economic growth. It was argued that lower tax rates would stimulate work effort, encourage enterprise and investment, discourage tax avoidance and evasion, and even generate additional revenue.

The study which follows, of the effects of the reduction in the United Kingdom income tax in 1988, is therefore of interest to all those countries where tax reform has taken place or is contemplated.

The Budget of 1988

In his 1988 Budget, Chancellor of the Exchequer Mr Nigel (now Lord) Lawson abolished all personal income tax rates above 40 per cent, thus bringing the top marginal rate in the United Kingdom down from 60 to 40 per cent. At the same time the standard rate of tax was reduced from 27 to 25 per cent and capital gains tax rates assimilated to income tax rates (though with their own separate threshold). The rates of personal income tax before and after the 1988 Budget are set out in the following table.

Table 9.1 Rates of United Kingdom Income Tax
1987-88 and 1988-89

	1987-88	1988-89
Basic rate	27	25
Higher rate(s)	40	{
	45	{
	50	{ 40
	55	{
	60	{

In introducing his proposals Mr Lawson referred to the fact that it was nine years since his predecessor, Sir Geoffrey (now Lord) Howe, had reduced the top rate from 83 per cent to 60 per cent and, since then, tax rates in other countries had fallen. He continued: 'The reason for the world-wide trend towards lower rates of tax is clear. Excessive rates of income tax destroy enterprise, encourage avoidance and drive talent to move to more hospitable shores overseas. As a result, far from raising additional revenue, over time they actually raise less. By contrast, a reduction in the top rates of income tax can, over time, result in a higher, not a lower, yield to the Exchequer.'

The Budget of 1988 thus offered the opportunity of a case study of the effects of the reduction in top rate income tax, with the possibility of testing out the Chancellor's claims.

Methodology of the Brown/Sandford Study

The effects of the 1988 income tax cuts were studied by interviewing over 300 partners, principals or sole proprietors in accountancy firms in three geographical areas - London, South West England and South Wales, and Central Scotland. Accountants were chosen because, even when not tax partners, they were knowledgeable about tax and could be expected to be sensitive in their behaviour to tax changes; they were used to dealing with figures, so they could be expected to answer questions precisely and accurately; they were in a better position than most workers to vary the amount of work which they did - especially sole proprietors (31 per cent of the sample) and other firms with only a single office (a further 27 per cent); a large proportion of them paid tax at higher rate; and they were in close contact with clients who paid tax at higher rate. The three geographical areas chosen, offered a good mix of accountants from the City of London, large provincial cities, like Glasgow, Bristol and Cardiff and small urban and rural areas.

The sample of interviewees was drawn according to a formula that combined cluster sampling (for reasons of economy) with random sampling. Offices in the selected areas were randomly chosen from the membership lists of the Institute of Chartered Accountants in England and Wales and the Institute of Chartered Accountants in Scotland, but with firms weighted by the number of partners to increase their chance of selection. Within a firm up to four partners, chosen randomly, were interviewed. To minimise interviewer bias all of the interviews were conducted by one or other of the authors. The findings relate to 316 interviews; after deducting from the original sample those who could not be contacted for various reasons (e.g. not known at this address, retired, seriously ill) the response rate was 69 per cent. Of the 316, 179 (or 57 per cent) had paid tax at 45 per cent or more in 1987-88.

Most of the questions sought to establish whether there had been any change in the respondent's behaviour between the fiscal years 1987-88 and 1988-89 i.e. the year before and the year after the 1988 Budget; e.g. had there been any change in the average number of hours worked each week. If there had been a change the reason for it was then sought. Respondents were not directly asked about the effects of tax on their behaviour until towards the end of the interview. The large majority of the questions related to the respondent's personal behaviour; but, later questions asked respondents about their perceptions of the effect of the cut in higher rate tax on the behaviour of their clients. Responses to questions about other people's behaviour are second hand evidence, which necessarily has less reliability than replies to questions about the accountant's own behaviour. However, because the questions were about matters which accountants would often implement on behalf of their clients, or at least would discuss with clients, they possess a much higher reliability than second hand evidence normally carries.

Incentives for Work and Enterprise

The Theory

Economic theory does not provide a clear answer about whether an increase in income tax rates reduces the willingness to work and a reduction in income tax rates increases it. A change in rates gives rise to two effects, working in opposite directions - an income effect and a substitution effect. An example will illustrate the point.

Consider a community with a proportional tax rate of 25 per cent. An individual 'A' works 40 hours per week at £10 per hour; his gross weekly wage is therefore £400; tax is £100; and his take home pay is £300. Now imagine that the tax rate is dropped to 10 per cent. If he continues to work 40 hours per week, his gross weekly wage is unchanged at £400; tax is now £40; and his take home pay is £360. He is better off by £60 and can afford more of those things he enjoys, which may include leisure i.e. he may decide to work less, say, working 38 hours - for £380 gross; tax £38; take home pay £342. The decision to work less following a tax reduction (or more, following a tax increase) arises because of the effect on income.

But the reduction in tax from 25 to 10 per cent has also had another effect. If he works an extra hour, the net of tax return on that hour is now more than before. When tax was at 25 per cent, an extra hour of labour yielded £10 gross, which was £7.50 net. With the reduction in tax, the net return to an additional hour of work is £9. Because of the higher return he may decide to work more i.e. substitute work for leisure. Putting the point another way, the cost of leisure has gone up. An extra hour of leisure now involves a bigger sacrifice of other things than before. When the cost goes up we tend to buy less.

Thus there are two opposing effects: the income effect of a tax reduction works in the direction of taking more leisure i.e. doing less work; the substitution effect works in the direction of taking less leisure i.e. doing more work.

Economic theory cannot tell us which of these two effects will predominate. For that we need empirical analysis. But theory can take us a bit further along the road. The income effect works through the change in aggregate income; the substitution works through the change in the terms on which income can be acquired at the margin. The bigger the reduction in marginal rate relative to the change in aggregate income, the more will be the incentive or the less the disincentive effect.

Of course, our example was oversimplified and the real world is far more complicated. Thus, many workers have little scope to vary their work effort. Tax rates are rarely proportional throughout the income range, but are more often progressive. Overtime rates may differ from normal rates. There is normally a tax threshold and changes in the threshold have an income effect without a substitution effect. Moreover, we need to ask what happened to make possible the income tax reduction. For example, if the cut in income tax rates was offset by an increase in commodity taxes, such that, in our example, the £360 take home pay would only buy what £300 had bought before, there would be no income effect. Similarly, however, the £9 from an extra hour of work would then only buy what £7.50 had bought before, so the cost of an hour of leisure would be unchanged and there would be no substitution effect either. Or the reduction in tax may have been paid for by a reduction in government expenditure; and, if this expenditure had added to the real income of individual 'A' e.g. provided services which he now has to pay for, there is an offset to the income effect of the tax reduction. To obtain an answer to the question whether a reduction in tax will stimulate work effort and enterprise we need an empirical study which takes account of the particular circumstances of the case.

Previous Studies

Most earlier studies, in the United Kingdom and the United States, have been concerned with the general population.[1] The overall conclusion from these studies was that, for most kinds of direct tax changes, the effect on hours worked by male earners would be minimal, although the evidence suggested rather more response from women who were secondary earners. However, few studies have been made of that part of the population subject to the highest tax rates and these studies were either out of date and/or flawed in some respects.

The best of the earlier studies is that of Professor George Break undertaken in England in 1955-56 (Break, 1957). He interviewed a sample of 306 accountants and solicitors, of whom two-thirds were subject to surtax. After discarding the doubtful cases he concluded that 13 per cent of his sample suffered disincentives as a result of taxation and 10 per cent worked more; for just over half of the latter, the incentive effect took the form of postponing retirement. His principal conclusion was that the net effect of tax on work effort 'be it disincentive or incentive is not large enough to be of great economic or sociological significance'.

In 1969 Fields and Stanbury (1971) repeated Break's study. They found that 19 per cent of the sample experienced disincentive effects and 11 per cent experienced incentive effects. These differences were statistically significant and also suggested that disincentive effects had grown over time. However, the conclusions were flawed in that, despite the claim of Fields and Stanbury to have replicated Break's study, they changed both the order of the questions and the wording of the key questions in ways that might bias the results towards a larger disincentive effect. (See Brown and Jackson, 1990).

Fiegen and Reddaway (1981) reported on a study, carried out under the auspices of the Institute for Fiscal Studies, on the incentives of senior managers in 94 companies (53 per cent of those approached) in 1978. In each company, interviews, lasting over one hour, were held with a senior

[1]For a summary of the earlier studies, see Chapter 17 of Brown, C. V. and P. M. Jackson, 1990.

manager - usually at Board level - and questions were asked about senior staff (defined as those earning more than £10,000 p.a. in 1978). Disincentive effects roughly matched incentive effects and, each way, were about 12 per cent. The authors concluded: 'Although a study of this type does not enable precise relative weights to be attached to the various effects of incomes and tax policies, it is clear that in total any disincentive effects that operated on senior managers had a minimal impact on the activities of British industry.'

The problem with this study is that all the evidence is second-hand; that some of the companies had over 100 senior staff, that not all would react in the same way and, even when the number was smaller, it must be doubtful if any one manager would know how all staff had behaved.

American studies of high earners (surveyed by Holland, 1977) also show little evidence of taxation reducing or increasing productive work, but rather more evidence of taxation causing businessmen to devote time to minimising their corporate and personal tax liabilities.

The Brown/Sandford Study

Whereas earlier studies had taken place in a static situation, the Brown/Sandford study was able to compare the before and after effects of a major change in higher rate tax. The interviews took place in the fiscal year 1989-90 and generally sought comparisons of 1987-88 and 1988-89. Interviewees were asked about any changes in hours normally worked each week, holidays taken, work turned down and work taken on outside the firm. The responses of 179 accountants who paid tax at 45 per cent or above in 1987-88, and thus had a cut in tax rate of at least 5 per cent as a result of the 1988 Budget, are set out in Table 9.2.

Table 9.2 Accountants' Short-term Changes in Labour Supply[1]
percentages

	Hours normally worked	Holidays taken	Work turned down	Work outside the firm
More in 1988-89	19	13	8	2
No change/don't know	72	80	92	96
Less in 1988-89	9	7	0	2
	100	100	100	100

[1]Based on 179 accountants who paid tax at 45 per cent or more in 1987-88.

The longer term effects, i.e. the changes in retirement plans for those of the 179 accountants who were 45 years or over, are given in Table 9.3.

Table 9.3 Changes in Retirement Plans[1] - percentages

Retire later	2
No change/don't know	88
Retire earlier	10
	100

[1]Based on 88 accountants who were at least 45 years old and who paid tax at 45 per cent or more in 1987-88.

Whilst, to take the most important question, there was a significant difference in the proportion of respondents working more, rather than less, hours the crucial issue is, of course, how far these changes were a product of the tax cut. No tax reasons were given for changes in the amount of paid work taken on outside the firm (in any case negligible), nor in reasons for work turned down. More than half of those turning down work gave pressure of work or more selectivity as their reason. The overwhelming reason for working more hours was 'pressure of work' and reduced pressure of work was the most common reason given for working fewer hours. But two respondents gave the reduction in marginal tax rates as the reason for working longer and one gave 'better off as a result of the tax cuts' as a reason for working less. One respondent also gave 'better off - tax cuts' as a reason for taking more holiday.

Turning to the longer term effects, no respondents gave taxation as a reason for postponing retirement, but two gave it as a reason for planning an earlier retirement.

Although the respondents whose tax rates were 45 per cent or more in 1987-88 are obviously those most likely to be affected by the reduction in income tax, respondents on standard rate tax or on the 40 per cent rate in 1987-88, might be affected, in particular any who felt inhibited in their income generation by the existence of rates above 40 per cent. If we apply the same analysis to the total sample of 316 accountants, in fact we find one other respondent who experienced an incentive effect as a result of the cut in income tax rates.

The direct evidence from the accountants about their own work response to the cut in higher rate tax is summarised in Table 9.4.

**Table 9.4 Incentive and Disincentive Effects on Labour Supply
of the Tax Reduction**

Incentive		Disincentive	
Longer hours 2/179	(3/316)	Shorter hours	1/179
		Longer holidays	1/179
		Earlier retirement	2/80

Thus only 7 respondents out of 316 (or 2.2 per cent) were affected in their work effort by a tax incentive or disincentive. If the analysis is confined to those whose 1987-88 tax rate was 45 per cent or more, the figure becomes 6 out of 179 or 3.4 per cent, with the effects working in both directions.

Thus the overall impression is that the tax changes had a negligible effect on hours worked by the respondents. The tendency for more hours to be worked by accountants was a demand side and not a supply side response. The impression of an unimportant supply side response is confirmed by an exploration of the demand side. Respondents were asked if there had been any significant change in the volume of business coming into the office. Seventy-two per cent reported that the work had increased in 1988-89 with only 6 per cent indicating a decrease (see Table 9.5). The main reasons for the increase (up to two given by each respondent) were an increase in economic activity (62 per cent), more work from existing clients (36 per cent) and the growing awareness of the services accountants could offer - all demand side reasons.

**Table 9.5 Changes in the Volume of Accountancy Work[1]
percentages**

Higher in 1988-89	Same	Lower in 1988-89
72	22	6

[1]Based on 179 accountants who paid tax at 45 per cent or more in 1987-88.

That the growth in business was from the demand side is further confirmed by the fact that 88 per cent of the respondents saw the increase in the volume of work as part of a trend that started before the 1988 tax cuts.

If there was such a big increase in volume of work, it may be wondered why the number of respondents working more hours was not higher. The answer is that accounting offices increased their staff. In 1988-89, 32 per cent of offices took on at least one new partner (with 5 per cent having fewer partners); 45 per cent took on more qualified accountants (with 4 per cent taking less); and 53 per cent took on more staff without accountancy qualifications (with only 5 per cent taking less).

The only piece of evidence which appeared possibly inconsistent with the conclusion of a demand, and not a supply, led expansion is that almost half the accountants subject to a 45 per cent or more rate of tax in 1987-88 said that their firm had put more effort into attracting new clients in 1988-89 than in 1987-88. Unfortunately, in the interviews, this question was not followed up to find out the reasons. However, subsequent discussion with accountants has led the researchers to believe that the increased effort to attract clients was part of a trend which pre-dated the tax cuts. It seems likely that a more formal effort to attract new business started with the relaxation of the advertising restrictions of the Institute of Chartered Accountants in England and Wales in 1985. There was much new business available because of the buoyant economy. Furthermore this was a period in which accountancy firms were moving into new areas of work, such as consultancy, areas which needed increased marketing effort compared with the more traditional recurring work like auditing. This interpretation is consistent with the finding of the survey that the increased effort to attract new business was highest amongst firms with more than one office and lowest amongst sole practitioners. Like the other changes, the increased marketing effort was not a supply side response to the tax changes.

Further indications of the effect of the tax changes on effort and enterprise are provided by the second-hand evidence. Respondents were asked two general questions about their perceptions of the behaviour of their clients in response to the tax cuts - inviting up to four replies in all. Four per cent of the accountants said that they had clients who worked harder as a result of the cuts whilst 3 per cent said their clients worked less hard, took more holidays or retired earlier.

In his Budget speech Mr Lawson had implied that his tax reduction would encourage 'enterprise'. He did not define the term. It can properly be interpreted as including increased work effort, but can also go beyond it. In the general questions towards the end of the interview when accountants were asked about the most important effects of the tax cuts on their own behaviour, less than one per cent indicated that the cuts had made them more enterprising or adventurous. If we turn to the second-hand evidence, 7 per cent of respondents considered that the tax cuts had made their clients more enterprising or adventurous and 9 per cent said that the economic environment was better or that their clients were more bullish as a result of the tax cuts.

Emigration/Immigration

Mr Lawson's Budget speech of 1988 referred to 'excessive rates of income tax (driving) talent to more hospitable shores overseas' and it has been a long-standing concern that high rates of income tax in the United Kingdom could drive people out of the country. Whilst there is much anecdotal evidence of pop stars and others who have moved abroad to escape tax, an earlier official study (Cmnd. 3417, 1967) of the brain drain - restricted in its terms of reference to qualified engineers, technologists and scientists - found little evidence to support the fear that tax was a main cause, and stressed other factors, such as better research facilities abroad, in explaining the brain drain.

Clearly, as the researchers had no way of contacting accountants who had actually moved abroad, they were restricted to asking respondents about total emigration from and immigration into their offices in the two tax years 1987-88 and 1988-89; and where there had been emigration or immigration, the reasons for it, if known to the respondents. There had been immigration (emigration) in 32 per cent (28 per cent) of the firms in which respondents worked. The overwhelming reason given for the movement in both directions was to gain experience in an accountancy office in another country. In no case was it suggested that a move was attributable wholly to tax reasons. In one case it was believed that an emigrant had departed 'partly for tax reasons'.

Tax Avoidance

Tax avoidance constitutes legal methods by which a taxpayer can reduce his tax bill, as compared with tax evasion which comprises illegal methods of tax dodging. However, for all the simplicity of its definition, tax avoidance is not a simple concept. We can distinguish intended methods of avoidance, where the policy-makers wished to encourage a particular form of activity, e.g. investment, or at least accepted that an activity was worthy of support e.g. charitable giving or pension provision; and unintended methods where the avoider is using a loophole in the law or/and engaging in some wholly artificial transaction to save tax (see Chapter 6). The unintended avoidance is clearly distorting and undesirable; but even the intended methods may also be undesirable.[1]   To quote the kind of example given to the researchers by interviewees: at the end of a financial year, a farmer, facing a high marginal tax rate may, often quite irrationally, decide to reduce his total tax liability and his marginal rate by spending many thousands of pounds on a new tractor which he doesn't really need; such an investment is wasteful in the sense that the same sum could have generated a much higher return from an investment elsewhere in the economy.

There must be a *prima facie* case for believing that lower marginal tax rates will reduce avoidance of the undesirable kind. It can be expected to reduce unintended avoidance because the return is lower compared to the cost of implementation, which may be considerable. Moreover the lower potential gain is less worth the risk that the method may be declared illegal in the courts, or made retrospectively illegal by new legislation. A tax reduction can also be expected to reduce intended but undesirable tax avoidance because it constitutes a smaller wedge between the real return and the return to the investor; in our example, the farmer will be much less inclined to buy an unnecessary tractor if his tax saving is much less.

The Brown/Sandford study looked at avoidance under three heads: changes in respondents' avoidance in their personal affairs; changes in respondents' professional activities in response to clients' avoidance; respondents' views about the most important effects of the cut in higher rate taxes on their clients' behaviour.[2]   Of the 179 accountants whose tax rate in 1987-88 was 45 per cent or more, 20 per cent said they spent more time in personal tax planning in 1988-89 and 8 per cent said they spent less. Up to two reasons were invited so that the responses sum to more than 100. Over three-quarters of those who said they spent more time on tax planning gave reasons unconnected with the tax change (like becoming a partner). About one-third cited the income tax change, but

---

[1]The distortions introduced by tax have been well documented by the Meade Committee (1978) and more recently by Hills (1984) and Saunders and Webb (1988).
[2]A fuller analysis of the responses than given here can be found in Brown and Sandford, 1990.

often the increase in time was for temporary matters, like making sure they got the maximum relief at the old tax rate on their pension contributions. In many cases the extra time spent on tax avoidance amounted to no more than the odd hour. Of those reducing the time spent on tax avoidance, 57 per cent gave the reduction in marginal tax rate as a reason. This suggests that the long term balance of the effects of the tax reduction may be in the direction of reducing avoidance.

Of the 316 accountants, 13 per cent said that they did more tax avoidance work for clients in 1988-89 and 18 per cent said they did less. The most numerous reasons for doing more were miscellaneous (e.g. a client inheriting money). But some were related to the tax change. On the one hand several respondents indicated that the increase was of a temporary nature because, in the light of the income tax changes, along with the capital gains tax changes, they needed to review their clients' portfolios. Others mentioned that, because of the reduction in income tax, some clients now had more money available which they wished to invest in tax efficient ways (a kind of income effect). The most important reasons given for decreased avoidance work for clients was the change in the tax rates, which were mentioned by four-fifths, and less scope for tax avoidance - with investment now for commercial rather than tax reasons - cited by nearly one-third.

In the general questions to accountants about their perceptions of their clients' behaviour in response to the tax cuts (the second-hand evidence) where up to four responses were invited, the most numerous response, from as many as 30 per cent of the 316 accountants, was less tax avoidance - savings and investment now undertaken more on their economic merits rather than on their tax saving capabilities.[1]

It is important that this finding emerges from the less strong, i.e. the second-hand, evidence. Moreover, the reduction in investment allowances of recent years would also work in this same direction - and there is a danger that too much might be attributed to the tax cut. However, bearing in mind that investment decisions would be an aspect of the business in which the accountant would often be closely involved, and taken with the responses in respect of tax planning (above) it does appear that an important benefit of the reduction in the higher rates of income tax was to reduce, at least in the longer run, the extent of tax avoidance and to improve the quality of investment.

---

[1] Although given in answer to a question on the cuts in income tax, this response may also owe something to the alignment of capital gains tax with income tax rates.

Revenue Effects

A strong supply side argument, used especially in the United States, has been that lower tax rates actually generate more revenue. As the quotation from his 1988 Budget speech made clear, this was also a contention on which Mr Lawson put strong emphasis.

The essence of the argument is that, if a tax is gradually increased from zero up to a point at which it becomes prohibitive, its yield begins as nil, then increases in stages until it reaches a maximum, after which it gradually declines until it again falls to zero. The sequence can be illustrated in Figure 9.1, which is commonly called a Laffer curve (after an American economist) although it actually goes back to a French nineteenth century economist, Dupuit. The most crucial issue, of course, is at what rate the curve turns back on itself i.e. how high is the maximising tax rate.

Figure 9.1 A Dupuit or Laffer Curve

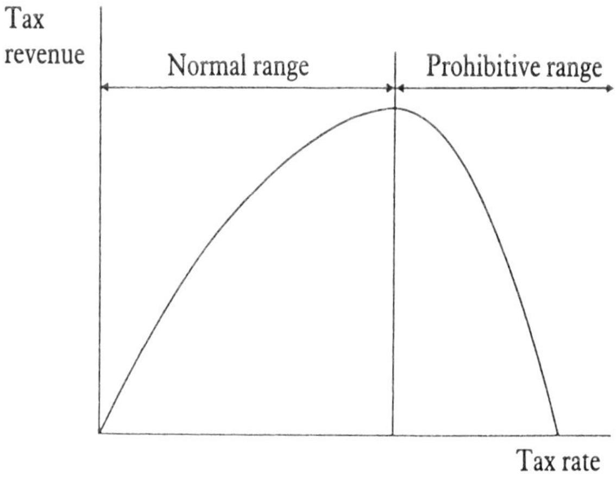

There are several possible reasons for cuts in tax rates to generate an increase in revenue. The tax reduction might lead people to do so much more work that they end up paying more income tax despite the lower rate. This possibility would normally require a very large labour response - much larger than anything remotely likely from the evidence.

For example, if someone worked 40 hours per week at £25 per hour, with a proportional tax at 60 per cent they would pay £600 tax. To pay more tax at a 40 per cent rate, they would have to work more than 60 hours. If the tax was not proportional and the tax cut only applied to the top marginal rate the increase in hours worked would not need to be as dramatic; but even so, it would need to be very considerable for a 20 point rate reduction.

Further possibilities are that the lower tax rate may reduce tax avoidance and/or tax evasion, including, what is often a form of tax avoidance, less payments in kind (fringe benefits which may or may not be taxed, and, if they are, may be taxed at preferential terms) and more in cash.

The Brown/Sandford study sought to shed some light on the revenue effects of the 1988 tax reduction by asking the 179 accountants who paid at the 45 per cent rate or above in 1987-88, what tax they paid in 1987-88, what they paid in 1988-89 and what they *expected* to pay (given that the interviews were taking place part way through the year) in 1989-90. As these were all people whose tax rates had fallen by at least 5 per cent, if the amount of tax they paid (or expected to pay) had *not* fallen, they were asked for (up to two) reasons why this was not so.

Table 9.6 sets out the changes in income tax paid in 1988-89 and Table 9.7 the tax expected to be paid in 1989-90, in each case by reference to the respondents' marginal tax rate in 1987-88.

**Table 9.6 Change in Income Tax Paid in 1988-89
Compared with 1987-88,
Analysed by Reference to Respondents' 1987-88 Marginal Tax Rate**

1987-88 tax rate		45%	50%	55%	60%	DK	Total
Less tax paid in 1988-89	N	9	12	17	48	0	86
	%	30	32	50	64	0	48
Same tax paid/DK	N	7	9	3	15	2	36
	%	23	24	9	20	100	20
More tax paid in 1988-89	N	14	17	14	12	0	57
	%	47	45	41	16	0	32
TOTAL	N	30	38	34	75	2	179
	%	100	100	100	100	100	100

Table 9.7 Change in Income Tax Expected to be Paid in 1989-90
Compared with 1987-88,
Analysed by Reference to Respondents' 1987-88 Marginal Tax Rates

1987-88 tax rate		45%	50%	55%	60%	DK	Total
Less tax expected	N	4	7	10	24	0	45
to be paid in 1989-90	%	13	18	9	32	0	25
Same tax/DK	N	8	8	8	23	1	48
	%	27	21	24	31	50	27
Less tax expected	N	18	23	16	28	1	86
to be paid in 1989-90	%	60	61	47	37	50	48
TOTAL	N	30	38	34	75	2	179
	%	100	100	100	100	100	100

Despite the fall in their tax rates, 32 per cent of the sample of 179 accountants paid more tax in 1988-89 than in 1987-88 and 20 per cent of the sample paid the same. As to expectations in 1989-90, as many as 48 per cent of the sample expected to pay more tax than they had in 1987-88 and a further 27 per cent expected to pay the same. On the face of things, these figures seem to bear out the contention of lower tax rates generating more revenue. But, of course, the vital consideration is the reason for more tax being paid. In respect of each year only 3 per cent of the respondents who paid more or the same amount of tax, gave working longer or harder as the reason. Overwhelmingly, (86 per cent of respondents in respect of 1988-89 and 95 per cent in relation to 1989-90) the reason given was increased pay/increased profits/promotion.

Once again, the predominant influence is a demand and not a supply side influence. In the cases of partners and principals in accountancy firms the effect of demand growth on profits is accentuated because of the 'gearing effect'. With demand growing, profits grow more than proportionately because the additional staff taken on make their own contribution to profits without the partners necessarily having to work harder or longer. The fall in tax rates may well have been followed by an increase in tax revenue to the Exchequer from higher-rate paying accountants, but the increased revenue was not *because* of the fall in tax rates. Had tax rates not been reduced, the increase in revenue would have been greater.

Conclusions

The Brown/Sandford study indicates that the reduction in higher rate taxes in the 1988 Budget had no significant supply side effects, save in one possible respect. They had a negligible effect of work effort and enterprise; they had no discernible effect on emigration and immigration; and on the supply side, did not increase revenue to the Exchequer. The one benefit to emerge is that they may have reduced tax avoidance and improved the quality of investment. If so this is a significant achievement.

The tax cuts will, of course, have added to the demand effects which were the predominant influence and were demonstrated by the increased pressure of work, the growth of accountancy firms and the increase in their profits. It is abundantly clear that the tax cuts coincided with a period of boom in the British economy - a boom which, by the end of the fiscal year 1989-90, was showing signs of weakening and which subsequently turned into a prolonged recession in which accountancy firms suffered reductions in demand and were led to dismiss many of the extra staff they had taken on in the boom.

The question which arises is how far the findings of the Brown/Sandford study can be regarded as applicable for reductions in high marginal tax rates at other times and in other places.

Certainly, much care should be taken in applying the findings elsewhere. Some of the complications which arise in actual situations are set out in the concluding paragraphs of the section on the theory of the effect of tax changes in work effort (above). We need always to take account of the particular circumstances of the case; for example, it is quite possible that the 1979 reduction in higher rate income tax in the United Kingdom from 83 to 60 per cent on earned income and from 98 to 75 per cent on investment income may have been responsible for higher revenue yield among those affected, especially because of a reduction in tax avoidance. (In other words, rates of 83 and 98 per cent were in the prohibitive range of the Laffer/Dupuit curve.)

Again, tax reform in some other countries had some different characteristics from that in the United Kingdom. Thus, in the United States, the reduction in the tax rates was accompanied much more by the removal or reduction of tax reliefs and tax shelters. In such a case, for the same hours of work, a high income individual may find himself paying the same total tax but with much lower marginal rates; then there is a substitution effect with no income effect and it is more likely that increased work effort will result. This situation contrasts markedly with the United Kingdom tax changes of 1988, which were the subject of the Brown/Sandford study, where higher rate taxpayers were not only affected by an income effect from the cuts in higher rate tax, but also by an income effect (without a substitution effect) from the concurrent reduction of two percentage points in basic rate tax covering a wide band of income.

However, if the findings of the Brown/Sandford study cannot be indiscriminately applied elsewhere, they do provide a cautionary tale that should reduce unrealistic expectations of supply side effects from tax reductions, and offer some indication of what may reasonably be anticipated.

References and Further Reading

Break, G. F., 'Income Taxes and Incentives to Work: An Empirical Study', *American Economic Review*, Sepember 1957.

Brown, C. V. and P. M. Jackson, *Public Sector Economics*, Blackwell, Oxford, 4th edition, 1990.

Brown, C. V. and C. T. Sandford, *Taxes and Incentives: The Effects of the 1988 Cuts in Higher Rates of Income Tax*, Institute for Public Policy Research, London, 1990.

Fiegen, G. C. and W. B. Reddaway, *Companies, Incentives and Senior Managers*, Oxford University Press for Institute for Fiscal Studies, London, 1981.

Fields, D. B. and W. T. Stanbury, 'Income Taxes and Incentives to Work: Some Additional Empirical Evidence', *American Economic Review*, June 1971.

Hemming, R. and J. A. Kay, 'The Laffer Curve', *Fiscal Studies*, March, 1980.

Hills, J., 'Savings Taxation: the Chancellor's Middle Way', *Fiscal Studies*, May, 1984.

Holland, D. H., 'The Effect of Taxation on Incentives in Higher Income Groups', in *Fiscal Policy and Labour Supply*, Institute for Fiscal Studies, London, 1977.

Meade, J. E. (Chairman), *The Structure and Reform of Direct Taxation*, Institute for Fiscal Studies, London, 1978.

Sandford, C. T., *Economics of Public Finance*, Pergamon, Oxford, 4th edition, 1992.

Saunders, M. and S. Webb, 'Fiscal Privilege and Financial Assets: Some Distortional Effects', *Fiscal Studies*, November 1988.

HMSO, *The Brain Drain - Report of the Working Group on Migration*, Cmnd 3417, HMSO, London, 1967.

CHAPTER 10

'GREEN TAXES' -
THE SCOPE FOR
ENVIRONMENTALLY-FRIENDLY TAXES

Stephen Smith*

Introduction

Environmental problems are becoming an increasing concern of government. Moreover, the scope and scale of the environmental problems that governments have to tackle is becoming wider. Although many countries have made considerable progress over the past two decades in controlling industrial effluents, new problems are emerging, many of them with a major international dimension, such as the problems of acid rain and the risk of global warming through the 'greenhouse effect'. The pressure for effective environmental policy measures no longer comes simply from domestic sources, but also arises from a series of international negotiations and agreements on environmental policy.

The commitments which many countries have undertaken to reduce emissions of carbon dioxide and other greenhouse gases require more far-reaching changes to patterns of production and consumption than previous environmental policies have sought to achieve. There is a growing awareness of the potential economic costs of environmental policy measures and growing interest in ways in which the economic costs of achieving environmental targets can be minimised. One aspect of this new concern has been an upsurge of interest in the potential of 'market mechanisms' in general, and environmental taxes in particular, for reducing the costs to the economy of a cleaner environment.

*Deputy Director of the Institute for Fiscal Studies, and Jean Monnet Senior Lecturer in European Economics at University College London.

Market Mechanisms in Environmental Policy

In most countries, the conventional method of pollution control for many years has been based on 'command and control' - the regulation of the choice of technology or the level of emissions either across the board or on a plant by plant basis. Economists, on the other hand, have generally been enthusiastic advocates of market-based solutions to pollution problems, based on pollution charges or taxes.[1] Instead of *overriding* market signals, pollution charges *correct* the signals to take into account the environmental costs caused by pollution. For example, a tax or charge may be levied, either on emissions of pollutants, or on the inputs to polluting processes, in order to reflect the environmental costs involved and to encourage reductions in the amount of pollution. The rationale, as we discuss in the following section, is that economic instruments promise to achieve a *given level* of pollution reduction, at a *lower* cost to national well-being, than would be achieved by regulation.

Environmental market mechanisms can take a number of different forms.

- Charges for measured quantities of pollution emitted. For example, emissions charges, directly related to measured emission quantities, are employed in a number of OECD countries (e.g. the Netherlands and France) to control water pollution, or to raise revenues to finance investment in collective environmental improvements..

- Subsidies for reductions in pollution or the installation of pollution control equipment. In a number of countries incentives are provided within the direct tax system, in the form of tax allowances, accelerated depreciation or other forms of 'tax expenditure' to encourage environmentally-beneficial investments.

- Tradeable emission permits. This approach has been used in the US, as an alternative to pollution taxation. Under a tradeable permits system, the government restricts the total quantity of pollution by issuing a limited quantity of emission permits, which have to be purchased by polluters if they continue emissions and which can be traded between potential polluters.

[1]The use of taxes to correct externalities was analysed by Pigou (1920); recent advocates of market-based incentives to control pollution have included Beckerman (1974) and Pearce (1989).

- Modifications to the system of indirect taxes (excise duties and VAT), to discourage the production or consumption of goods or services associated with pollution. Large-scale applications of such taxes are rare, although a number of European countries have introduced environmental excise duties on certain products (e.g. fertilisers, lead and cadmium batteries, plastic bags, etc.) and some countries have introduced carbon taxes, related to the carbon content of fuels, with the aim of reducing carbon dioxide emissions. Increasingly, too, decisions about the rates of existing taxes, such as those on petrol and motor vehicles are being taken with environmental considerations in mind.

In this chapter we consider the potential for more extensive use of the final group of possible market based instruments, based on the use of the system of taxation to control pollution. We leave on one side the issues involved in direct pollution charging, such as charges for metered discharges of pollutants and the introduction of road pricing, where new systems of monitoring and control would be required. Our focus of attention is instead on the existing taxation system and on the scope for fiscal restructuring to achieve environmental objectives.

In the next section the general issues which are involved in formulating policy measures to restrict environmental pollution are outlined. Then follows a section on the strengths and weaknesses of using market-based environmental policy measures in preference to direct regulation are compared. The following section outlines some issues which are raised by the use of the fiscal system for environmental policy and a further section then suggests a number of areas of tax policy where environmental considerations could usefully influence the design of the tax system. The penultimate section contains some comments about implementation strategy, while the final section draws some conclusions about the potential of fiscal instruments in environmental policy.

'Efficient' Environmental Policy

The need for public intervention to control environmental pollution arises because of the 'externalities' involved in pollution - the costs that the polluter imposes on other members of society. Without government intervention, a polluter may have no reason to take these external costs into account. In particular, the atmosphere and water systems may be treated as free methods for disposing of unwanted waste products, despite the fact that unrestricted pollution of the atmosphere, or of rivers and seas, may impose costs on other firms or individuals.

From an economic point of view, the objective of environmental policy should be to ensure that these external costs of pollution are fully taken into account by those responsible for causing the pollution. An optimal environmental policy would require a balance to be drawn between the costs of pollution and the costs of controlling pollution. Ideally, pollution should be restricted up to the point where the benefits to society as a whole from further reductions in pollution are less than the costs of pollution control devices or the curtailment of polluting activities, or, in other words, where the marginal damage of pollution equals the marginal benefit of polluting activities.

For a single polluting firm (for example, a firm discharging organic matter into a river) we can draw Marginal Abatement Cost (MAC) and Marginal Damage Cost (MDC) functions as shown. The marginal abatement cost will generally rise (strictly will not fall) with more stringent control, since the MAC curve assumes a ranking of measures, such that the least costly are implemented first. Often the marginal damage cost will also rise with emissions, reflecting a tendency for large amounts of pollution to cause proportionately greater damage to the environment than small amounts of pollution. This might be the case if the environment has some natural assimilative capacity - as in the case of the ability of water systems to assimilate organic matter. In the diagram, E* represents the efficient level of pollution control. At E*, the marginal abatement cost and marginal damage cost are equal, at a level C*.

The implication of this argument is that environmental policies need to be informed by a careful appraisal of the costs of pollution control and the benefits of a cleaner environment. Whilst there may be some forms of pollution which it would be desirable to eliminate entirely, this will generally be the exception rather than the rule. In most cases, the costs of totally eliminating all polluting emissions will be greater than the benefits and whilst it may be desirable to reduce emissions, this should only be done up to the point at which the costs of reduced emissions can be justified in terms of the benefits. In practical terms, this means that environmental policies cannot rely on simple all-or-nothing forms of intervention, but instead must be able to accommodate a more complex balance between different considerations.

Figure 10.1

An Economic View of the Efficient Level of Pollution Abatement

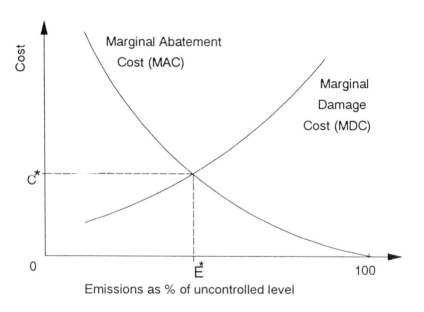

Valuation of the damage done by pollution, in order to determine the optimal level of pollution abatement, is both difficult and controversial, although considerable advances have been made in developing valuation methods in recent years.[1] In practice, most pollution policies still proceed from targets or objectives set by the political process. Even though the target level of pollution may differ from the economic optimum, the question still arises of efficiency in the attainment of environmental objectives. Where should reductions in pollution be made, to achieve the target level of pollution at least economic cost? It is this issue that the use of market instruments in environmental policy seeks to address.

[1]See Johansson (1990) for a survey.

The Case for Market Instruments

In principle, any given pattern of pollution reduction could be achieved either by regulations, restricting polluting emissions to a given level, or by the use of pollution taxes or charges to provide an appropriate incentive to reduce emissions to the same level. However, there may be considerable differences between polluters in the costs of reducing pollution - some firms may, for example, be able to install pollution control devices more cheaply than others. Minimising the cost of pollution control may then require differences between firms in the extent to which they contribute to the overall reduction in pollution. Although regulations could be devised which achieved pollution reductions at least economic cost by specifying greater reductions in pollution where they can be achieved most cheaply, the amount of information required about individual polluters would be substantial.[1] And, where the costs of pollution control differ between polluters, applying a single uniform rule to all would clearly be inefficient.

A system of pollution taxes or charges, on the other hand, has the attraction that it is not necessary to collect detailed information about individual polluters to achieve any target level of overall pollution at minimum economic cost. A tax on polluting pesticide use, for example, will make it *unprofitable* for those who have a *low* return to pesticide-use to continue using pesticide. They will, therefore, cut back on their use, whereas those applications of pesticide which have a high return will still be profitable and can continue. The authorities do not need to know the behavioural responses of *individual* pesticide users to generate the economically efficient outcome; all they need do is raise the price of pesticide and normal market pressures will ensure that some applications of pesticide which were profitable will no longer be so.

The information needs of an environmental policy based on market instruments are thus substantially less than of an equivalent policy based on regulation. Looking at this another way, the limited amount of information available is likely to make it difficult for a regulatory policy to take adequate account of the varied circumstances of individuals or firms. Regulations requiring all polluters to restrict emissions to the same extent or to use certain specified processes and techniques will be a

---

[1]There may indeed be difficulties in obtaining the necessary information, since polluters would have an incentive to misrepresent their costs of reducing pollution.

more costly way of meeting given environmental objectives than market instruments with the same overall impact.

In addition, market instruments have three further attractions. Firstly, charges or taxes on pollution provide a continuing incentive to *innovate* in order to reduce polluting behaviour. Taxes give firms a financial inducement to invent ways to reduce emission of pollutants even *below* the target level, whereas regulation only requires the minimum necessary changes in order to comply with the rules.

Secondly, an important practical consideration is that a policy based on market instruments may be less vulnerable to *regulatory capture*. Because regulators need to understand their industry in great detail in order to set sensible pollution targets, there is a tendency for the regulators to become too closely identified with the interests of the industry itself, rather than operating for the general interest. Regulatory personnel are often recruited from, and often leave to work in, that industry. In contrast, taxes are relatively immune from the effects of special pleading by particular firms, because one tax rate applies throughout an industry. Of course, successful lobbying by an industry as a whole may result in little pollution control, but similar problems arise in the case of regulation.

Thirdly, some market mechanisms such as taxation, raise additional fiscal revenues as a by-product of their role in providing better incentive signals. These revenues may allow other taxes, which may have economic costs (e.g. distorting taxes on labour or capital supply) to be reduced, giving an overall reduction in the economic costs of raising revenue.

Problems with the Use of the Tax System

Much economic analysis of market instruments in environmental policy implicitly assumes that a system of measurement or metering can be used to charge polluters for each unit of pollution emitted. Improvements in the technologies available for monitoring concentrations and flows of particular substances in effluent discharges are undoubtedly increasing the scope for pollution charging of this sort, based on direct measurement. However, direct charging for measured emissions will remain impracticable in many instances, for example, where there are many emission sources, or no single point where emissions can be monitored. Thus, for example, the huge number of emission sources of carbon dioxide (motor vehicles, domestic heating appliances, industrial energy combustion, etc.) rule out the use of direct metered charging. Similarly, direct measurement of the contamination of water systems by excessive use of agricultural fertilisers is infeasible, since there is no single point source of the pollution at which metering equipment could be used. In addition to these technical limitations, direct pollution charging would also require the establishment of new administrative procedures with associated administrative costs.

The existing tax system offers a range of possibilities for fiscal changes to pursue environmental ends. *Direct* taxes can be used to give incentives to people or companies to perform specific acts. For example, investment by households in energy efficiency might be made deductible for income tax and companies might be given more rapid depreciation allowances if they invest in energy-saving technology. However, the use of direct taxes would normally require new administrative mechanisms for the enforcement and verification of individual entitlements to the incentives. Conditional incentives within the direct tax system have the further disadvantage compared with the use of indirect taxes that they allow taxpayers less flexibility in how they respond. Whereas direct tax changes encourage a specific one-off act, an indirect tax could give the same incentive to invest in energy-efficiency (albeit the investment would be to avoid paying tax rather than to gain advantage of a subsidy), whilst offering households and companies the alternative of reducing their tax bill in some way other than investment in energy-efficiency, for example, by reducing their overall demand for energy services.

Environmental restructuring of the indirect tax system provides an alternative route for the introduction of market-based incentives for pollution control, which can make use of existing administrative procedures and apparatus. Rather than direct charging for each unit of pollution emitted, using the existing tax system to pursue environmental objectives would involve indirect incentives, making use of the relationship between polluting activities and the various transactions which are currently taxed. Thus, instead of taxing the pollution output from car exhausts, additional tax may be levied on petrol purchases, on the assumption that all this petrol will be burned and the amount of pollution is proportional to the amount of petrol burned.

The fact that indirect taxes are levied on *transactions* raises a set of issues concerning the *linkage* between the tax burden and the pollution which the policy seeks to control. The linkage between the taxed transaction (e.g. industrial input purchases) and pollution may be imprecise and may change over time, for example, as production technologies change.

Taxes on production inputs may discourage the use of polluting materials in production, but provide no incentive to clean up effluents from the process. A tax on sulphurous coal in an attempt to curb acid rain may cut the amount of such coal used, but it would not encourage those who continue to use it to do so in a way which minimises the resultant effluent, for example by fitting 'scrubbers' (Flue Gas Desulphurisation units, or FGDs) to coal-fired power-stations. A tax on petrol may discourage car use, but it would not encourage the fitting of catalytic converters, which substantially reduce the emissions of certain types of pollutant from car exhausts. This suggests that the use of input taxation as an instrument of environmental policy will be most appropriate where relationship between input use and pollution is stable and where the basic technical choices affecting pollution do not involve the possibility of effluent cleaning. Environmental taxes may thus, for example, be more appropriate to deal with carbon dioxide emissions, where effluent cleaning is not an option, than with sulphur emissions, where important effluent cleaning technologies are available.

In addition to the question of technological linkage, there are further issues about how well the tax incentive is linked to the value of pollution abatement. Market-based instruments may be less effective than regulation as a means of pollution control where the *concentration* of pollution, either in particular localities or over certain time periods, is an important objective of policy. Some level of trade effluent discharges into a river system may, for example, be acceptable if it is a constant flow which is consequently diluted to a sufficient level as to be relatively harmless, but would be extremely toxic if discharged all at once. Similarly, four different companies discharging effluent into four different river systems may be deemed more or less acceptable than one firm discharging the same amount of effluent in one river. In these questions, the *assimilative* capacity of the environment must be considered.

The market instruments required for managing these types of pollution problems are much more complicated than for situations where the concentration of emissions is irrelevant. A straightforward tax per unit of effluent discharge (or more generally, pollutant emitted) would not adequately discourage geographic or temporal concentrations of pollution.

Where the tax is based on measured emission quantities, it may be possible to design more complex tax structures, reflecting the fact that pollution in particular localities or at certain times causes greater damage. But it is not usually possible to do this with indirect taxes, which are not based on any direct link to measured pollution. Where the timing or geographical distribution of pollution is of significance, we can no longer be certain that taxes would be *at least as* good as the regulatory alternative, in terms of achieving a given level of pollution abatement at least economic cost. Market instruments, on the other hand, would appear particularly relevant to a number of the global environmental problems currently causing concern. In the case of CFCs or greenhouse gases, the *concentration* of pollution emissions is unimportant - all that matters is the *total level* of emissions.[1]

Policy Options for Green Taxes

The implication of the above discussion is that there will often be a trade-off between the accuracy of the signals given by an environmental policy instrument and the administrative costs of operating the system. The choice will depend on the importance of accuracy and on the likely administrative costs of the various signals. Different types of environmental market mechanism are thus likely to be appropriate in different circumstances.

Emission taxes, levied directly on the amount of polluting effluent, are likely to be appropriate in some circumstances. Where effluent discharges to the water system or the atmosphere can be readily observed and measured, direct effluent charges can make a significant contribution to the control of pollution. Improvements in measurement technology are increasing the number of effluent problems where precise and continuous measurement is feasible and where taxes can be levied in direct proportion to each source's contribution to environmental damage. However, alternatives to direct emissions charging, making use of the existing tax system, will often be worth considering.

---

[1] Some greenhouse gases, notably carbon monoxide and hydrocarbons, have localised pollution effects where the concentration is important (for example, in smog formation). However, their impact upon global warming depends only on the total level of emissions rather than their concentration.

Changes to VAT and Excises

Changes to the structure of the existing indirect tax system (sales taxes and VAT) will in other cases provide a more cost-effective way of introducing market incentives for pollution control. It may also be possible, at relatively low cost, to create incentives for reduced pollution by the introduction of new indirect taxes on products which are associated with environmental damage (e.g. on batteries and pesticides).

One potential gain is that such measures can use, or extend, the existing administrative apparatus. Whilst there is for this reason potentially a saving in administrative cost, differentiating the existing tax structure to reflect environmental objectives may introduce greater complexity into the tax system, especially where the existing structure of indirect taxes is based on a simple rate structure, and this may increase the costs of administration and compliance.

However, the use of taxes on products or production inputs has the disadvantage that it provides only 'approximate' incentives to reduce pollution. The tax paid is not calculated according to the actual level of polluting emissions, but depends on an assumed relationship between the tax base and emissions. Sometimes the assumed linkage between tax base and pollution may be weak - for example, the incentive will be poorly targeted where input taxes are used and effluent cleaning represents an important option in pollution control.

The scope for the introduction of environmentally-motivated changes in the existing indirect tax system is likely to be quite limited; taxes on actual emissions would generally be better targeted. VAT will usually be an inappropriate instrument for environmental incentives, since businesses registered for VAT do not perceive VAT on inputs as a cost. Also, VAT is paid on the value of products, whilst the environmental damage is usually related to quantities; hence, the linkage may be poor. Finally, in many countries, considerations of administrative and compliance cost will limit the amount of complexity which can be accommodated within the indirect tax structure.

Most of the product taxes specifically introduced to achieve environmental objectives have taken the form of specific excise taxes, rather than VAT changes. They have included taxes on the following goods.

Fertilisers. Taxes are levied on agricultural fertilisers in a number of countries, including Austria, Finland, Norway and Sweden.

Batteries. In Norway and Sweden environmentally-harmful batteries are taxed more heavily.

Plastic carrier bags. In Italy a tax of 100 Lire (five times the manufacturing cost) has been levied on non-biodegradable plastic bags.

Drinks sold in disposable containers bear environmental taxes in Denmark, Finland and Sweden. In some countries, taxes levied on disposable drinks containers are refundable if the container is recycled.

Pesticides in small quantities (i.e. for retail sale) are taxed in Denmark at 20 per cent of the producer price.

Some gases used as aerosol propellants (e.g. CFCs) are subject to environmental taxes in Denmark, Finland and the USA.

Carbon Tax

In most countries, the existing pattern of taxation of energy sources varies widely between different forms of energy. Only rarely has any attempt been made to tax all sources of energy on a consistent basis and very large differences in tax rates for different types of energy can be encountered, reflecting balance of payments considerations domestic political pressures (low taxation of coal in some countries), or the desire to reduce the tax burden on fuels predominantly used as industrial inputs. Systematic taxation of fuels according to their environmental characteristics is a comparatively recent idea, but the subject of considerable recent discussion.[1]

The principal option which a number of countries have considered is the carbon tax. This is a tax on the carbon content of different energy sources, which is intended to reflect the contribution that the use of energy makes to the emission of carbon dioxide, a major 'greenhouse gas' contributing to the risk of global warming. Using an excise duty to provide an incentive to reduce carbon dioxide emissions has some advantages over emissions taxation - taxing measured emissions of carbon dioxide would be impractical because there are many sources. Also, the geographical location of greenhouse gas emissions is irrelevant - what matters is simply the total stock of greenhouse gases in the atmosphere, so the tax rate does not need to vary between taxpayers in different localities. The carbon tax also scores well on technological linkage: cost-effective effluent-cleaning technologies do not appear to be in prospect.

[1]See Barrett (1991) and Pearson and Smith (1991).

A carbon tax would need to be levied at high rates to make much impact on carbon dioxide emissions. Large revenues would be obtained and the distributional incidence of the additional tax payments could be a heavy burden on poorer households in some countries, where fuel has the characteristics of a 'necessity'. As with other environmental taxes, its introduction would be more feasible as part of a package of measures.

Road Transport Taxation

There are a range of important externalities associated with road transport. These include environmental externalities - noise, atmospheric pollution and the effect of new road-building on the natural landscape. In addition, road use involves accident and congestion externalities and the wear and tear that road use causes to the (usually publicly-owned) fabric of the road system. As the volume of road traffic grows, these external costs are becoming of greater concern to policy-makers and the search for effective measures that can improve the situation is likely to include careful consideration of the potential of tax measures.

Road transport is already the subject of a number of different taxes in most countries. There is accordingly considerable scope for environmental objectives to be reflected through the restructuring of existing taxes rather than the introduction of wholly new ones.

Existing taxes include the following:

(1) *Sales taxes on new motor vehicles*, which are in many cases higher than on other goods, or imposed in addition to the general sales tax. Thus, for example, in the UK motor cars are subject both to VAT at the standard rate and also to a special car tax at 10 per cent on five-sixths of the list price of a new car.[1]

(2) *Recurrent annual charges* for the registration or use of motor vehicles. These may be an annual lump sum tax (e.g. the British vehicle excise duty (VED) of £100 per annum), or may be related to certain characteristics of the motor vehicle, such as engine capacity. In most countries, annual charges for the use of commercial vehicles differ from those for private motor cars; in the UK, VED on

---

[1]Since this paragraph was written, the special car tax has been abolished as a measure to stimulate the car industry - Ed.

commercial freight vehicles is higher than that for cars and related to vehicle weight. In some countries the annual registration charge is a local tax, either in the sense that the revenues accrue to local governments, or that the tax level is determined at a local level.

(3) *Motor fuel taxes.* Motor fuel is usually taxed at a higher rate than other goods and may be subject to additional, product- specific taxes or duties. In many cases, these additional taxes are quantity-related (i.e. specific duties), rather than *ad valorem* taxes related to price. Different rates of tax may be applied to different motor fuels. Diesel fuel is frequently taxed at a different rate to petrol (usually a lower rate, reflecting the greater use of diesel fuel by commercial vehicles) and a number of countries have already introduced a tax differential in favour of lead-free petrol.

Possibilities exist for the modification of each of these taxes for environmental purposes.

(1) Petrol taxes could be increased across the board, to reflect concerns about global warming or vehicle congestion - possibly as an alternative to the current annual lump sum taxes on motor vehicles, which may be less effective at discouraging vehicle use. This policy has been referred to in the Netherlands as the 'variabilisation' of motoring costs.

(2) The tax on new cars and the annual charges for registration could be differentiated according to the 'environmental' attributes of different vehicles. A tax incentive could be introduced for 'clean' cars (e.g. cars meeting certain emissions standards, or fitted with catalytic converters) and the taxes could be differentiated by engine size or other factors affecting fuel use.

(3) Fuels could be taxed according to their environmental characteristics. Where lead free petrol is taxed at the same rate as leaded petrol, a discount could be introduced. The differential between diesel fuel and petrol could be set at a level reflecting the environmental characteristics of the two fuels.

Implementation Strategy

The use of tax-based environmental policies creates a need for close co-ordination between different arms of government - between Ministries of Finance and of Environment. Tax-based environmental policies have the potential to improve both the fiscal system and the environment, but they are unlikely to be fully effective without co-ordination. The environmental gains may be low if revenue considerations are allowed to dictate the choice of tax rates. Also, if environmental taxes are introduced without considering their implications for the overall balance of the fiscal system, they may encounter political opposition that could be avoided with better co-ordination and other linked fiscal measures.

Lack of co-ordination of tax and environmental policies in the past may have created problems which need correcting. A review of the potential for tax-based environmental policies should consider whether non-environmental provisions of the existing tax system have had negative effects on the environment. The tax treatment of agriculture, forestry, land use and road transport may all contain elements with undesirable environmental consequences and a joint assessment of these issues by the relevant ministries would be a good starting point for the consideration of future tax-based environmental policies.

Those countries that have gone furthest in implementing tax-based environmental policies have generally done so in the context of a strategy or programme comprising a range of measures. Explicitly linking the introduction of environmental taxes to a package of expenditure and tax reduction measures, for example, to stimulate research and development of pollution control technologies or to offset undesired distributional effects, will help to offset political resistance, the lobbying of particular groups affected by each measure, or public concerns that the revenue may be used to increase the overall burden of taxation.

In practice, there has been a widespread tendency for countries to earmark the revenues from environmental taxes to particular environmental expenditures. This may reflect the political and presentational realities that decision-makers face. Also, in certain circumstances, it may be an appropriate way of organising the collective provision of environmental measures, for example, effluent treatment facilities for a particular sector or locality. However, the dangers of earmarking should be recognised. In general, earmarking the revenues from taxes designed to provide pollution abatement incentives to expenditures on environmental purposes is in the long run likely to introduce undesirable rigidity into public budgetary decision-making: the need for revenue, rather than environmental costs, may dictate the choice of tax rates, whilst environmental spending may be determined simply by the availability of earmarked revenue.

There are important international dimensions to environmental tax policy-making. Many of the major pollution problems that taxes would address cross national boundaries (global warming, acid rain, marine pollution), whilst environmental policy measures taken by individual countries can affect trade and competitiveness. Some countries have seen the introduction of environmental taxes as a demonstration of their commitment to the process of international negotiation on these problems. However, where the international linkages are significant, it is unlikely that countries will wish to introduce environmental taxes at the efficient level until international agreement has been reached on the objectives of policy.

Conclusions

This chapter has set out some of the areas where restructuring of the existing tax system could play a part in environmental policy and some of the limitations of the tax approach. The main limitation on the use of the indirect tax system, rather than direct pollution charges based on the metering of emissions, concerns the linkage between the transactions to which the tax is applied and the pollution which policy seeks to control. Where the linkage is imprecise, a policy based on taxes may not always encourage pollution reductions in the most efficient form. In particular, where the technological options for pollution control include effluent cleaning technologies (as in the case of the sulphur emissions that contribute to acid rain), input taxes will not provide any encouragement to deal with pollution by effluent cleaning.

As with all market-based instruments, environmental taxes are most straightforward where the location or concentration of pollution is not a concern of policy. This suggests that they may be of particular value in dealing with non-localised environmental problems, including the global problems associated with greenhouse gases. Moreover, the close linkage between the carbon content of individual fuels and the carbon dioxide emissions which result from industrial and household fuel use (and the absence of any significant technology for 'cleaning' carbon dioxide emissions) is a further reason why carbon taxes may be one of the more appropriate uses of fiscal instruments.

Such taxes would involve substantial additional tax payments by both industries and households. However, the additional revenue would then be available to ameliorate some of the adverse effects - on industrial profitability and international competitiveness (through reductions in other company taxes), on prices (through reductions in other indirect taxes), or on the standards of living of particular income groups (through offsetting changes in income tax and social security).

Although environmental taxes, like other market-based instruments, offer the potential for reducing pollution at lower cost than regulatory policies with equivalent effect, the overall package of measures introduced needs to be assessed as a whole. One reason for this is the potential for using the revenues to compensate for certain adverse or undesired effects. Policy-making will thus need to be carefully co-ordinated between the government departments and agencies responsible for environmental policy and for fiscal policy.

References and Further Reading

Barrett, S., 'Economic Instruments for Climate Change Policy' in *Responding to Climate Change: Selected Economic Issues*, OECD, Paris, 1991.

Beckerman, W., *Pricing for Pollution*, Hobart Paper No. 66, Institute of Economic Affairs, London, 1974.

Johansson, P. O, 'Valuing Environmental Damage', *Oxford Review of Economic Policy,* Vol. 6, No. 1, 1990.

Pearce, D., 'The Role of Carbon Taxes in Adjusting to Global Warming', *The Economic Journal*, Vol. 101, No. 407, pp.938-48, 1991.

Pearson, M. and S. Smith, *The European Carbon Tax: An Assessment of the European Commission's Proposals*, Institute for Fiscal Studies, London, 1991.

Pigou, A. C., *The Economics of Welfare*, Macmillan, London, 1920.

Smith, S., 'Taxation and the Environment: A Survey', *Fiscal Studies,* Vol. 13, No. 4, November, 1992.

CHAPTER 11

POLICY PERSPECTIVES ON INTERNATIONAL TAXATION

Donald J.S. Brean*

Introduction

Until recently international tax issues were primarily the concern of the relatively small, arcane group of lawyers and accountants who advise multinational corporations on how to minimize their global tax liability - so-called international tax planning. Tax policy, unlike practice, did not have a mission so well-defined. Research on international aspects of tax policy was scarce, and what there was was unfocused and seriously lacking in either economic or empirical content.

The situation is changing dramatically due to the rapid economic integration of nations. Concern for competitiveness and heightened awareness of the potential for one nation's taxation to affect other nations' economic welfare underlies the new awareness of international aspects of taxation. In recent years a corpus of theory has been brought to bear on substantive international tax policy issues while the depth and breadth of empirical analysis has grown steadily.

Like domestic tax policy, the international dimension focuses on *allocation* (or 'efficiency'), *revenue* and *distribution*, and *administration*. In each respect, international issues are more complex than domestic issues. The international interaction of national tax systems in the face of economic openness and the mobility of factors together with practical limitations on tax administration leave nations with fewer realistic objectives and more formidable constraints on tax policy.

*Professor of Finance and Economics, Faculty of Management, University of Toronto.

This chapter presents an overview of recent developments in international aspects of taxation. The purpose is to summarize significant economic and legal issues and to illustrate policy through selected examples.

A recurring theme of the chapter concerns the process of policy - how international tax policy is designed and implemented. Two alternative approaches are explored. The first is the unilateral/bilateral approach characterized by the international extension of national tax laws in conjunction with a network of tax treaties. The second approach, illustrated by recent developments in the European Community, is multilateral. This latter approach seeks consensus among nations and encourages convergence.

Trade, Foreign Investment and Taxation

Tax takes on an international dimension in the presence of trade and cross-border movement of factors, especially capital. Tax enters the policy calculus as nations strive to expand and capture national gains from trade and foreign investment. At the same time, nations are reluctant to allow international considerations to compromise internal fiscal objectives.

The policy instruments that nations use to manage their international economic affairs have changed in the modern era. Tariffs are virtually a thing of the past. Explicit barriers to international investment are crumbling. As a result, trade and foreign investment are now relatively more exposed to taxes that touch international commerce. Questions of how taxation affects international trade and cross-border investment now have a more prominent role in international tax affairs. These are the so-called 'allocative' issues.

The development of policy with respect to allocative issues divides into *indirect* and *direct* taxation. This division conveniently corresponds to international trade and cross-border investment, respectively - the structure adopted in the following sections.

Indirect Taxation – Fiscal Barriers of a Physical Form

In a world of free trade, the touchstone of tax policy - dubbed the 'destination principle' - calls for goods and services to enter world markets free of tax. Export taxes are anathema. Nations usually levy indirect taxes on imports, however, consistent with taxation of domestic consumption and also to offset the potential advantage of the tax-free status of goods on world markets. Imports typically face indirect taxes at rates that would apply if such goods or services were produced in the importing nation.

Many problems that stem from the effect of indirect taxes on trade have been successfully addressed in recent years either by nations acting individually or collectively. In an example of unilateral initiative, Canada in 1991 replaced its archaic and highly distortionary manufacturers sales tax with a comprehensive goods and services tax. This change was motivated by, among other things, the fact that the manufacturers sales tax penalized exports and favoured imports. Other nations, including Indonesia, Israel, Mexico, New Zealand, the Philippines, South Africa, and Thailand also independently revamped and rationalized their indirect tax systems in recent years consistent with more efficient international trade.

There are also counter-examples. The United States, Japan and Australia encountered domestic resistance to sales (or similar) tax reform. Reasons vary from the difficulty of achieving agreement within a federal system (especially in the United States), concern about the regressiveness of a sales or value added tax (Australia) and fear that a flush of revenue would lead to undue government expansion (Japan). In these countries, adverse trade effects of the *status quo* in tax do not weigh heavily against internal political and administrative considerations.

Europe illustrates collective action on indirect taxes with a view to efficiency. A proper course was set in 1957 with the signing of the EEC Treaty in Rome. That treaty provided a clear juridical basis for indirect tax harmonization in the interests of the common market. Turnover taxes in particular were targeted (Article 99). The initiative to replace these cascading levies lead eventually to the present common system of value added taxes including a harmonized basis of assessment.

The intent of Article 99 is recast in The Single European Act of 1986 - the foundation of '1992' - which has the explicit aim of ensuring that taxation and its attendant red tape are not a residual reason for retaining checks at the frontiers. This goal is at hand. From 1957 to 1992, Europe has progressed from policy that minimizes collective damage to policy that maximizes collective gain - and the key is Community commitment to value-added taxation.

Collective objectives in tax policy are viable only if the required adjustments at the nation-level are consistent with nations' domestic objectives. VAT meets the test. It is a buoyant revenue source that is closely linked to changes in domestic consumption. It is a preferred alternative to sales tax and it may also be a substitute for income taxation. For its shortcomings, VAT is most commonly criticized on equity grounds, for being at most proportional and at worst regressive.

The European Community's approach to tax harmonization requires *unanimity* in changes that affect all EC members. Some scope remains for diversity, especially on the question of rates. Currently the European Community has agreed to minimum rates while espousing the view that competitive pressures tend to constrain impetus for higher rates. The important point for the international dimension is that, in the European model of economic integration, the potentially disintegrative effects of indirect taxation are addressed by Community-wide endorsement of arrangements that member states find sound (and acceptable) in their own right but which are also consistent with the EC internal market.

Value-added taxation was once associated only with Europe. It is now a common choice in tax reforms around the world. Although most nations that have adopted VAT may not have done so primarily for external considerations - but, rather, for reasons of internal efficiency, revenue, and administration - the widespread adoption of VAT nevertheless has resulted in significant reductions in tax distortions of international trade[1].

Moreover, the continuing development of this system of taxation is likely to deal more with international aspects. Discussions will centre on coordination in common markets and federal countries, on the most appropriate rate structure, and the means to include international trade in services - such as banking and insurance - in the base. When several countries address policy in concert, as in the European Community, gains in both efficiency and administration are enhanced for individual nations and *a fortiori* for the group as a whole.

This conclusion requires a caveat. The distribution of revenue and welfare effects of VAT harmonization depend critically on assumptions concerning international differences - or similarities - in economic behaviour. National savings and investment propensities, the composition of spending, import and export elasticities, and factor substitutability in production ultimately influence the international distribution of gains in a transition to a more efficient world economy

---

[1]For details of the widespread adoption of VAT and on the means for ensuring trade neutrality under a destination or origin based VAT, see above, Cnossen, Chapter 4.

(Frenkel *et al*, 1991). Some countries adjust more readily, more extensively, and more productively than others. And, of course, when some win more than others, conflict can ensue.

Direct Taxation

The greatest challenge in international taxation concerns taxation of income earned on mobile capital. The problem is to mitigate the distortive effects of tax on cross-border investment without compromising the integrity of the domestic tax system, without undue loss of revenue, or without imposing unreasonable demands on tax administration.

Every nation harbours its own objectives concerning cross-border investment. Each nation's preferred tax policy would have implications for efficiency, revenue, and administration. However, unconstrained national objectives seldom arise in polite discussion of international tax policy. In the case of investment, for example, if truth be told an individual nation would not prefer arrangements to achieve an internationally efficient allocation of capital - wherein pre-tax marginal returns to capital are equal across countries. Rather, each nation would prefer tax to distort investment in its favour. Likewise, since each nation would prefer to have more tax revenue than less, each would choose to tax on both source and residence basis as opportunities dictate.

A nation that is oblivious to the rest of the world would provide no relief of foreign taxes paid by residents on their foreign-source earnings, thus raising the cost of capital exports. Such countries would have no compunction to treat earnings of imported capital in a preferential or a discriminatory manner, depending on national needs for investment or tax revenue.

Nations are not so cavalier. On international tax matters, especially with respect to capital, each nation's policy invariably involves careful consideration of policies of other nations and regard for the inevitable clash of national systems. Each nation's approach to taxation of internationally mobile capital reflects a view of the merits of economic efficiency - including how much merit an individual nation can extract from a more efficient world - together with a pragmatic regard for other nations' powers to tax.

Risk of retaliation is cause for circumspection if not cooperation. 'Principles' of international taxation, such as they are, generally reflect discrete attitudes of individual nations in a competitive, integrated world. These principles are not forged in heaven, but perhaps in Paris or Brussels.

Above all, nations know the first axiom of tax incidence: the greatest burden of tax is born by the least mobile factors. Mobile factors, like capital, migrate from taxation. Immobile factors, like labour and land, are left to bear the burden.

At a practical level, most nations are intent on maintaining a tax system wherein international investment decisions, involving either in-bound or out-bound capital, are not driven by tax considerations. This can be achieved - again, in principle - if, from the perspective of each individual nation, its investors incur the same rate of tax on domestic and foreign investments. Under these circumstances capital will flow to the source of highest pre-tax return and in this sense it will be allocated efficiently throughout the world.

The problem of so-called international double taxation, and the resulting distortion of international investment, arises when *both* countries - the (source) country in which the investment income is earned and the residence country of the investor - levy tax on the same investment income. One investment, two taxes.

The interaction of two tax systems can be made consistent with a more efficient allocation of capital in alternative ways. A simple and obvious resolution of 'double taxation' is for countries *not* to tax income earned on foreign investments. This option generally falls to the residence country. Twelve OECD member nations, including Canada, France, and the Netherlands, have adopted this 'territorial' or exemption approach in the case of foreign-source dividends.

Alternatively, the residence country may include foreign-source income in its residents' tax base and then allow credit for taxes paid to foreign governments. Eleven OECD nations, including the United States, the United Kingdom, and Japan, tax the worldwide income of their residents in this fashion and grant 'foreign tax credit'.

Table 11.1 summarizes the tax treatment of foreign source income by OECD member nations in their respective roles as residence nations.

The efficient international allocation of capital is an illusive objective. Economists advocate it on grounds similar to the argument for free trade - *viz*, the world is wealthier as a result. Unfortunately many practical considerations get in the way.

To explore such problems, perhaps the first thing to note is that international capital takes various forms. Taxation makes a fundamental distinction between 'portfolio' and 'foreign direct' investment. The following discussion recognizes this split.

Portfolio Investment

Portfolio investment refers to foreign bond issues and non-controlling equity. Portfolio investment income is thus in the form of interest and dividends earned abroad. The bulk of portfolio income is earned by financial institutions such as banks, trust and insurance companies, and pension funds.

International portfolio investment does not require a foreign corporate presence. Financial institutions may trade in foreign securities and thus manage an international 'portfolio'. On the other hand financial institutions may operate through foreign branches (as opposed to subsidiaries). Foreign branch income is ordinarily consolidated with residence income and taxed on a current basis.

Most countries include property income, rents, and capital gains on securities in foreign source portfolio income. Intra-firm non-arm's-length payments of interest and dividends arising from active business income - for example, within non-financial multinational enterprise - is generally *not* considered to be portfolio income.

The *net* volume of international capital flows represents the financial counterflow of external (trade) imbalances among nations. Nations that consume more than they earn (or invest more than they save) must import capital from nations that earn more than they consume (or save more than they invest).

International portfolio investment is the most rapidly growing dimension of the economic integration of nations. While trade imbalances drive net portfolio investment, the ever-increasing gross volume of cross-border flows is driven by investors' quest for diversification and speculators' pursuit of arbitrage profit. The gross volume of cross-border lending increased from $324 billion in 1981 to $7.5 trillion in 1991. To put these figures in perspective, cross-border lending in a decade increased from a volume equal to 4% of OECD GNP to 44%. Daily turnover in foreign exchange is $900 billion. Between 1980 and 1990 the volume of worldwide cross-border transactions in equities alone grew at a compound rate of 28% per year, from $120 billion to $1.4 trillion per year. The technical sophistication of international bond markets, including a highly efficient global communications network, facilitates this spectacular growth.

Table 11.1 Treatment of Foreign Source Income from Treaty Countries[1]

Resident country	Dividend income	Interest income
Australia	exemption[2]	worldwide credit
Austria	exemption	credit by source
Belgium	exemption of 90% of gr. div.	worldwide credit[3]
Canada	exemption	credit by source
Denmark	exemption[4]	credit by source[5]
Finland	exemption	credit by source[6]
France	exemption of 95% of gr. div.	credit by source
Germany	exemption	credit by source
Greece	credit by source	credit by source
Iceland	worldwide credit	worldwide credit
Ireland	credit by source	credit by source
Italy	credit by source	credit by source
Japan	worldwide credit	worldwide credit
Luxembourg	exemption	credit by source
Netherlands	exemption	credit by source
New Zealand	credit by source	credit by source
Norway	credit by source	credit by source
Portugal	credit by source	credit by source
Spain	credit by source[7]	credit by source[8]
Sweden	exemption	credit by source
Switzerland	exemption[9]	credit by source
Turkey	credit by source	credit by source
United Kingdom	credit by source	credit by source
United States	worldwide credit[10]	worldwide credit

[1]Based on a 100 percent ownership of subsidiary.
[2]Only for treaty countries designated having corporate tax systems as Australia.
[3]Worldwide credit based on deemed withholding tax of 15%.
[4]Dividend from a foreign subsidiary (minimum 25 per cent holding) in a country with a corporate tax similar to Denmark's; also applies to non-treaty countries.
[5]Denmark exempts interest payments from Portugal and Spain.
[6]Finland exempts interest payments from Spain.
[7]Spain exempts dividends from Switzerland.
[8]Spain exempts interest payments from Portugal.
[9]Strictly, Switzerland does not have an exemption system. However, total dividends received from abroad are divided by total income, and this ratio is then used to reduce the Federal income tax. The net effect is exemption. .
[10] Credit separately calculated (worldwide basis) for some categories of income.

International investors compare (and equate) international net-of-tax returns. When portfolio income is taxed in one country and not taxed in another, the pre-tax yield on the taxed investment must exceed the yield on untaxed investment in order for after-tax returns to be equal. A change in taxation, perhaps by elimination of an exemption or by a change in the tax rate, disturbs equilibrium pre-tax yields which in turn prompts an international reallocation of capital to restore equilibrium based on (equal) after-tax yields. Although foreign tax relief could mitigate the effects, taxes at source are often 'final' taxes for international financiers.

These financial and technical points have direct implications for a nation's scope to tax income from international portfolio investment. The high sensitivity of capital movements to tax means that interest income on mobile capital is generally an elusive and, indeed, an ill-advised base for taxation.

Nations are nevertheless inclined to exercise their sovereign right to make mistakes in international tax matters. An especially perilous policy involves withholding tax on interest income. A quick review of experiences in a cross-section of countries illustrates the pitfalls.

Withholding Taxes

Australia had a frenzied turnaround in withholding tax policy in a remarkably short period of time. The Treasurer announced the elimination of exemptions to a tax on bond interest in July 1986. Following an outcry from borrowers, he abruptly reversed his position in August. Perhaps the Treasurer feared a wrenching of financial markets. Regardless, he realized that he had underestimated the political price of policy that raises tax on mobile capital.

In 1990 Belgium reduced the rate of a withholding tax (the *precompte mobilier*) - from 25 per cent to 10 per cent - levied on interest earned by Belgians on their domestic savings. Foreigners are exempt, and foreign-source interest earned by Belgians is also exempt. Following the rate reduction, Belgian banks were less interested in maintaining complex international arrangements - involving a circular flow of Belgian savings to Luxembourg or Holland and back to Belgium - that they had devised for Belgians to circumvent the tax.

In 1987, Germany announced a 10 per cent withholding tax on interest paid on German bonds issued in Germany. Foreign bonds issued in Germany and German bonds issued abroad were exempt. Following the change in policy, German interest rates rose sharply and domestic bond issues fell as German corporations turned to foreign sources of bond finance. In less than two years, the new withholding tax was repealed and German yields and financial patterns promptly returned to their previous state.

In 1975 Canada removed a withholding tax on interest paid to foreigners. As a result, Canadian corporate costs of borrowing fell significantly and new Canadian bond issues sold to foreigners rose sharply.

The United States in 1984 changed withholding tax policy that affected a huge volume of international finance. As part of the Deficit Reduction Act, the US repealed a 30 per cent tax on interest paid to foreigners. Consistent with the fact that international finance flows freely around taxes, however, this change had little impact on US tax revenue or the cost of borrowed funds. The tax had been almost entirely avoided by means of a well-known route to the Euromarkets through the Netherlands Antilles which had uniquely favourable tax relations with the United States. The repeal of the withholding tax had the relatively inconsequential result of shifting the registration of a huge volume of US bond issues from Aruba to Wall Street.

These illustrations of policy changes and their consequences lead to certain conclusions concerning the economic, financial, and fiscal effects of withholding taxes on income earned on internationally mobile capital.

(1) Withholding taxes, if effectively applied, increase the cost of borrowing via taxed securities.[1]

(2) Withholding taxes lead to significant distortions in the domestic/foreign composition of portfolio capital.

(3) International financial accommodation of withholding taxes mitigates their real effects and also reduces the revenue such taxes might otherwise generate.

(4) International financial adjustments are rapid.

[1]This is so in the case of small open economies that have no independent influence on world interest rates. On the other hand, a large country whose demand for and supply of capital are determining forces in world financial markets - perhaps, for example, the United States - could conceivably use withholding taxes in a strategic fashion to lower its cost of foreign capital. See Goulder (1990).

Policy developments around the world appear to reflect increasing regard for the fact that withholding taxes on interest income involve uncertain revenue and certain inefficiency. Adverse effects are greater at high rates of withholding tax and especially when the rate in one country substantially exceeds rates elsewhere. Constructive developments in policy include the pan-European initiative to harmonize all withholding taxes in the EC (at rates close to previous minimum rates), and unilateral corrections as we have seen in the cases outlined above.

Direct Investment

Direct investment is synonymous with multinational enterprise. Multinational enterprise is the vehicle of technology transfer and it is a driving force in the internationalization of production. Moreover, a substantial amount of international trade - more than half of all trade - takes place within multinational enterprise. The industrial organization of the world has been re-structured by multinational enterprise and, in consequence, traditional concepts of distinct nationality are muted. What, for example, is the nationality of IBM Japan? Who has the right to tax IBM Japan?

Taxation of foreign direct investment is closely linked to domestic corporate taxation. Indeed, most countries generally extend 'national treatment' to foreign investors, which essentially means that foreign-owned firms are treated like domestic firms for tax purposes. This also means, of course, that source countries have primary taxing power over multinational enterprise. Residence countries, with secondary taxing power, face the formidable challenge of taxing residents' income earned abroad - if they choose to tax on a worldwide basis. As mentioned, the matter of foreign tax relief also rests with the residence country.

Company taxation in general, even without explicit regard for international complexities, is problematic in several respects, including the following.[1]

---

[1] For each of the following points, the first reference to the literature is pertinent to the general or domestic point of view. The second reference takes an international perspective. Investment: Feldstein (1987) and OECD (1991); Finance: Auerbach (1983) and Alworth (1988); Organisational Form: Gravelle and Kotlikoff (1989) and inter alia OECD/BIAC (1990), Integration: McLure (1979) and Bird (1987); Inflation: Jenkins (1985) and Sinn (1990).

(1) *Investment.* Corporate taxation affects the level and composition of capital spending by driving a wedge between investors' after-tax rate of return and the economic (or pre-tax) rate of return on capital. Investment is further distorted by differential tax effects on different categories of investment. Tax distortions translate directly into efficiency losses and reduced output.

(2) *Finance.* Taxation affects corporate financial decisions by favouring debt over equity. Taxation also affects the timing and pattern of corporate retentions and dividends. Such influences on corporate finance distort the allocation of risk between the government and the private sector and within the latter.

(3) *Organisational form.* Corporate taxation (especially *vis-a-vis* tax on unincorporated business) influences the legal and organizational form of business, and thus affects merger activity, corporate concentration, *et cetera.*

(4) *Integration.* Tax is ultimately born by persons and not corporations. The overlap of corporate and personal taxes has implications for effective tax rates and, especially, for taxpayer equity. The lack of proper integration of corporate and personal taxation creates an additional layer of complexity (of the economic sort) and potentially introduces further distortion of savings and investment decisions.

(5) *Inflation.* Inflation generally erodes tax revenue and adds variance to effective tax rates in an unindexed corporate tax system. Depreciation on the basis of historical cost raises the effective corporate tax rate while the deductibility of nominal (inflation inclusive) interest on debt reduces it.

Every problem involving corporate or capital taxation is heightened in the international context - where both income and capital move readily across borders, where the weight of taxation is determined by complex interaction of two or more tax systems, where countries are enticed to tax competition, and where costs of tax administration inevitably increase with distance.

Moreover, these problems pose a clear challenge to fiscal sovereignty. On the one hand nations cannot effectively cast their tax nets beyond their borders. On the other hand economic openness compromises domestic tax objectives. The forces of international economic integration may mean, for example, that the corporate tax has been surpassed by events. The demise of the corporate tax appears to run parallel to the demise of the residence principle (Gordon 1992).

A uniquely international tax jargon illustrates the tension between tax authorities and the illusive, amorphous global income that is their target. Terms such as income shifting, transfer pricing, tax havens, treaty shopping, thin capitalization, and tax arbitrage refer to financial or accounting maneuvers that affect the international allocation of the tax base quite independently of where production in fact takes place.

That is not to say, however, that multinational tax minimizing strategy does not involve production-location decisions. In certain types of business, taxation may be a crucial factor in deciding where to produce. The American pharmaceutical industry, for example, conducts most of its expensive research and development in the United States where the tax write-off is more valuable. Income-generating production is often shifted to low-tax sites, such as Puerto Rico.[1]

Multinational corporations are well-suited to exploit international differences, even very small differences, in tax rules, rates, and regulations. Fiscal diversity among nations is at odds with market forces, mobile factors and global competition. This raises the basic question of whether solutions to international tax problems are better approached through coordination - which inevitably involves complex legislation and formidable administrative challenges - or through resignation to the market forces that underlie economic integration in the first place, forces that are likely to render some tax bases inappropriate or inaccessible.

Two Paradigms of Policy

Two paradigms of policy have emerged in connection with taxation of multinational enterprise. Neither model is entirely new, but each is infused with new vigour. The first approach, led by the United States, entrenches the residence basis with worldwide taxation, foreign tax credits and so on. The second approach is distinctly European. It respects fiscal sovereignty but - in cooperative fashion - it focusses on a process to identify and deal with the sources of fiscal disharmony by means of directives from the centre.

---

[1]The US courts take a dim view of such arrangements. The legal precedent, known as the 'Eli Lilly' ruling, requires that gross margins from domestic operations be at least as great as the gross margin from foreign operations.

The American way is a way that perhaps only America can pursue. The United States has the strongest motive to tax resident corporations' foreign-source income, and is the only country likely to have the administrative means to do so. Americans control the largest stock of foreign direct investment abroad and, naturally, the merits of the residence-basis of taxation are more obvious from that vantage point. Effective taxation of foreign-source corporate income requires technically sophisticated tax administration capable of tracing income to its source. This must be coupled with a legal system capable of creating and enforcing laws to prevent the inherent arbitrariness of international accounting from prevailing against the residence country. Despite firm US resolve, there is some question of whether its tax and legal systems, let alone those of any other nation, are up to the task, as we shall see presently.

The European way, in particular the intra-European way, is multilateral and cooperative. It has guidance from the centre. The key to the European approach is the recently enshrined 'principle of subsidiarity'. This principle, expressed in Article 3b of The Treaty on European Union, states:

> 'The Community shall take action, in accordance with the principle of subsidiarity, only if and insofar as the objectives of the proposed action cannot be sufficiently achieved by the member states and can therefore, by reason of scale or effects of the proposed action, be better achieved by the Community.'

The principle of subsidiarity can be invoked in all manner of policy within Europe. On matters of direct taxation, subsidiarity implies harmonization if necessary, but not necessarily harmonization.

Commissioner Scrivener:

> 'The Commission has chosen not to interfere in every field of economic life, but to intervene only when it is necessary to attain the specific objectives agreed by the member states...... For the rest, market forces play.'[1]

---

[1]Christiane Scrivener (1990), p.207.

The unilateral approach and the European multilateral approach represent a contrast in policy process in the international dimension of taxation. The form, the stability, and the economic consequences of each approach, including the extent to which policy is congruent with world economic developments - e.g. the increasing mobility of capital - are likely to differ under the alternative regimes.

There is also a question of whether taxation is a tie that binds. Europe is more fiscally centralized today than it was in the past. The Community has moved in this direction with caution. Europe intends to determine its degree of fiscal centralization by design. America and the rest of the world are decentralized by default.

The next section outlines the current difficulties with the unabashed residence approach. This is followed by a brief summary of directives guiding the European approach. It appears that the unilateral/bilateral system is not achieving all that national tax authorities would want. On the other hand, in Europe where the framework for coordinated policy is still under construction, little is known of how policy will work.

Taxation of Residents' Worldwide Income

A country that includes foreign-source income of (resident) corporations in its tax base does so for three distinct reasons: efficiency, equity, and protection of the domestic tax base. With respect to efficiency, residence countries that favour capital-export neutrality (wherein resident investors face similar tax on domestic and foreign investments) must reconcile this objective with their secondary power-to-tax by including foreign-source income in their tax base and granting credit for foreign taxes. The second policy reason, equity, recognizes that foreign-source income ought to be included in a comprehensive definition of residents' income. The third reason, protection of the domestic tax base, reflects practical regard for the risk of income being diverted to low tax countries.

Taxation of residents' worldwide income, where 'residents' for the most part are resident-based multinational enterprises, falls short of achieving each of these policy objectives. Based on the American experience, residence countries are generally unable to contain violations of capital export neutrality, and they collect very little revenue from off-shore earnings of resident multinationals. The United States and other countries also have had limited success in shoring up the domestic corporate tax system - controlling the erosion of the domestic tax base by international tax arbitrage.

Problems faced by residence nations are due partly to policy design and partly to administration. The difficulties stem from the deferral provision, the upper limit on the foreign tax credit, and transfer pricing. Deferral means that foreign-source income is usually taxed only upon repatriation; *i.e.* it is not taxed on an accrual basis. Limitation means that the foreign tax credit is generally not extended beyond the tax liability that would otherwise apply in the residence country. Finally, *via* transfer pricing, foreign investors have significant scope to shift income from one country to another for the purpose of avoiding (or evading) residence tax.

Residence-based taxation of multinational enterprise, together with deferral, foreign tax credit and limitation, is linked to various economic and fiscal consequences with little counterpart in domestic corporate taxation. These tax effects have implicationsfor capital-export neutrality as well as for the division of tax revenue between the source and residence countries. Some of the key points include the following.

(1) *Capital–export Neutrality I.* Residence taxation generally does not sustain capital-export neutrality. Multinational corporate investors do not face the same effective rate of tax on domestic and foreign investments. There are two main reasons. First, if the source tax rate is less than the residence tax rate, the multinational corporation has an incentive to defer repatriation, perhaps via re-investment, so as to avoid the residence tax. In so doing, the (lower) source tax becomes the relevant tax rate in (re)investment decisions. Second, if the source tax rate is above the residence tax rate, the limitation on the foreign tax credit results in less-than-full relief of the foreign tax and thus the effective tax rate on foreign investment exceeds the rate on domestic investment.

(2) *Capital–export Neutrality II.* When foreign direct investment is financed out of retained earnings - as in fact is the case for the bulk of such investment - the residence tax on foreign source income is not a determining factor in the investment decision. Residence tax affects only repatriated earnings, not the earnings themselves. (Hartman 1984, 1985).

(3) *Transfer Pricing.* Multinational corporations use transfer pricing and financial arrangements to minimize their global tax bill. The tax revenue of the source country is less at risk than that of the residence country, especially if the source tax rate is less than the residence rate. Corporations have considerable scope to shift profits to tax havens (Hines and Rice 1990). Global tax planning governs whether multinationals borrow locally or from the parent firm as well as the form and timing of intra-firm payments including dividends, interest, royalties, and management fees (Scholes and Wolfson 1991).

(4) *Residence Tax Revenue.* Further to (3), residence countries collect relatively little of revenue from the off-shore earnings of resident (multinational) companies. In the US experience, foreign subsidiaries effectively link the timing of foreign earnings repatriations to the availability of foreign tax credits in order to virtually eliminate any residual US tax (residence) liability (Altshuler and Newlon 1991).

(5) *Domestic and Foreign Investment – Are They Substitutes or Complements?* When a change in the general level of corporate taxation induces a change in domestic investment, foreign investment changes in the same direction. In the United States, for example, a tax-induced increase of one dollar of domestic investment has been estimated to bring with it between eight and twenty-seven cents of new (inward) foreign direct investment (Boskin 1987). There is some question of whether the increased domestic investment plus the new foreign investment corresponds to a reduction of (outbound) foreign direct investment.

In summary, it appears that the residence system may lead to its own undoing. Worldwide taxation together with the foreign tax credit and deferral invites policy adjustments in source countries (Bossons 1987, Tanzi 1987) and financial adjustments by multinational enterprises that stymie the objectives of residence policy. Source countries have an incentive to tax income of foreign-owned enterprise at the residence rate or somewhat less since tax that they collect is credited in the residence country. With a lower source tax rate, multinational enterprise has an incentive to defer repatriation by reinvesting abroad.[1] The overall result is *de facto* source-based taxation (Devereux and Pearson 1989). Deferral means forever. Residence countries generate virtually no revenue from the off-shore earnings of resident-based corporations.

The remaining role for worldwide taxation is to protect the integrity of the domestic tax system. Whereas the residence principle appears thwarted with respect to corporate income, its greatest relevance may be with respect to personal income. Indeed, as McIntyre (1989a, 1989b) argues, the United States, during its rise to international economic power, negotiated tax treaties and drafted domestic legislation that steadily relinquished source jurisdiction over foreign enterprises in order to strengthen residence jurisdiction over US persons.

Regardless, on the corporate side the United States has addressed weaknesses in its residence-based system in the Tax Reform Act of 1986. In addition to broadening the corporate tax base, reducing investment incentives, and lowering the corporate tax rate from 46 to 34 percent, the United States also tightened up rules pertaining to foreign-source income. The United States is now more vigilant with respect to transfer pricing, the tax treatment of intangibles - especially research and development (Hines 1991) - and the international allocation of interest expense. These developments have general relevance beyond the United States insofar as other nations emulate US policy or as they play host to US-based foreign direct investment.

The European Approach

In Europe, the principle of subsidiarity has quelled the sense of urgency to harmonize taxation among member states. By invoking subsidiarity, national tax authorities and Eurocrats are able to step back and ask whether harmonization achieves a preferred result that could not be achieved in some other, less centralized way. Subsidiarity does not compromise the goal of internal economic efficiency. Rather, in tax

---

[1]The after-source-tax earnings may be re-invested in the source country or elsewhere. As a result, source countries face a complex optimisation problem. A low corporate tax rate results in less (source) tax revenue but a larger flow of re-investable earnings. If the after-tax funds flow out of the source country, however, regardless of whether it is to the residence country, this capital service payment is in effect a capital outflow from the source country. It could otherwise have been tax revenue. A rationale thus emerges for low corporate tax rates together with withholding taxes on out-bound corporate dividends and intra-firm interest.

matters at least, subsidiarity reconciles efficiency at the Community level with sovereignty at the level of member states.

Europe can draw on the policy experience in the less cooperative, traditional mode. With a better understanding of the more troublesome areas in international taxation, Europe is able to identify specific reasons why decentralized arrangements lead to distortion and inefficiency. As these interjurisdictional problems are properly and effectively addressed, the need for additional central intervention on tax matters is lessened.[1] This process distinguishes Europe from the rest of the world.

The EC Commission in the past three years has issued a number of directives dealing with intra-European aspects of company taxation.[2] The thrust of these directives is to correct tax problems that impede the establishment of the EC internal market, in particular where such problems are unlikely to be resolved by independent action at the level of the member states. The directives deal with intra-EC corporate organization, source versus residence rights to tax (especially with respect to dividends, interest, and royalties), arbitration of double-tax disputes, and the treatment of intra-EC losses within a corporate group.

In our review of international issues in taxation, the European policy initiatives provide a convenient, sharply focussed summary of key problem areas along with promising solutions.

The Merger Directive[3]. The aim of this directive is to remove, as much as possible, the tax costs of cross-frontier corporate reorganization. Such costs may involve taxation of capital gains when assets are transferred from one country to another, taxation of reserves, or the denial of loss carry-forward. Within member states, the tax consequences of these types of transactions are generally addressed by rollover provisions whereby the tax liability is transferred to the reorganized corporation.

Mergers and corporate acquisitions are integral to a properly functioning market for corporate control. Corporate reorganization is often part of more efficient productive arrangements that capture economies of scale or scope.

---

[1]Various 'European tax issues' and their solutions have counterparts in fiscal arrangements within federal states such as Canada. See, for example, Boadway (1989).

[2]Easson (1992) provides an excellent review and critical commentary on the evolution of European direct tax policy from 1957 until the present. The following synopses of EC directives draw selectively from Easson.

[3] European Council Directive 90/434/EEC of 23 July 1990, OJ 1990 L 225.

The EC Merger Directive calls for relief from immediate taxation arising from corporate reorganizational transactions. At the same time the right of member states to impose tax is preserved in the event of any subsequent disposal of transferred assets. In effect, capital gains and depreciation that may be rolled over for domestic tax purposes may now be rolled across internal borders within Europe.

The Parent–Subsidiaries Directive.[1] The purpose of this directive is to eliminate double taxation of dividends that cross borders within Europe. To this end the directive first provides for the abolition of withholding tax on (out-bound) dividends paid by subsidiaries to parents in other EC member-states and, second, it calls for exemption of tax on (in-bound) dividends or residence taxation with credit for foreign taxes paid. The first form of relief, abolition of source withholding tax, is the more significant development of tax policy. The latter - residence exemption or foreign tax credit - is broadly established either under domestic legislation or through tax treaty (Table 11.1).

The Arbitration Convention.[2] This convention addresses a thorny issue in international taxation that arises from inherent arbitrariness in the allocation of income within a multijurisdictional enterprise. Each nation reserves the right to reassign income of multijurisdictional business especially when accounting for such income involves non-arm's-length (or intrafirm) transfer prices with a corporate affiliate in another country. However, unilateral assignment of taxable income generally does not trigger a corresponding adjustment in the other member state and hence in such cases income may become taxed in one country and remain taxed in the other - double taxation. The purpose of the Arbitration Convention is to establish procedures to arbitrate between EC member states concerning such matters.

The Directive on Interest and Royalties (Proposed).[3] This directive complements the parent-subsidiary directive that exempts cross-border dividends from withholding tax by extending the exemption to intra-firm interest and royalties. A significant difference, however, is that the

[1]EC Council Directive 90/435/EEC, 23 July 1990, OJ 1990 L225.
[2]Convention 90/436/EEC, 23 July 1990, OJ 1990 L 225.
[3]Proposal for a Council Directive on a Common system of Taxation Applicable to Interest and Royalty Payments Made Between Parent Companies and Subsidiaries in Different States; 28 November 1990, Doc. COM (90) 571 final, OJ 1991 C 53/91.

exemption applies to interest and royalties that flow in either direction - from subsidiary to parent and vice versa. Otherwise, complex cross-lending and proprietary rights within multinational enterprise encounter potential tax penalties that have no counterpart in domestic company taxation.

Like dividends, cross-border intra-firm interest and royalties are at risk of double taxation. In the case of interest, this is largely because tax is levied on gross payments whereas foreign tax credit is generally restricted to interest on a net basis (the spread between the intrafirm interest rate and the cost of borrowing). Royalties, on the other hand, often are not eligible for foreign tax relief.

At present, even when the source country grants an exemption from withholding tax under treaty, the tax is typically collected and a claim must be made for refund. Abolishing withholding taxes on interest and royalties means that such cumbersome administrative arrangements can be dismantled.

The Directive on Intragroup Losses (Proposed).[1] In consolidated accounting, losses in one division of a company offsets income in another division. When divisions of a corporate group are in different countries, however, such intragroup offset of losses is generally not available. This becomes an impediment to foreign direct investment, especially since foreign start-up operations typically involve losses.

The resolution of this problem inevitably involves some form of 'international consolidation' such that business losses in one country lead to a reduced tax liability in another. There is little incentive for a unilateral solution, notwithstanding the fact that the required redistribution of income is within the country that provides the relief of foreign-source losses, *i.e.*, from its treasury to the one of its resident corporations.

Conventional law also tends to prevail against consolidation inasmuch as (foreign) subsidiaries are legal entities in their own right. Ordinarily, a parent company is not taxed on the income of the subsidiary but only on income from the subsidiary. The legal distinction similarly precludes international consolidation and loss offsets.

The proposed *Directive on Intragroup Losses* sees through the legal distinction between parent company and its subsidiaries and, consistent

---

[1]Proposal for a Council Directive Concerning Arrangements for Taking Into Account by Enterprises of the Losses of Their Permanent Establishments and Subsidiaries Situated in Other Member Stateses; 28 November 1990, Doc. COM (90) 595 final, OJ 1991 C 595.

with an efficient internal market, the directive calls for EC member states to take an economic perspective on enterprise that spans Europe's internal borders.[1] The thrust of the directive is to allow parent companies to deduct losses incurred by subsidiaries in other member states. If and when the subsidiary generates taxable income, such income shall be reincorporated into the parent's taxable income to the extent of the losses previously deducted.

As a group, the EC directives on company taxation address pan-European problems that individual member states would be unwilling or unable to pursue independently. The objective is to remove tax influences on decisions of European firms to establish operations in one EC member state or another. The directives do not substantially 'harmonize' company taxes. For instance, they do not deal directly with tax rates or bases of company taxation in member states. The directives focus on adverse effects of the interaction on member state systems.

If the intent of the directives is achieved in respect of the specific issues that they address, then the differences in EC member company taxation are brought into sharper relief. At that point pressures for more fundamental convergence come into play, with the prerogative for change resting with the member states themselves. Indeed, that process may well have begun.

Concluding Remarks

Taxation is a nation's sovereign right. Nevertheless, the compelling forces of international economic integration significantly reduce national degrees of freedom in tax matters.

Nations do themselves damage when tax policy decreases or deflects potential gains from international trade and foreign investment or when revenue is eroded by international tax arbitrage. Nations must learn to deal with a span of tax policy that overruns their borders. Equally, each nation must be aware that what other countries do constrains their own tax policy and may vitally affect their own tax reforms.

---

[1] The 'economic perspective' recognises that multinational enterprise involves shared technology, integrated production, co-ordinated marketing, centralised finance, and joint risk taking. The greater the degree of trans-border corporate integration, the more difficult it is to assign costs or revenues (and thus income) to one location or another.

References and Further Reading

Altshuler, Roseanne and T. Scott Newlon, *The Effects of U.S. Tax Policy on the Income Repatriation Patterns of U.S. Multinational Corporations,* NBER WP No.3925; Cambridge, Massachusetts, 1991.

Alworth, J. S., *The Financial, Investment and Taxation Decisions of Multinationals,* Blackwell, Oxford, 1988.

Auerbach, A. J., 'Taxation, Corporate Financial Policy and The Cost of Capital', *Journal of Economic Literature* Vol.21(3), pp.905-40, September, 1983.

Bird, R. M., 'Personal-Corporate Tax Integration', in ed. S. Cnossen, *Tax Coordination in the European Community,* Kluwer, The Neths., 1987.

Bird, R. M. and O. Oldman, eds., *Taxation In Developing Countries,* Johns Hopkins University Press, 4th Edition, Baltimore, 1990.

Boadway, R., 'Corporate Tax Harmonisation: Lessons From Canada', in ed. M. Gammie and B. Robinson, *Beyond 1992: A European Tax System,* Institute of Fiscal Studies, London, 1989.

Bossons, J. D., 'The Impact of The 1986 Tax Reform Act on Tax Reform in Canada', *National Tax Journal,* Vol. 40(3), 1987.

Boskin, M. J., 'Tax policy and the International Location of Investment', in ed. M. Feldstein, *Taxes and Capital Formation,* University of Chicago Press and NBER, Chicago, 1987.

Brean, D. J. S.,'Here or There? The Source and Residence Principles of International Taxation', in eds. R. M. Bird and J. M. Mintz, *Taxation To The Year 2000 And Beyond,* Canadian Tax Foundation, Toronto, 1992.

Brean, D. J. S., R. M. Bird and M. Krauss, *Taxation of International Portfolio Investment,* Institute for Research on Public Policy, Ottawa, 1991.

Devereux, M. and M. Pearson, *Corporate Tax Harmonisation and Economic Efficiency,* IFS Report Series No.35, Institute for Fiscal Studies, London, 1989.

Easson, A., 'Harmonization of Direct Taxation in the European Community: From Neumark to Ruding', *Canadian Tax Journal* Vol. 40(3), pp.600-38, 1992.

Feldstein, M., ed. *The Effects of Taxation on Capital Accumulation,* University of Chicago Press and NBER, Chicago, 1987.

Frenkel, J. A., A. Razin and S. Symansky, *International VAT Harmonisation: Economic Effects*, IMF Working Paper wp/91/22, International Monetary Fund, Washington, 1991.

Gammie, M. and B. Robinson, eds., *Beyond 1992: A European Tax System*, Institute for Fiscal Studies, London.

Gordon, R. H., 'Can Capital Income Taxes Survive In Open Economies?', *The Journal of Finance* Vol. 47(3), pp.1159-80, July, 1992.

Goulder, L. H., 'U.S. Withholding Taxes on Foreign Interest Income', in ed. L. H. Summers, *Tax Policy and the Economy*, MIT Press and NBER, Cambridge, Massachusetts, 1990.

Gravelle, J. G. and L. J. Kotlikoff, 'The Incidence and Efficiency Costs of Corporate Taxation When Corporate and Noncorporate Firms Produce The Same Good', *Journal of Political Economy* Vol. 97, pp.749-81, 1989.

Hartman, D. G.,'Tax Policy and Foreign Direct Investment in the United States', *National Tax Journal* Vol. 37; pp.475-87, 1984.

Hartman, D. G.,'Tax Policy and Foreign Direct Investment', *Journal of Public Economics*, Vol. 26, pp.107-21, 1985.

Hines, J. R., 'On The Sensitivity of R & D To Delicate Tax Changes: The Behavior of U.S. Multinationals in the 1980s', NBER Working Paper No. 3930, Cambridge, Massachusetts, 1991.

Hines, J. R. and E. M. Rice, 'Fiscal Paradise: Foreign Tax Havens and American Business', NBER Working Paper No. 3477, Cambridge, Massachusetts, 1990.

Jenkins, G. P., 'The Impact of Inflation on Corporate Taxes and the Cash Flow of Business', *Canadian Tax Journal* Vol. 33, pp. 759-85, July-August, 1985.

McIntyre, M. J., 'A Critique of the Source Principle', *Tax Notes International*, pp.261-2, September, 1989.

McIntyre, M.l J., 'The Demise of US-Source Jurisdiction', *Tax Notes International*, pp.371-3, October, 1989.

McLure, C. E., *Must Corporate Income Be Taxed Twice?* Brookings Institution, Washington, 1979.

McLure, C. E., *The Value Added Tax: Key to Deficit Reduction?* American Enterprise Institute, Washington, 1987.

Newbery, D. and N. Stern, eds., *The Theory of Taxation for Developing Countries*; Oxford University Press for The World Bank, Oxford, 1987.

Sinn, H.-W., 'The Non-Neutrality of Inflation for International Capital Movements', NBER Working Paper No. 3219, Cambridge, Massachusetts, 1990.

Scholes, M. S. and M. A. Wolfson, *Taxes and Business Strategy: A Global Planning Approach*, Prentice-Hall, Englewood Cliffs, New Jersey, 1991.

Scrivener, C., 'Corporate Taxation in Europe and The Single Market'; *Intertax* Vol. 4, pp.207-8, 1990.

Tanzi, V., 'The Response of Other Industrial Countries to The U.S. Tax Reform Act', *National Tax Journal,* Vol. 40(3), 1987.

OECD / BIAC, 'Obstacles to International Flows of Capital', Bulletin of *The International Bureau of Fiscal Documentation*, IBFD, pp.161-79, Amsterdam, April, 1990.

OECD, *Taxing Profits in a Global Economy: Domestic and International Issues*, Paris, 1991.